306.84   Janda, Louis H.
JAN
           The second time
           around.

$17.95

DATE			

© THE BAKER & TAYLOR CO.

The Second Time Around

THE SECOND TIME AROUND

Why Some Marriages Fail While Others Succeed

by Louis H. Janda, Ph.D.
and Ellen MacCormack

A Lyle Stuart Book
Published by Carol Publishing Group

A Lyle Stuart Book
Published by Carol Publishing Group
Lyle Stuart is a registered trademark of Carol Communications, Inc.

Editorial Offices: 600 Madison Avenue, New York, N.Y. 10022
Sales & Distribution Offices: 120 Enterprise Avenue, Secaucus, N.J. 07094
In Canada: Musson Book Company, a division of General Publishing Company, Ltd.,
    Don Mills, Ontario M3B 2T6

Queries regarding rights and permissions should be addressed to Carol
Publishing Group, 600 Madison Avenue, New York, N.Y. 10022

Carol Publishing Group books are available at special discounts for bulk
purchases, for sales promotions, fund-raising, or educational purposes.
Special editions can be created to specifications. For details contact:
Special Sales Department, Carol Publishing Group, 120 Enterprise Avenue,
Secaucus, N.J. 07094

Manufactured in the United States of America
10 9 8 7 6 5 4 3 2 1

Library of Congress Cataloging-in-Publication Data

Janda, Louis H.
    The second time around: why some marriages fail while others succeed / by Louis
H. Janda and Ellen MacCormack.
        p. cm.
    ISBN 0-8184-0557-0
    1. Remarriage—United States.   2. Remarried people—United States—Psychology.
3. Stepfamilies—United States.   I. MacCormack, Ellen.   II. Title.
HQ1019.U6J36   1991
306.84—dc20   91-19329
                                                                          CIP

To Our Parents
Stanley and Lorraine Janda
and
John and Nancy MacCormack

Contents

Preface

IT IS IMPOSSIBLE to live in our society and not be at least curious about second marriages. Second marriages have become almost commonplace. If we have not had one ourselves (and one of us, EM, is about to take the big step), we certainly know friends and relatives who have. As clinical psychologists, we were probably more curious than most about people who, as the cynical epigram suggests, "allowed hope to triumph over experience." We saw more and more clients over the past ten years who had given up on one marriage and were trying to make a second one work.

But information about the experiences of these men and women has not kept up with the dramatic increase in the numbers of people who are marrying for the second time. The professional as well as the popular literature does offer many examples of the types of problems such couples face, but there is little information that tells us about the struggles and the successes of men and women who are on their second marriage and who never have occasion to seek professional help.

We were grateful for the opportunity to satisfy our curiosity when our local newspaper invited us to do a survey of couples who were in second marriages. We received replies from more than one hundred people, most of whom included long letters with their survey responses, and several of whom talked with us at length about their experiences. Their descriptions of the challenges and joys of their second chances were often poignant, sometimes amusing, but always informative. Let us tell you a little about the men and women who provided much of the material for this book.

The women ranged in age from twenty-four to fifty-two with an average age of thirty-five. The ages of the men were from twenty-three to sixty-two with a mean of thirty-six. For 16 percent of the women, their current marriage was their first (they qualified as a stepfamily because it was their husband's second marriage), for 69 percent of the women, it was their second marriage, 8 percent of the women were on their third marriage, and the remaining 7 percent were on their fourth, fifth, or sixth marriage. Fourteen percent of the men indicated that their current marriage was their first, for 68 percent it was their second, none were in their third marriage, and 9 percent were in each of the fourth or fifth marriage categories. The average length of the current marriage ranged from six months to thirty-four years for women with a mean of five years, while for men the range was six months to thirty-five years with an average of six years. Seventy-three percent of the women and 78 percent of the men had children from a previous marriage.

On the whole, our respondents were satisfied with their second chance. Fully 83 percent of the men and 87 percent of the women said they would marry their present spouse again if they had it to do over. There was, however, a wide range of marital satisfaction. We heard from people who were more miserable than they could have ever imagined as well as from those who never knew that marriage could be so gratifying. As is the case with most surveys, we cannot state with any confidence how representative our sample is, but we can say that our respondents provided us with a wide diversity of experiences.

Along with the experiences of our respondents, we have drawn upon the professional literature and our own clinical and personal experiences in collecting information for this book. Our goal is to provide you, the reader, with an up-to-date overview of what behavioral scientists have learned about second marriages and to share with you the experiences of hundreds of men and women who have taken their second chance so that you may avoid some of the pitfalls they have had while maximizing your odds of sharing their success.

We wish you the best of luck!

Acknowledgments

We wish to thank all those couples who took the time to respond to our survey. Not only did they answer numerous questions that only psychologists could think to ask, many of them included lengthy and informative letters with their survey responses. We are especially grateful to those couples who agreed to talk to us in depth about their second marriages. These men and women were willing to share with us their difficult times as well as their successes in adjusting to their stepfamilies. Without their help, this book would not have been possible.

The Second Time Around

CHAPTER 1

In Search of the Brady Bunch

JOHN AND MICHELLE suspected something would come of their relationship within hours after their first meeting. Michelle had just moved to a new city to put some distance between herself and her first husband, and she took a job at the same midsized insurance agency where John worked. One need talk to Michelle for only a few minutes before her competence, intelligence, and professionalism show through, but there is something about her that doesn't quite fit. Perhaps it is her appearance. Michelle is slender and has a nice figure, but she could be so much more attractive if she invested a little attention in her attire and makeup. It's almost as if she wants to remain unnoticed. Also, for someone who speaks with such authority, she finds it difficult to look others in the eye. Could her apparent self-confidence be hiding a sense of shyness she is trying to overcome? Or has her first marriage left her wary of making contact with other men?

In some ways, John is Michelle's counterpart. On first meeting him, one might think his soft voice and quiet manner reflected bashfulness, but John can talk easily to anybody. And his natural openness and curiosity about people often inspire others to share secrets with him that have been tucked away safely for years. John is like Michelle, though, in his apparent lack of concern for his appearance. He gave up artfully combing his hair to conceal his encroaching baldness years ago, and he would laugh should someone suggest he get a toupee. He always dresses neatly and appropriately, but the fact that styles change every few years or so is not a sufficient reason for John to buy new clothes. He gives the impression of a somewhat eccentric college professor rather than of the successful insurance salesman he is.

John was still married to his first wife when Michelle came to work in his office—a marriage of twelve years that he had regretted since his honeymoon. Whether because of his dissatisfying marriage or because of his sensitivity to the subtle signs that Michelle was not as comfortable in her new situation as she would have liked others to believe—John is not even sure what his inspiration was—he asked Michelle to lunch that first week.

Before a year passed, John separated from his wife. After another year, Michelle moved in with him, and six months later they married. Now, nearly a decade has passed and neither John nor Michelle has ever given a thought to the possibility that their marriage will not last forever. They have made the best of their second time around, and they are grateful for the opportunity.

Not all stories have such a happy ending, however. Jan, for instance, had made a very successful adjustment to her divorce and her life as a single mother. She was a real estate agent in the Washington, D.C., area, and she was good enough at it that she was able to buy her own three-bedroom house in the suburbs and do pretty much as she pleased. She is a friendly, outgoing woman and attractive in a quiet, elegant sort of way, so she found it easy to meet men—so easy that she had to set limits on her social life so as not to deprive her young son of the attention he needed.

Jan's life changed one morning, in ways she never could have foreseen, when she dropped her son off at the day-care center. On that fateful day, she happened to catch Robert's eye when he was depositing his son, who was only a few months older than Jan's boy. Robert was a young attorney on his way up in the federal government, and he had just separated from his first wife. He was interested in female companionship, and Jan was just what he was looking for. He asked the owner of the day-care center to introduce him to Jan, and he was waiting for her at six that afternoon—the time Jan usually came to pick up her son. The owner was forthright. She told Jan that Robert had asked to meet her because he found her very attractive. Jan was flattered. Years later she would describe that first meeting: "I had met lots of men through my work but this was the first time a stranger had ever gone out of his way to get to know me. And Robert was impossibly handsome and the most charming man I had ever met. Something clicked inside of me that very first afternoon."

Despite her infatuation, Jan was sensible enough to proceed with caution. She talked with Robert on the phone half a dozen times before she agreed to meet him for dinner, but her resistance soon evaporated. Within weeks of that first evening together, they were seeing each other every night and spending most weekends together. She was smitten, and she had every reason to believe he was too.

They were married four years later after an off-again, on-again courtship. The only constant during that period was the passion and intense attachment each experienced for the other.

Thirteen years have passed since their marriage, and Jan and Robert are separated for the third and, Jan insists, final time. They have had three children together, and Robert sees them perhaps every three or four months. Jan is trying to survive on the sporadic child-support payments Robert sends. She wonders how she can possibly make it.

A mere generation ago, stories like that of Michelle and John, and of Jan and Robert, were rare. Stepfamilies were an oddity, almost a curiosity. But the nature of the American family has changed. For the first two hundred years of our history, the question of what makes a family never came up. Everyone knew the answer. A man and a woman married, they had children, and they lived together ever after—perhaps happily, perhaps not, but they stayed together.

But things began to change during the middle to late 1960s. Over the preceding century the divorce rate had remained relatively stable. It did show a slow, steady increase, but divorce was still considered unusual by 1960. Many of us who grew up in the 1950s and early 1960s cannot recall having a single friend who came from something other than a traditional family. That was simply the way things were. Moms and dads didn't divorce, unless there were truly exceptional circumstances.

The 1960s marked the beginning of a revolutionary change in family life. From 1950 to 1960, there was a 2 percent increase in the number of divorces in our country. Over the ten-year period ending in 1970, the increase was 80 percent. Ten more years passed with another increase of 68 percent. The divorce rate has increased more over the past twenty-five years than it did over the preceding two hundred years. As we enter the final decade of this century, we have reached a point where marriage, an institution that we once thought of as forever, has about a fifty-fifty chance of survival.

But we Americans are the marrying kind. Just because a first marriage does not work out does not mean that we give up on the institution. About 80 percent of divorced men and women will try it again. According to the National Center for Health Statistics, 46 percent of all marriages are remarriages for one or both partners, 23 percent are remarriages for both. We have reached the point where every day thirteen hundred instant families are formed when a man and a woman, at least one of whom has children from a previous marriage, tie the knot convinced that they have learned enough from their past painful experiences to make their new family a success.

These instant families have become so commonplace that social scientists have added a new term to their lexicon—bi-nuclear families. Current estimates are that before they reach age eighteen, one third of American children will experience a bi-nuclear family and have to shuttle between Mom's house and Dad's house.

Bi-nuclear families, or stepfamilies as they are more commonly called, are invariably formed with the highest of hopes. No matter how many painful or disappointing relationships have preceded it, the new marriage provides an opportunity to begin again, to atone for past mistakes. As long as they have enough love, patience, and understanding, couples like Michelle and John and Jan and Robert are convinced they can make their new families work. All they need is a chance.

But good intentions and determination are not always enough. Despite the glib solutions offered by TV stepfamilies like the Brady Bunch, the reality of stepfamilies is too complex to ensure an effortless, blissful future. Indeed, more than 60 percent of the men and women in second marriages we surveyed reported that it was much more difficult than they had anticipated. And even when they were committed to their own second marriages, fully 46 percent of women and 35 percent of men said they would not recommend to a friend that he or she marry someone with children. It can be hard, very hard. And many couples discover, like Jan and Robert, the happiness offered by a second marriage is nothing more than an elusive ideal. The painful fact is that second marriages are even more likely to fail than are first marriages. It is estimated that of every ten second marriages, six will end in divorce.

What distinguishes those who make the most of their second chance and those who fail? Why are some couples like John and Michelle able to resolve the problems that threaten to undermine their relationship while couples like Jan and Robert seem destined for failure almost from the very beginning?

There is nothing mysterious about some of these factors. As you will see in the following chapters as we tell you more about these two couples, there was plenty of evidence available to Jan that marriage to Robert was fraught with potential pitfalls. Her friends saw it and tried to tell her, but she would hear none of it. Jan, unlike her friends, was not an uninvolved, outside observer. She was in love with Robert, and she could not see, and sometimes chose to ignore, the damning evidence.

But it is not always so clear-cut. Many of Michelle's and John's friends quietly predicted that their marriage wouldn't last two years. After all, John had numerous affairs in his first marriage, and both of them moved directly from their first marriage into their second. If the old cliché "You have to learn to live with yourself before you can live with anyone else" had universal validity, it would eliminate any chance this couple had of making a success of their second chance. Yet their marriage of ten years is rock-solid and truly satisfying for both of them.

One of our goals in writing this book is to help you learn to make use of the obvious factors (this is harder than you might think—as Jan would attest) and to acquaint you with the not-so-obvious factors that can influence success. After reading this book, we hope you will never have cause to say what so many men and women who responded to our survey told us: "I wish I had only known!"

DIFFERENCES BETWEEN FIRST AND SECOND MARRIAGES

We've heard people say that there aren't really any important differences between first and second marriages beyond the obvious factors of stepchildren and money. While we don't accept this, it is a point of view that does contain an element of truth; namely, all of the ingredients (we can't think of a single exception) that contribute to the success of a first marriage also are important in a second marriage. Men and women have to be reasonably well adjusted and mature if they are going to have a successful relationship. They must bring a sense of commitment and a willingness to see the other's point of view if they are to have a chance. Negotiation and compromise have to be more important to both than being "right" or getting one's own way if the marriage is to be "until death do us part." Second marriages do have much in common with first marriages. This much is obvious.

But knowing the obvious is not always enough. We have heard countless people say something to the effect of, "I learned from my mistakes in my first marriage, so I'm prepared to have a successful second marriage." We would have more confidence in such optimistic prognostications if it were not for the fact that we have also heard people say, "I have learned a lot from my mistakes in my first four marriages, so now I'm ready to make good with the next one." The truth will set you free only if you're prepared to accept it and deal with it.

Some, perhaps quite a lot, of what we will be telling you in the following chapters will seem obvious to you. But we would not bother repeating the obvious if we did not feel it vitally important for men and women contemplating second marriages to hear it again, and more importantly, to use the information to make their second chance a success. As Jan, with her hindsight, would tell you, it is not easy to make use of plain and simple truths. It can be exceedingly painful to acknowledge one's own failures and limitations. And it can be even more difficult to set about making the necessary changes to increase the odds of succeeding in a second marriage. So when you come across a section that "seems obvious," don't skim over it. Take a long, hard look at yourself and ask in what ways the information may apply to you, what it tells you about the choices before you. We will provide you with the information you will need to be successful the second time around, but it is up to you to make use of this information. As emotionally taxing as self-exploration and change can be, it is easier than having another failed marriage.

So what are the differences between first and second marriages? Yes, stepchildren and money are the big ones. They are, as most everyone knows, the two leading causes of failed second marriages. But once again, knowing that these are important—no, crucial—issues is not always enough. We know one woman, a licensed clinical social worker, who has specialized in treating families for the past fifteen years. Because Janna has seen hundreds of step-families in therapy, she was confident that she would be effective with her husband's daughter once she remarried, but nothing could prepare her for the emotional blow she experienced when she had her first major confrontation with her eight-year-old stepdaughter. As she tells it: "I never would have guessed how devastated I would be the first time I tried to discipline Kimberly. She thought I wasn't being fair, and she told me in a hateful voice, 'I want to go live with my *real* mother.' I was crushed. I'd tried so hard to make my new family work, and it all seemed to fall apart in a matter of minutes."

Janna was able to fall back on her knowledge and her own personal maturity to work out the problems with her stepdaughter and make her second marriage a success, but she learned firsthand that knowing the challenges of stepparenting is not always sufficient to deal with them effectively.

Money issues often work the same way. Sharon knew that Fred's financial obligations to his former wife would make things tight for the two of them, but she was certain that their love for each other would make a spartan budget a trivial concern. Barely a year after her marriage she told us, "I didn't realize how hard it would be. It seems like a new problem comes up every day. Most of the time it seems worth it, but sometimes when I pay the bills, I can't help but wonder. It takes almost my entire take-home pay to make Fred's alimony and child-support payment, and it's at those moments when I think to myself, 'And I have to work full-time to earn the right to be this miserable?' "

We will provide you with numerous examples of how successful couples negotiated the dangerous waters of stepchildren and money problems. To be forewarned is the first step to being forearmed.

Let us give you a brief preview of the many other important differences between first and second marriages that we will be discussing in the chapters that follow.

In a second marriage one, or perhaps both, of the spouses brings a marital history into the relationship. Obviously, there were elements of the first marriage the individual did not like, but nonetheless the person did develop certain expectations about what it means to be married. Clara, for example, divorced her first husband because of his remote, cold nature, but she was accustomed to having a partner who was a whiz at home and yard maintenance. She married Sam, whose first wife always called a repairman at the first sign of problems. A trivial difference? Perhaps, unless you happen to be Clara or Sam, who couldn't understand why the other spouse didn't care enough about the marriage to take care of such mundane matters.

Then there are the scars left by a bad first marriage. Courtney divorced because of her husband's incessant womanizing. She was leery of marrying again, but Randy convinced her that he was as committed to monogamy as she was. But the first time he came home late for dinner, her old fears immediately surfaced. The second time it happened, she refused to talk to Randy for three days. Six months later Randy was ready to move out unless Courtney agreed to do something about her suspiciousness and jealousy.

In-law problems can be challenging enough in a first marriage but they can't hold a candle to the potential complications in a second marriage. Imagine the most negative stereotype of a meddlesome mother-in-law and then add to this a mother-in-law who blames you for breaking up her son's first marriage. Or consider grandparents who distinguish between the "real" grandchildren and the step-grandchildren, who are viewed as little more than intruders who are best ignored. An unsympathetic, angry extended family can cause strains in the most solid of second marriages.

A second marriage almost always means there is at least one "ex" in the picture. As much as one would like to forget that one's spouse was once married to someone else, legal obligations, and often emotional bonds, usually make this impossible. Dealing with a hostile mother-in-law may seem like a picnic in the park compared to dealing with a vindictive former spouse. We heard from many couples whose finances and emotional stability were strained past the breaking point by an angry ex who regularly demanded that problems be resolved in the courtroom.

Because it is a second marriage, it means that at least one of the partners has given up on a previous union. And once one has divorced a first time, it is a little easier to do it a second time. The average duration for first marriages is eleven years, but for second marriages it drops to seven years.

We certainly do not want to paint a dismal picture of second marriages, but the problems are real, and few of us are so rational and logical that we can anticipate all of them. More than 70 percent of the women in our survey and 52 percent of the men said that their second marriage was more difficult than they had expected.

But the rewards can be great. A majority of our respondents indicated that while they had more problems than they expected, and that they were continuing to work on making their new family work, they were pleased with their choice to give marriage a second chance. Fully 83 percent of the men and 87 percent of the women said they would marry their spouse again if they had it to do over. And 74 percent of the men and 67 percent of the women predicted that their present marriage would last forever. There is good reason to be optimistic about a second marriage, and if you're concerned enough about your relationship to be reading this book, the odds are probably even better for you. We are confident that we can be of some help in making your second chance a big success.

CHAPTER 2

Looking for Prince Charming

"LISA IS THE FIRST woman I've ever truly been in love with," said Ted, whose ecstasy over his "first, true love" is tempered by the agony of being married to Marion, a woman he likes and respects, and his ties to his two children, whom he adores. Ted is perplexed, and more than a little angry, that he could find himself in this situation where several people are probably going to experience a great deal of pain. "I thought I did everything right. I waited until I was almost twenty-nine years old until I got married. If there was one thing I wanted to avoid, it was rushing into marriage the way so many of my friends did. I had known lots of women, but it was different with Marion. We hit it off right from the start, I could talk to her about anything, and she was the only woman who could give me a run for my money when we played tennis. I was sure I loved her. How could I have been so wrong?"

The intensity of his feelings for Lisa is conclusive evidence for Ted that he made a mistake with Marion. There is no convincing him that it might be something else about his life that is causing his feelings of despair. Perhaps his disappointment with his stagnating career (at least in his mind) as a sales manager for a business machines company could be a factor. Or Marion's devotion to their children and her tendency to put him second could play a part. And then there is the fact that his time with Marion is usually spent talking about juggling bills, or arranging for piano lessons and baseball practice—conversation that doesn't make for the most romantic of relationships. Perhaps his feelings for Lisa have more to do with his routine, and yes, sometimes stultifying home life than with romantic concepts such as true love. But Ted will hear none of this.

"How could you say such a thing?" Ted protested. "Just look at Marion. She's a good person, but she's hardly the kind of woman a man can have a special feeling for. She's gained twenty-five pounds since we married, she's only interested in talking about the kids, and although she says she wants to go back to work now that Elliot and Donna are in school, she says she can't find anything that interests her.

"Lisa, on the other hand, cares about her appearance. She has the figure of a twenty-year-old even though she's three years older than Marion. She also has drive and ambition, qualities I admire in a woman. And we never talk about the boring, mundane details of living that Marion is so preoccupied with. Sure, the sex is great with Lisa, but if that's all there was to our relationship, I'd settle for a little fling. I really do love Lisa, and I'm convinced we are meant for each other."

Ted spent almost a year vacillating between the two women. Every time he thought he had summoned enough courage to leave Marion for Lisa, he would be overwhelmed with guilt about what he was doing to his family. When he would resolve to cut Lisa out of his life, he would become so depressed, he could scarcely function. He wondered how he could live without her.

During one of these periods when he wasn't seeing Lisa, he took Marion out to dinner and to a movie, hoping to revive some of the romance in his marriage. He made it through dinner with a façade of cheerfulness and good humor, but once in the darkness of the movie theater, he began to sob uncontrollably. He moved out of the house that night.

For the first year following his separation—and Lisa's—Ted was convinced he made the right decision. Yes, there were problems. His children couldn't understand why he left them and their mommy, and money was tight now that he had to support his old house along with his efficiency apartment near the oceanfront. But it was all worth it, no doubt about it.

By the end of the second year, Ted was beginning to have second thoughts. He and Lisa were married and living with Lisa's three children, whom Ted believed were spoiled beyond belief. Because Ted left his wife for another woman, the judge awarded Marion generous alimony and child support. Lisa, on the other hand, received no alimony and minimal child support because of her involvement with Ted prior to her divorce. Ted and Lisa were drowning in unpaid bills in their futile attempt to maintain their former lifestyles.

By the end of the fourth year, there was no doubt left in Ted's mind that he had made a mistake. "I don't know how I could have been so stupid. I knew Lisa and I would have a lot of obstacles to overcome, but I really believed our love for each other would make it easy for us to do whatever had to be done. Now we argue constantly—about her kids, about money, about one damn thing after another. And Lisa is a vicious fighter; she's not nearly as kindhearted as Marion was. To top it all off, our sex life is virtually nonexistent. I wish I could have my old family back."

Ted's story is hardly unique. Estimates point out that nearly half of all divorces involve a third party waiting in the wings—the quest for "true love" is a common occurrence in today's world. Many of these people do leave unsatisfying, even destructive, marriages for Prince or Princess Charming, but all too many men and women confuse a novel body and fresh conversation with a "love that was meant to be."

This search for the perfect partner, for unending passion and romance, and the subsequent divorces and remarriages, is actually a rather recent development in our society. We don't have to go back too many generations to discover that our ancestors had more sense than we do. Prior to the twentieth century, love, passion, and romance had nothing to do with marriage. Finding a man or woman of good character, a spouse who could provide economic stability or healthy children was what mattered. The idea of marrying for love would appear hopelessly foolish to our forefathers.

According to social scientist Bernard Murstein, it wasn't until the later part of the 1800s that we Americans began to replace economic security with romantic love as the raison d'être for marriage. Murstein has argued that this derived from the industrialization of our country and that as people moved from farms to cities, from plowing fields and milking cows to jobs in factories and shops, marriage became less important for economic survival. People no longer had to have a spouse, who was necessary to make a go of the family farm. The decline of the importance of economic motives for marriage left a vacuum, and it soon began to be filled with notions of Princes and Princesses.

By the turn of the century, the transition was nearly complete. Women's magazines, such as the *Ladies' Home Journal*, began to offer advice such as, "No high-minded girl and no girl of truly refined feeling . . . ever . . . admits the advisability of marriage without love." But as is the case for all movements, the silent majority lagged behind in their views. A survey of one hundred young women conducted in 1903 reported that "strength of character" was the most important quality in a prospective husband. "Love" came in a weak fourth behind "business ability" and "respect for women."

The tide had turned, however, and by the late 1920s the connection between romantic love and marriage had gained a solid foothold. Themes of love, heartbreak, and eventual happiness in radio soap operas, novels, and movies all began to reflect the general population's growing obsession with love. We had arrived at a new age—one in which we became convinced that if only we could find the right person, we would fall in love, get married, and live happily ever after.

By the late 1960s this proposition about true love and marriage had been amended so that if we began to experience marriage as nothing more than a deadening routine, it must mean that we had married the wrong person. If only we could find the right person, we would feel alive once again. So we've reached a point where countless people move from marriage to marriage looking for their Prince or Princess rather than taking a close look at themselves.

A LOOK AT LOVE

We Americans may have decided that romantic love was both a necessary and sufficient justification for marriage by the early twentieth century, but that did not mean we had a very good idea of what it was all about. Shortly after the turn of the century, a social scientist named Finck wrote, "Love is such a tissue of paradoxes, and exists in such an endless variety of forms and shades that you may say anything about it that you please, and it is likely to be correct."

It has only been about two decades since one could justifiably take issue with this assertion. Around the late 1960s and early 1970s a handful of psychologists decided that it might not be impossible to unravel some of the mysteries of love and began to conduct research on the topic. We are far from having all the answers, and we probably never will, but we do know a lot more about this often frustrating, sometimes delightful emotion than we did a generation ago. Many of the answers we've obtained have confirmed folk wisdom, but others have been surprising—some might say distressing. With the hope that knowledge is power—power that will allow us to make decisions that serve us well—let us take a brief look at what the social scientists have learned about love.

MYTHS ABOUT ROMANTIC LOVE
Falling in love tells us that we've found the right person.
Love goes along with other feelings, such as liking and respect.
True love lasts forever.
As long as two people love each other, they can solve anything
    that might come up.

Let's take a closer look at these myths about romantic love.

Do We Always Like the Person We Love?

Jan, the woman we introduced in the first chapter, certainly believed that her intense feelings for Robert meant that she had found the right person. Countless other men and women have come to the same conclusion. Could there be any truth to this?

Except for those occasions when we are in its grasp, most of us know that this is utter nonsense. We can look at our friends and see immediately that the person they are in love with is not right for them, but when it comes to ourselves, we have little doubt that our loved one is the person we have been searching for our entire lives. After all, we could not fall in love with anyone who was not perfect for us in every way, could we?

Psychologist Zick Rubin was among the first to collect evidence to show that being in love did not guarantee that we would even like the object of our passion. He painstakingly constructed tests, based on careful observation and questioning, to measure liking as well as loving. He then brought dating couples into his laboratory, observed their behavior, and administered the tests measuring their feelings for each other. Lo and behold, he found that liking a steady date and feelings of love for that person were only modestly related. While some individuals both liked and loved their partner, others actually disliked the person they were in love with.

Ellen Hatfield and Elaine Walster, who have researched interpersonal attraction and love extensively at the University of Wisconsin, have also pointed out that liking and loving do not necessarily go together. They make frequent presentations to various community groups about their work, and they have said that the one question they are most commonly asked is "Can you love someone and hate that person at the same time?"

Their answer is yes. Liking and loving seem to lie on different dimensions. We may like someone greatly, but if the spark isn't there, love will never blossom. On the other hand, we can fall passionately in love with someone we hardly know. And indeed, this has happened countless times.

Let us take a closer look at Jan's romance with Robert. As you may recall from the previous chapter, Jan felt the spark of love upon first meeting Robert. He seemed so kind, witty, sophisticated, and interesting. And it didn't hurt that he was one of the most handsome men that Jan had ever dated. It only took a few weeks before she decided she was hopelessly in love and that Robert was the man she wanted to spend the rest of her life with. The intensity of her feelings convinced her she was right about this.

But less than two months after being introduced to him at the day-care center, Jan was left hanging. After seeing each other almost daily, Robert missed a date and did not call for two weeks. Jan couldn't stand it. "I was sure our relationship was special, if not unique. When he stood me up, I was so angry that I vowed not to call him. I managed to hold out for two weeks, but after not hearing a word from him, I gave in and called. His number at this apartment had been disconnected, so I called him at work. He told me, in a very cool and distant way, that he had decided to try to make a go of it with his wife and moved back in with her. I couldn't believe it. He had led me to believe his divorce had been final for some time."

Jan is a very bright, very logical, down-to-earth kind of woman. One might expect that such an experience would destroy any illusions she might have had about Robert. But her feelings of love were so strong that she was defenseless when he called three months later to tell her he had once again left his wife—for good this time. She promptly took up where she had left off, convinced that everything would be fine now that Robert was serious about proceeding with his divorce.

Their courtship stumbled along in a rocky fashion, with Robert returning to his wife one more time, and dropping out of sight for two more three-month periods. Jan learned much later that he had been having relationships with other women during these times. After four years of alternating between unimaginable bliss and excruciating pain, Jan decided she had had enough. Robert had taken a job two hundred miles away, they were not seeing each other very often, so she decided the time was right to make a clean break. "I knew I was in for a lot of nights crying myself to sleep, but I had to break it off. It was destroying my life. I called to tell him but before I could get the words out, he asked me to marry him. What is so incredible to me now, I didn't even hesitate. I said yes in a flash. He told me he would call me later in the week to arrange for me to come down for the weekend."

Jan thought her days of heartbreak were over, but they were just picking up steam. As Jan tells it: "When I didn't hear from Robert by Thursday night, I called him—after all, I had to arrange for a baby-sitter if I was going away for the weekend. He apologized for not calling sooner, but after hemming and hawing, he said that it turned out that the weekend wasn't good for him. I couldn't believe it! He had asked me to marry him four days earlier and he couldn't make time for me on the weekend!

"In the past I was always understanding—at least I pretended to be—when he gave me his excuses about not having time for me, but this time I exploded. He finally told me that he had met a woman since he had moved and before he asked me to marry him, the two of them had made plans to go to Nags Head for the weekend. 'She was so sensitive,' he said, that he couldn't cancel on her out of the clear blue sky. He would use the weekend to let her down easy. I could understand why he had to handle it that way, couldn't I?

"Believe it or not, I said I could. I was devastated, of course, but I guess I thought we were so close to being married that I didn't want to do anything to rock the boat. And I was sure that everything would be fine once we were finally married."

The horrors of Jan's courtship were not over, however. "About a month later, Robert asked me to move down and live with him. We were to be married in a couple of months as soon as his divorce was finalized, but he said he couldn't stand to wait that long to be with me. So like a fool, I quit my job, sold most of my furniture at a garage sale, and moved to Virginia Beach. Robert had a one-bedroom apartment near the oceanfront, so my six-year-old son had to sleep on the couch.

"Two weeks later, Robert told me he had to go back up to Washington for a few days to help his attorney prepare his case against his wife—he was trying to get custody of their son, Jeremy, who was also six years old. Robert had smashed up his car in an accident, so he had to take mine. So there I was, stranded with a restless, angry six-year-old boy, in a city where I didn't know a soul, and with no car when the nearest grocery store was more than a mile away.

"A few days turned into five weeks. When I would call to ask him to send money for the rent, utilities, and groceries, he would scream at me, saying that he had more important things on his mind. By the time he finally returned, the electricity had been turned off (he had 'forgotten' to pay the bill the previous two months) and the landlord was threatening to evict us. I was scared to death at what I had done—I did have a good job and a comfortable life in Washington—but I still believed everything would turn out okay once we were married and Robert settled everything with his ex-wife. I told myself he was under a lot of stress and I had to be as patient and understanding as I could."

Jan did marry Robert despite all that had happened. She was beginning to have doubts about him, but the passion overrode her good sense. She really believed that their love for each other would conquer all, and that theirs was a love that would last forever.

Does True Love Last Forever?

Jan's optimism notwithstanding, we have learned that Kipling's words from "The Lovers' Litany," "Love like ours can never die," are little more than a hopeful fantasy. Psychologist Dorothy Tennov, who interviewed and queried more than one thousand people about their love experiences, has concluded that, on the average, romantic love can be expecxted to last somewhere between eighteen months and three years. This does not mean that a man and a woman will not continue to love and cherish one another once their three years are up, but it is true that the nature of the bond that keeps them together will change.

Psychologists have coined the term companionate love to describe the feeling that keeps a man and a woman together over the long haul. It is a feeling of caring, respect, and liking for someone with whom our life is deeply intertwined. It does not have the fire of romantic love, but it can be a very special feeling that gives the relationship meaning. Companionate love is what couples who have been together for many years are talking about when they say they love each other.

But back to romantic love. Like any other emotion, it thrives on uncertainty and novelty. When we first begin to have the feeling that we might be falling in love with another person, it makes everything seem fresh and new. We want to tell our loved one our every thought. We want to share our dreams as well as our fears. Events that have occurred in the past, that at one time seemed ordinary enough, take on a new meaning as we fill in our lover on our history. We want to make sure that he or she knows everything about us and that we know everything about him or her.

But as time passes, the novelty of the relationship inevitably begins to wear off. For couples who are able to make the transition to companionate love, this will not pose much of a problem. But those who were counting on romantic love to sustain their attachment to each other are in for some rough times. While at one time, they could not wait to tell each other about every last detail of their day, they reach the point where it feels all too boring to talk about. A friend of ours once commented that he thought that the end of romantic love was in sight once the couple ran out of stories about their past to tell each other. Couples whose relationships thrive over time have an ability to continue to appreciate sharing their thoughts, but all too many people end up like the countless couples all of us have seen at restaurants, sharing a meal without exchanging a word. Without the impetus of romantic love, they are left with nothing to say to each other.

Uncertainty, the other champion of romantic love, serves to make any emotion more intense. Just as fear is likely to be especially strong when we do not know what the outcome of some dreaded event will be, our feelings of romantic love will be strongest when we are not completely confident that we have a secure bond with the person we so desperately desire. Jan's passionate love for Robert was undoubtedly strengthened by her uncertainty about his commitment to her. The peaks of ecstasy associated with being in love usually occur before we are certain that our feelings of love are reciprocated and when we see some evidence that perhaps the other person does indeed feel about us the way we feel about him or her. It is sad, even tragic at times, but as we begin to feel more secure with a relationship, the intensity of our feelings about it are likely to diminish. Perhaps it is a perverse quirk of human nature, but we do seem to want most the things we cannot have or are not sure we do have.

Tennov observed that virtually all of the people she interviewed who reported that their feelings of romantic love for their partner did not fade with time never felt completely secure with their relationship. Barbara, for example, claims that she is every bit as much in love with her husband after twelve years of marriage as she was on the day she became engaged to him. "It may seem kind of silly, but I still get a little nervous around the time I expect him to get home because I'm so excited to see him. I do all kinds of little things to try to please him, like making his favorite dinner or dessert, or getting the children to play outside so he can read the paper in peace. He can still make me melt after all these years just by smiling at me."

For those of you who might be feeling envious, consider the other side of the coin. As Barbara tells it, "Sometimes I get disgusted with myself for trying so hard to win his love. I suppose it's because I've never felt certain that he won't just walk out one day—after all, my first husband did. Sometimes he seems to appreciate the things I do for him, but other times he just scowls and won't talk to me. I'm thirty-six years old, but lots of times I feel like a teenager who is having her first crush on a boy. I'd give anything for a normal marriage. I'd gladly trade the passion I feel for Doug when things are going well for a sense of security, even if it meant things would be a little dull."

Indeed, Tennov described one man who was "in love" with his wife for over thirty years. The marriage ended with her death and he subsequently remarried. Although he took his second wife for granted and described the relationship as "boring at times," he preferred it to his first marriage. The feelings of security and trust he experienced with his second wife were much more comfortable than the emotional roller coaster he was on in his first marriage.

Romantic love could be the icing on the cake if people only did not take it so seriously. But many of us have succumbed to the myth that if only we find the right person, if only we could meet our Prince or Princess Charming, our love would indeed last forever. Every semester I (L.H.J.) ask the one hundred and fifty students in my Human Sexuality class to write anonymous responses to a variety of questions and issues. Last semester, after presenting the evidence regarding the ephemeral nature of romantic love, I asked them how they felt this would affect their relationships. Many of the students had what I would call realistic expectations. One twenty-year-old woman, for instance, wrote, "I've been living with a man for two years, and already the intensity of the relationship isn't what it used to be. But I think knowing that there is another person in the world that you can always count on more than makes up for the excitement of being in love. We plan to get married as soon as we graduate, and we have promised each other to work hard on our relationship so we don't lose what we have."

But a majority of the students, who are of prime marrying age, subscribe to the myth that romantic love can last forever if only you find the right person, and many of them are downright angry at my suggestions to the contrary. My favorite example came from a twenty-two-year-old man who wrote, "I think this theory about romantic love lasting only three years is a bunch of shit. When I get married, if I ever feel that I am no longer in love with my wife, I'll know I made a mistake and should get a divorce." Unless he changes his ideas, he would be well advised to find a good divorce lawyer and put him on retainer.

Perhaps saddest of all are those responses that come from married students who are beginning to feel unhappy because the intensity has gone out of their relationship when they had expected it to last forever. For instance, a twenty-three-year-old woman wrote, "I've been married for three years and the excitement is gone. I miss it terribly. I'm going to work on trying to recapture the romance, but I don't know what I'll do if I can't get that old feeling back." Unless she can change her views about the relation between romantic love and marriage, she will probably be contributing to the divorce statistics within a few years.

No, contrary to Kipling's suggestion, romantic love does not last forever. Perhaps European social critic Denis de Rougemont was closer to the mark when he wrote that the notion of marrying for love "is one of the most pathological experiments that a civilized society has ever imagined, namely, the basing of marriage, which is lasting, upon romance, which is a passing fancy."

LOOKING PAST LOVE

"How do you know when you've met the right person for you?" we've asked numerous men and women. The most common answer: "You've got to trust your feelings."

Perhaps we psychologists are partly to blame for this clichéd advice. We're always telling people that they have to pay more attention to their feelings but when it comes to selecting a spouse, especially when it means leaving an existing marriage for someone new, men and women would be well advised to look past their feelings, to trust their intellect and their reason. Few of us would be interested in marrying someone for whom we did not have strong feelings, but passion and romance should be viewed as icing on the cake rather than the sole justification for making such an important decision.

Remember John and Michelle from the previous chapter? Theirs wasn't a particularly intense romance, but they gradually gained a sense of confidence that they were right for each other, that they could have a satisfying life together. As John tells it: "Something clicked with me the first time I met Michelle. I knew right from the start that I could have very special feelings for her. I know it sounds stupid, but we were on the same wavelength, we could really talk to each other. With my first wife, it always seemed like we were competing with each other, even when discussing the simplest things. But with Michelle it was different. I felt I could trust her with even my deepest, darkest secrets."

Michelle has much the same view of how their relationship has unfolded. "Although my first marriage wasn't terrible, I knew I would never be very happy in it, so I left. Perhaps it is a somewhat cynical view, but I wasn't looking for my 'one and only.' I believed there were probably thousands of men out there with whom I could have a satisfying marriage.

"John seemed to fit my ideal right from the start. He was always interested in what I was thinking or feeling, something that my first husband was incapable of even feigning. I liked John when I first met him, and my feelings for him just gradually grew stronger. I don't know if there was ever a particular moment when I thought to myself, 'I'm in love with him,' but as time passed I became more and more confident that he was a man I could be with for the rest of my life."

If their story doesn't sound particularly romantic, consider what they have to say after ten years of marriage. When we asked them if they had one particular reaction to their second chance, John replied, "I'm just grateful that I have found someone whom I can love so much." Michelle's response was similar. "I used to think I could be happy with any number of men who had the qualities I was looking for, but now, corny as it may sound, I believe that John and I were meant for each other. We seem so compatible in every way that I don't believe there is anyone else I could be happier with."

John and Michelle refuse to accept any credit for being especially wise about making the most of their second chance. They attribute much of their success to good fortune—they were lucky, so they say, to find a partner who was good and decent, and easy to live with. But they were smarter than their modesty allows them to admit. John, for instance, acknowledges being attracted to women who are nothing like Michelle. "I have had fantasies about being with a tall, not-too-smart, very uninhibited blonde. I've met a few women who fit the bill, but a part of me knew I would never be happy with such a woman for very long." It is rare for people to recognize that the type of person they are attracted to may not be good for them in the long run. Most of us have a tendency to adjust our beliefs to make them consistent with our emotions. John was too smart for that.

Michelle was equally wise. Because of her unhappy first marriage, she developed a very clear sense of the qualities she wanted in a second husband, and she didn't waver. "When I would meet a man after my divorce, I always would ask myself if I could live with the qualities I didn't like in him. Would I be able to stand his irritating habits ten years down the road? I had learned enough from my first marriage to know that I couldn't change anyone by marrying him, no matter how much we loved each other, so I had better be sure I knew the difference between what I could and could not tolerate. John was the first man I met for whom the answer was yes—that I could live with his irritating habits over the long run. There were a couple of things about him that bothered me—for instance I didn't like his feeling so free to tell me about all the other women he found attractive. He still does it, and it still irritates me after all these years, but it's not something that I can't live with. It may not sound very romantic, but John had all the positive qualities I was looking for in a husband, and none of his less desirable qualities were intolerable."

John and Michelle both prepared a mental checklist of the qualities they were looking for in a spouse. They had learned from their first marriages that it isn't safe to rely on feelings alone—indeed, it can be downright dangerous. Liking one's partner is more important in the long run than passion.

Love can be blind, so it is not always the easiest thing in the world to determine if we really like the person we are in love with. How can you tell the difference? Psychologist Zick Rubin's test, designed to measure liking for one's partner, provides useful clues. Based upon the items in his scale, there are several important questions one should ask before deciding to marry. First, do you consider your partner to be unusually well adjusted? Do you admire how he or she handles problems, reacts to stressful situations, deals with others who are angry or upset? Or, do you find yourself making excuses for your partner—such as, "She's upset now, she didn't really mean what she said," or "He's been under a lot of pressure lately, he's usually not like that." If you can answer yes to the former, it's a good sign that you like your partner. If you find yourself making the excuses, then your feelings of passion may be coloring your judgment.

A second important consideration is how your family and friends react to your partner. Do you look forward to introducing your prospective spouse to those close to you, confident they will like him or her as much as you do? Is your partner the type of person who most people react favorably to after a brief acquaintance? If the answer is yes, then you're on solid ground. However, if you find yourself dreading the prospect of your partner meeting your friends, you may be in trouble. If you find yourself thinking "They won't understand him like I do" or "They won't be able to appreciate all her wonderful qualities like I can," you may be allowing your passion to interfere with your judgment. We tend to be proud of the people we like. If we feel defensive, embarrassed, or ashamed of a prospective spouse, the relationship will be in real trouble once the passion begins to fade.

Third, it is important to consider how similar one is to one's prospective spouse. It may be romantic to believe that "opposites attract," but psychological research has made a very strong case to show that "birds of a feather flock together." Dating couples tend to be similar on a wide variety of characteristics, including socioeconomic background, religious and political values and attitudes, personality style, intelligence, and physical attractiveness, to name just a few. It also has been established that couples who stay together over the long term are more similar than couples who divorce.

Determining how similar one is to a partner can be a tricky thing, because we all tend to be more aware of differences than similarities. We've heard lots of people say, for example, "My husband and I are completely different. He is very quiet and likes to stay at home, while I'm outgoing and prefer to be on the go." What these people often forget is that they have very similar values about raising children, religion, or politics, they may enjoy the same type of movies or books, or they may agree about how to plan for their later years. In other words, differences are always more salient than similarities.

It may be difficult to evaluate similarities and differences, but it is not impossible as long as one is willing to take a hard look at one's relationship. With the aid of hindsight, Jan wishes she hadn't ignored the differences between Robert and herself. "While we were dating, there wasn't really one thing we enjoyed doing together except having sex. He would grudgingly agree to go to a play with me, or I would go to a basketball game with him—which I hated—and then we'd rush back to his place to make love. We even had a whole list of topics we agreed not to discuss because we'd always end up in an argument. And to top it off, it wasn't until after we were married that I found out how different we really were."

Everyone hopes to find their Prince or Princess Charming, whether it is in a first or a second marriage. The problem, it seems to us, is that our society has come to place such importance on feelings, on passion and romance, that it is all too easy to become beguiled by the Prince's armor or the Princess's gown and to forget that real Princes and Princesses have more substance. They are people we can share our innermost thoughts with over the years, they are people who will always have our best interests at heart, they are people who will share our triumphs and comfort us when we are down. Feelings of passion and romance, while wonderful, are not enough to allow us to see past the superficial.

We are all too aware of how easy it is to advise others to be rational and logical when selecting a spouse, but, oh, how difficult it is to do it while under the spell of intense emotions. Perhaps it is not the best solution to this dilemma, but we admire the decision a friend of ours, Debbie, made to ensure that she would not make a mistake with her second chance. As she tells it: "I got married the first time when I was twenty for the usual reasons—I was in love and no one could tell me that Bill wasn't right for me. It only lasted for two years.

"I was thirty-two when I met Don, and it happened all over again. The feelings I had for him were incredibly strong. He wanted to get married after we had been dating for a few months, and I was pretty sure it was right, but I was determined not to make the same mistake a second time. So we agreed to live together. After about a year, the passion and romance were at manageable levels and I could begin to see his faults more clearly. We would have arguments and times when we wanted to be alone, but I still had the sense that our relationship was very strong. That was when I knew it was right to get married. You might say we got married as soon as we fell out of love."

Debbie will never be accused of being an incurable romantic, but she continues to be happily married after eight years, confident that her Prince Charming is there for the long term.

CHAPTER 3

Estranged
Bedfellows

STEPHANIE GAVE HERSELF an admiring look in the mirror. "Not bad," she said to herself, "for someone who's thirty-something." She knew she looked sexy in the black cocktail dress, even though her husband, Bob, would have a fit when he saw how much cleavage it revealed.

She had mixed feelings about their plans to go out to dinner. Based on eight years of oh-so-tedious experience, she knew her husband would be monitoring her behavior closely. She would get one of those icy glances every time she ordered another drink, every time she got excited and talked too loud, or every time she laughed too enthusiastically. She could count on his playing his refined, genteel, stick-in-the-mud role to the hilt. If nothing else, he was predictable.

On the other hand, she was looking forward to the evening out because they were meeting their neighbors Chris and Gloria. It was rare that they socialized with anyone other than her in-laws, so it was a real treat to be going out with friends. Gloria wasn't all that much fun—she was too much like Bob—but Chris was another story. He was witty and irreverent, much like herself. She didn't know him all that well, but he had just won the neighborhood round-robin tennis tournament that Stephanie had helped organize. The four of them were going out to celebrate, and she was confident that Chris would put some life into the evening.

Stephanie and Bob made it through the twenty-minute ride to the restaurant without any overly harsh words. There was the predictable "Do you think you're dressed appropriately for a woman who's the mother of three children?" and her usual rejoinder, "I know you want me to look like a nun, but I don't care to." But Stephanie kept her temper, and Bob was too civilized to start a full-fledged fight. As the hostess led them to their table, Stephanie was glad to see Chris and Gloria were already there. It would spare her any more dreary remarks.

Stephanie gave Gloria a perfunctory hug before turning to Chris. "Well, if it isn't the neighborhood tennis champion. Congratulations, Chris," she said as she gave him a kiss on the cheek.

"Thank you, thank you," Chris said as he hugged Stephanie just a little more tightly than politeness allowed. "But my skills as a tennis player, suspect as they are, pale in comparison to your skills as an organizer. I should be the one thanking you. I was lucky enough to win, but we all had a great time, and it wouldn't have happened had it not been for you."

Stephanie continued to smile at Chris as she took her seat across from him. Perhaps he was so interesting because he was a study in contrasts. He was approaching his fortieth birthday, but his beard was already almost completely gray. He looked like a svelte Kenny Rogers. His appearance, taken together with his soft, Southern drawl, made him seem like the kind of man who should be spending his weekends at stock car races rather than winning tennis tournaments. But shortly after meeting him at the beginning of the summer, Stephanie knew he was an extremely intelligent, literate man, and best of all, he didn't take himself very seriously. She had to force herself to take her eyes off him.

She was lost in her own thoughts for several minutes, but in the background she could hear Bob talking about the weather. "Not nearly as muggy as it usually is during late August," he was saying. Good ole Bob. You could always count on him to drag out the tired and trite.

"How about another drink, Steph?" Chris's inquiry brought her back to reality. "Sure, another gin and tonic," she said to the waitress. Bob passed (one drink was his limit), Gloria ordered a second tonic water with a slice of lemon, and Chris asked for another scotch and water. The somewhat strained small talk continued until Chris interrupted, "I feel like dancing. How about it, Gloria?"

"No, not right now," his wife answered, as he knew she would. She hadn't danced with him since their wedding.

"Bob, would you mind if I borrowed your wife for a few minutes?" Chris asked.

Before Bob could answer, Stephanie rose and said, "I'd love to."

As soon as they reached the dance floor, Chris asked, "Do you know what the best part of the tennis tournament was?"

"Of course, winning the trophy," Stephanie said with a laugh.

"No," he answered in a low, serious voice, "it was getting to know you. Until this summer I've only been able to admire you from afar. But now, I'm actually holding you in my arms. I think you are the most beautiful, most desirable woman I've ever known."

Stephanie's heart started to pound furiously. A little innocent flirting could be fun, it could add a little spice to the evening, but this was going too far. After all, she was a married woman. . . . But, she admitted to herself, a married woman who was feeling very attracted to this man who was so different from her husband. Maybe that's why she felt so scared.

The rest of the evening was a blur for Stephanie. She remembers laughing at Chris's jokes, him laughing at hers, and the stony silence from Bob and Gloria. She felt younger, more alive, and more beautiful than she had for years. Was it Chris, she wondered, or would a little attention from any man have had the same effect?

Stephanie felt sad on the ride home, and it had nothing to do with the sarcastic comments from her husband. After all, he wouldn't be happy unless she wore a veil when she went out in public. No, it was something more. She knew the clock had struck midnight and she was back to her humdrum existence.

She awakened the next morning when Bob kissed her on the cheek. She looked up, surprised to see him fully dressed. "What time is it?" she asked.

"It's almost nine. I knew you'd be tired so I got the kids off to school. I've got to run—see you around six." He was silent for several seconds before adding, "I love you."

After she heard the front door close, Stephanie dissolved into tears. Her husband was a good man, she knew he loved her, and he tried so hard to make her happy. Why then did she feel so miserable? Why could she barely stand it when he touched her? She knew she had to endure her life with Bob—after all she had three young children who loved both their mommy and daddy and whom she couldn't support on her own—but how could she go on?

She had to forget about last night. She would shower and then get busy with the housework. Keeping busy always helped to dull her pain.

When she stepped out of the shower, the phone was ringing. She thought about not answering; it might be Bob. He was always especially attentive when he sensed she was in one of her funks. But if it was him and she didn't answer, there would be a thousand questions to answer later that night. She picked up the receiver, ever so tentatively, and said, "Hello."

"Good morning, my fair lady. This is the champion of your neighborhood tennis association calling to thank you for a wonderful time last night."

It was Chris. Her heart began to pound. "Good morning. This is a surprise." She tried to keep her voice pleasant, but neutral.

"Actually, I'm calling to apologize. I came on a little strong last night, and I'm sorry if I made you feel uncomfortable."

His unexpected apology lowered her defenses. "No, no, I had a wonderful time. If it hadn't been for you, Bob would have talked about the weather and politics all evening."

Half a minute passed in silence. "Will you have lunch with me today?" Chris blurted out.

Stephanie's heart pounded harder than ever. "I . . . I don't think that's such a good idea."

"Please, just this once. For the past two years I've seen you around the neighborhood, and I've been trying to figure out a way to meet you. Now that I have, I'm completely bewitched. Maybe if I could talk about this with you, I could regain my sanity. Won't you do it for me, to keep an aging tennis champion from being institutionalized?" Chris said, trying to lower the tension with his joke.

"Okay, but just this once."

Six months after their lunch, Chris left his wife, Gloria. Two months later, Stephanie left her husband and children and took an apartment in the same complex where Chris lived. They were married seventeen months after that. Eight years after their wedding, they continue to have, in Chris's words, "A knock-your-socks-off love for each other."

WHEN IS LEAVING A MARRIAGE FOR A SECOND CHANCE A MISTAKE?

Unfortunately, there are no simple answers to the very difficult question of when is it best to forgo a relationship with a new love and stay with one's spouse. There are so many variables involved that researchers have only begun to examine how the most obvious factors influence the success of a second marriage. The many subtle variables involved in the case of Stephanie and Chris remain largely a mystery.

We do know that it is common for both men and women to leave a first marriage because they have met someone new, someone who promises a more satisfying life. But we also know that a majority of these affairs do not result in a second marriage. It seems that the "third party" may serve to provide emotional support for someone who finds it difficult to leave a dissatisfying marriage, but when the leaving is finally accomplished, the nature of the affair changes, and it often ends within months following the marital separation.

Grace provides a good example of how this can work. "I knew I had made a mistake six months after I married Larry, but I felt I had to make the best of it. No one in my family had ever been divorced, and I was sure it would kill my parents if I left my husband. I endured for six years but then I met Hale. He came to work for the company where I was a receptionist. At first we were friends, having lunch now and then, but then it became drinks after work, and within a few months we were having an affair. It was wonderful. It showed me what I had been missing all those years. Hale wanted me to leave Larry so we could be married, and I was sure it was the best thing to do.

"Six months after I separated, I could hardly stand the sight of Hale. I discovered he was incredibly possessive—he couldn't stand it when I joked around with the other salesmen, and he would have a fit even if I talked to my mother on the phone for more than two minutes. So I had to tell him I couldn't see him anymore.

"I felt a little guilty because I wondered if I used Hale as a way out of my first marriage. I probably wouldn't have had the courage to do it if it weren't for him. Could I really have ever cared about him if I came to dislike him so much in such a short time? I don't know if I'll ever understand what happened, but I am grateful to be single again."

Grace was fortunate. Things did work out for her. But her ability to unequivocally state that her first marriage was a mistake comes with the advantage of hindsight. And hindsight isn't always so kind.

Remember Ted and Lisa from Chapter 2? In the midst of his affair with Lisa, Ted was also convinced that his marriage to Marion was a mistake. A few months after meeting Lisa he said, "Lisa showed me what I was missing. It was after I met her that I realized I had never really been in love with Marion."

You may also remember that after being married to Lisa for a few years, Ted wondered where he had gone wrong. "Life wasn't very exciting with Marion, but it was a hell of a lot easier than life with Lisa," he concluded with the aid of his hindsight.

Why did things turn out so well for Chris and Stephanie and so badly for Ted and Lisa? Were there warning signs that Ted ignored, signs that should have told him that he was making a mistake to leave Marion for Lisa?

We, too, are speaking with the aid of hindsight, but there does appear to be a pattern among the people we have interviewed. Before anyone leaves a first marriage for their "true love," it is crucial to determine whether they are leaving a marriage that is simply stale, one that has a few minor problems that could be fixed with a little effort, or one that is truly dissatisfying and beyond repair.

This is rarely easy to do. Consider Stephanie's description of her first marriage: "Bob was a good man. He was always kind to me, always trying to make me happy, and he bought me anything I wanted. And he was a wonderful father, the kids adored him. But we were just so different. He was the most serious man I've ever known. He didn't even recognize jokes much less think they were funny. I've never been able to take anything too seriously for very long. I want to laugh, to enjoy life. But Bob thinks that anyone who is having a good time isn't taking his responsibilities seriously enough.

"The worst part of our marriage was our social life. We spent almost every Sunday afternoon for eight years with his parents. If I would invite a few couples over for dinner, Bob would be so sullen and uncomfortable that I'd always regret it. Sometimes I'd feel sorry for him, but the last few years of our marriage I almost hated him for isolating me from the rest of the world. I was starting to drink more than I should, and I think there was a chance I would have developed a real problem had I not met Chris when I did."

In contrast, consider Ted's account of his marriage before he met Lisa. "I assumed Marion and I would always be married. Sure, there were times when I craved more excitement, but I really liked Marion. We got along well most of the time, and we agreed about all the important issues. We used to spend hours talking about all the traveling we'd do once the kids were on their own.

"There were a few things about her that annoyed me. For instance, I wished she would have been more serious about a career—we could have used the money—and I was always nagging her to exercise more—she seemed to be letting herself go. After Lisa and I got started, I saw these as fatal character flaws, but I have to admit, before I met Lisa, I was pretty content with my life, even though there were plenty of times when I felt as though I were missing out on something."

We do know from research that one of the best predictors of parital satisfaction is similarity. Couples who are alike in their values, their attitudes, their interests, and a whole multitude of other characteristics are more likely to have a successful long-term relationship than those couples who differ in important ways. So it is doubtful that Stephanie would ever have been very happy in her marriage to Bob, no matter how much counseling they tried. They were just too different. They couldn't agree how to spend their time, their money, how the children should be disciplined, how to behave in public, and a myriad of other things. As Stephanie puts it, "I know there must have been things we enjoyed doing together. Why else would I have married him? But I honestly cannot remember the last time I even wanted his company, much less enjoyed it."

Perhaps Stephanie could have salvaged her marriage to Bob, but it would have been a marriage in name only. They didn't have a relationship; they had no foundation for their marriage. Remaining married to Bob would have meant enduring the rest of her life, rather than living it.

Ted and Marion, on the other hand, had much more in common than Ted could recognize after he became involved with Lisa. Both Ted and Marion were former schoolteachers who shared the same vision for their children's future. They rarely disagreed about any major issue, and indeed, enjoyed taking long walks together during which they talked over their dreams of the future. Like many couples, they did not share too many specific activities, but they did enjoy going out to dinner and taking in a movie or an occasional play or baseball game.

In other words, Ted and Marion were like any number of other couples who had basically satisfying marriages. True, the intensity of their relationship had dimmed over more than a decade of marriage, but the bond that held them together was solid—until Lisa entered the picture. It was only then that Ted began to view Marion's shortcomings as unforgivable flaws. It was only then that Ted began to see his wife as directionless, dull, and matronly. It was only then that Ted decided he did not like his wife anymore.

The old cliché that suggests that third parties cannot break up sound marriages is simply not true. We've seen too many cases where, with the aid of several years' perspective, men and women wished they had stayed with their first spouse instead of opting for a new, intensely passionate love. But where did Ted make his mistake? How could he have known he would have been happier over the long run had he stayed with Marion rather than leaving for Lisa?

His first and biggest mistake was trusting his feelings rather than his reason. He was in love with Lisa. He couldn't bear to have a day go by without seeing her, or at least talking to her on the phone. And their physical relationship was so intense. "It isn't just sex," Ted protested at the time, "it is the tenderness, the affection. I love to simply hold Lisa in my arms, smell her hair, caress her hand." While in the grasp of his passionate love for Lisa, Ted convinced himself he had never felt that way about Marion.

On the other side of the coin, Ted found that he could barely stand to be around Marion once his affair with Lisa began to gather momentum. He believed she couldn't carry on a conversation for more than ten minutes without finding something critical to say about him. And their sex life was little more than a mechanical act to relieve physical tension. He didn't like it when she caressed him, and he couldn't stand to touch her any more than he had to.

Everything was clear enough to Ted. His feelings for Lisa were so intense, so completely positive, while his feelings for Marion—what was left of them—were so negative that there was no doubt about what he must do if he was to have a chance at a happy life. He would be forever miserable if he stayed with Marion, while Lisa promised a chance for happiness, for fulfillment.

Ted did not stop to consider (and would not have believed it even if he had) that the intensity of his feelings for Lisa had as much to do with their situation as it did with any of her personal qualities. They were, after all, having an affair. They were stealing precious minutes from their families and their jobs to be together. They were worried about being seen together in compromising situations. There was always an edge of anxiety, if not outright fear, to their assignations.

This fear and conflict served to heighten the intensity of their get-togethers. We have learned from research that the experience of love can be both heightened and prolonged if it is associated with conflict. Often, once the conflict is removed, the intensity of the love diminishes in short order. This is why so many passionate affairs fizzle as soon as those involved leave their spouse to be with their "true love."

Ted also failed to consider that his negative feelings for Marion might have something to do with his affair. He was basically a decent man who wanted to do what was right. He was not the sort of person who could have a casual extramarital encounter. If he was involved with someone else, it had to be because there was something wrong with his marriage. His conscience forced him to rationalize his affair with Lisa, and the easiest way to do this was to find the flaws in his relationship with his wife. He did not stop to consider that Marion's "nagging" may have had something to do with all his unexplained late nights at the office. He did not wonder if his negative feelings toward Marion might be explained, at least in part, by the fact that they had to resolve any number of difficult problems together—as do any husband and wife. They had to decide which bills could be paid in full that month, what to do about their daughter's failing algebra grade, if they could live with the peeling paint on the windows another year, or if they should borrow the money to hire a painter. On the other hand, when Ted was with Lisa, all they had to talk about was how much they loved each other and when they could arrange to be with each other next. There were no nagging little problems for them to solve which might put a damper on their time together.

Ted also failed to evaluate his relationship with Marion B.L.—before Lisa. Had he done so, he would have concluded that he liked Marion. She was rarely moody, and most of the time he enjoyed her company. He was comfortable with her, even when they did nothing more than watch a movie on television. He knew he could always count on her to have his best interests at heart, that she would never kick him when he was down. Few women, Ted realized, were better mothers than Marion. She genuinely liked her children but, at the same time, was an effective disciplinarian. Had he been objective, Ted would have realized that his problem wasn't his marriage to Marion, it was his vague feelings of restlessness and his need for more excitement.

And because he was in love with her, Ted was not able to be objective about Lisa. In retrospect, he realized he should have seen the signs. There were many occasions when Lisa would tell Ted about how angry she was with her husband when Ted didn't see that her husband had done anything all that bad. But Ted was in love and Lisa was the perfect woman, so, he thought at the time, he probably didn't understand the full picture. Lisa wouldn't have become so angry unless she had good reason to be. Needless to say, Ted's opinion changed once he was married to Lisa and he became the object of her periodic furies. With hindsight, Ted is able to say, "Lisa treats me the same way she treated her first husband. How could I have been so naïve?"

None of us is capable of choosing our feelings, of selecting the people we are drawn to. But all of us are capable of utilizing our reason and our logic to decide what we want our future to be. We can use our intellectual powers to determine what will be best for us and for those we care about in the long run. It is never easy to be objective about matters of the heart, and it certainly is not merely a matter of intelligence. Ted is a very bright man, but being in love can make the smartest among us appear to have a terminal case of stupidity. Had Ted stopped to consider his situation rationally, it might have given him the strength to get past his attachment to Lisa and mend his damaged relationship with Marion.

We all know the divorce rate in our country is higher than it has ever been, and we all have heard any number of experts provide their analysis of this. We live in an age of instant gratification, we're told, and people no longer have the will or self-discipline to work through their problems. At the first sign of marital problems, we dispose of an old spouse and search for a newer, better model. The implication of many of these expert analyses is that we've experienced a change in our character, a change for the worse that has made the institution of marriage and family less stable.

We're not so sure this is true. It seems likely that other changes have occurred in our society that make it easier for couples to terminate unhappy marriages. The most important of these is the number of married women who work. A generation or two ago, it was almost unheard of for a married woman with children at home to be employed, while now nearly 60 percent of such women bring home their own paycheck. This means, of course, that men and women who are unhappily married can afford the option to set up separate households—an option their parents did not have.

There is little doubt that any number of men and women have abandoned marriages too soon, before trying to work out problems and giving the relationship a chance to work. But as clinical psychologists, we're more impressed with the men and women who come for marital counseling who have little hope of ever having a marriage that is even remotely satisfying. We suspect that for every couple who have given up on marriage too soon, there is at least one, and perhaps several, who have stayed with hopeless marriages and given up their second chance for happiness.

Some of these couples are easy to spot. Arlene, for instance, insisted that Ray, her husband of more than twenty years, accompany her to marital therapy. Arlene presented their problems as centering on her husband's temper. "Ray rarely talks to me or our two daughters unless he's angry about something," she explained in a meek voice. "He is yelling at the girls constantly, and sometimes he gets physically abusive with me. I insisted we come in when he shoved me around our bedroom until I fell."

"She's exaggerating," protested Ray in an angry voice. "Yes, I do lose my temper more than I should but it wouldn't happen if she didn't constantly undermine my authority with the girls. I punish them, and they run to their mother because they know she'll let them off the hook. It infuriates me, but I want to work this out. I want to stay married."

After six months of therapy, things were no better between them. Ray would go as long as two weeks without becoming angry, but something would set him off and he reverted to his old ways. Arlene became harsher in her evaluation of their marriage and finally she asserted, in her husband's presence, "I'm not coming back for therapy. I hate him, and I've hated him for at least fifteen years. As soon as I get things arranged, I'm going ahead with a divorce." The therapist agreed that for six months they had tried hard to work things out with no improvement, so perhaps a separation would help them both to sort things out.

Two years later Ray called the therapist because he and Arlene had an argument about a comment the therapist made during one of their sessions. Arlene insisted the therapist said that Ray was completely responsible for their problems, while Ray remembered the therapist saying they shared responsibility equally. Ray reported that he still wanted to work out their problems, and that while Arlene continued to insist on a divorce, she had done nothing to initiate it. "We're getting along about as well as usual," he said without enthusiasm.

We've seen any number of couples like Ray and Arlene, couples who have serious and long-standing problems. The problems may focus on alcohol abuse, physical abuse, frequent infidelities, or complete financial irresponsibility. The couple may have tried several private therapists, talking with their clergyman, or various community agencies, all to no avail. But for one reason or another, they stay together. Perhaps it is fear of the unknown, perhaps it is an unwillingness to lower one's lifestyle, or perhaps it is a vague sense of obligation to the children or even the parents. Who can know for sure? But there are lots of men and women whose first chance has come up empty but who still cannot bring themselves to try a second time.

It is easy to decide what is best for couples like Ray and Arlene. Their only possibility for happiness is a second chance since their marriage is beyond repair. But for others, the best course is not so obvious. Ken and Jeanette, for example, are both in their early sixties, and they both wish they had opted for a second chance years ago. Now they simply feel it is too late for them, that life has passed them by. Ken and Jeanette spend no more than thirty minutes together each day—the time it takes them to eat dinner. During this time they discuss any business that needs attending to, but as soon as dessert is finished and the table cleared, Ken retreats to his study and Jeanette to her bedroom. They do not see each other until dinner the following evening.

When asked how she managed to get herself into such an empty marriage, Jeanette can only shrug. "It was a gradual thing. I thought of myself as happily married for the first eight or ten years, but Ken and I slowly grew apart. Neither one of us is very good at fighting, so when we would have a disagreement, we tended to avoid each other. For the second ten years of our marriage, we would periodically talk about doing something to make things better, but a few months would go by and things would be back to usual.

"I still remember my forty-fifth birthday. I knew by then my marriage was dead and our youngest son was in college, so I decided the time was right to make a change. I talked to Ken about it and he agreed. But every time I thought about calling a lawyer, something would stop me. I worried about how our kids would react—even though they were all adults. I worried about losing my friends—I wouldn't be able to keep up with them financially once I was on my own. I thought about it a lot, and I've come to the conclusion that things just weren't that bad between Ken and me. We were usually polite to each other, we continued to go out with other couples, and we had a very comfortable lifestyle. But now I can't help but be bitter and angry at myself. I've had no one to love or to love me for almost thirty years, and now it's too late for me. I've wasted my life."

Sad as Ken and Jeanette's situation is, it is understandable. There was never a single point where their marriage was so unambiguously bad that they could be certain that divorce was the best option. Yes, they were unhappy, but it was a passive unhappiness born from clear and serious problems. Their marriage provided a certain degree of comfort, of stability. But their indecision precluded the possibility of either of them having a second chance.

Remember John from Chapter 1? While married to his first wife, Helen, he was afraid his life could take the same direction Ken's and Jeanette's did. He began to wonder if he had made a mistake a few months after marrying Helen, but he realized he had no way of knowing for sure. Yes, he felt confined by Helen's demanding to know where he was every moment he was gone from their apartment, and yes, he resented Helen's constant complaining about his casual (in his view) approach to housework, but maybe that was just what marriage was like. Perhaps any woman would have the same complaints about him. It could be that all he needed was a little time to adjust. How could he know for sure? He had never been married before.

A few months turned into ten years and John still wasn't sure how he felt about his marriage to Helen. He was completely miserable at times, but they had a seven-year-old son, and John felt a strong responsibility toward him, to provide him with a stable home. On the other hand, John was terrified by the prospect of living his entire life without knowing the feeling of being glad to return home from a day's work. He had to be missing something.

John found the courage to ask Helen to try marital therapy with him. It was difficult for him because, as he predicted, Helen was at first shocked and then angry that he should suggest such a thing. As far as she was concerned, everything was fine between them. If John would just take his responsibilities around the house more seriously and try to be a little more pleasant, their problems would disappear.

They went through three therapists without finding one that Helen approved of. She would become furious at any mention of the possibility that she played some role in John's dissatisfaction and would refuse further sessions.

Finally, John decided to try therapy on his own. After six months of biweekly sessions, he knew that he should try a separation, but he was still reluctant to bring this up with Helen. She would be furious, and he didn't know how it would affect their son.

After six more months of therapy and six more months of wishing he could find the courage to move out, he met Michelle. It wasn't love at first sight, it wasn't an intensely passionate affair, but the rapport and intimacy he experienced with her were completely new to him—and wondrous. He moved out of the house ten months later.

To John's acquaintances, who did not know about his situation in detail, it appeared that he had left his wife for another woman. But John had done everything he could to give his first marriage a chance. He tried therapy with her, he tried therapy on his own, he tried several marital enrichment courses offered by the church and community groups, he even tried forcing himself to be especially attentive and romantic with Helen, hoping his feelings would follow the lead of his behavior. Near the end he was as confident as one could be that a separation was the best course of action, but still, it took Michelle to provide the impetus that allowed him to follow through.

Even after John moved out of the house, he tried to give his marriage a chance. He limited his contacts with Michelle (he did not see her at all for one four-month period) to see if any feelings for his wife might surface. He continued with his personal therapy to give himself every chance of making the right decision.

After a year passed, John no longer had any doubts. He found that it was a relief only to have to talk with Helen about their son's concerns. He never missed her, even when he was feeling intensely lonely. Given his Catholic background, leaving Helen was the hardest thing he had ever done, but he could tell himself truthfully that he had given his marriage every chance and that his decision was best for him.

John was fortunate to have had the resources to seek professional help, but even those who believe they cannot afford therapy can usually find a competent counselor through community agencies at little or no cost. Often, a close friend, whose judgment you trust, may be as helpful as, and perhaps even more helpful than, a professional therapist. A friend who knows your situation and who is willing to be honest with you may be able to provide you with fresh insights as to whether it would be better for you to leave your spouse to search for something better. But be prepared for the possibility that you will be told that you're being foolish risking what you have by indulging in a love affair. Your friend may not be completely right, but you probably should listen carefully. Friends often have the luxury of an objectivity that we usually do not have.

We hear a great deal about how selfish and self-centered people are nowadays, that the divorce rate would only be a fraction of what it is if we could really care for others. But as we discussed earlier, we're often impressed with how many people will sacrifice their own happiness to avoid hurting others. John and Stephanie are far from unusual. They both endured years of misery before leaving their spouses, because, at least in part, they couldn't bring themselves to hurt them. They were both lucky to meet someone who helped them to see that it was okay to take a second chance.

One fear that people like John and Stephanie have is that if they do leave their marriages, their spouses will be alone in the world and will never be happy again. They don't want to be responsible for the misery of a person they once cared about. This does happen but it is far from inevitable. John's first wife, Helen, remarried two years after John did, and based upon his infrequent contact with her, John concludes that she is happier with her second husband than she ever was with him.

Stephanie's story is even more dramatic. After she left Bob and Chris left Gloria, Bob and Gloria got together to share the cost of a private detective. They reasoned that if they could gather evidence that their spouses were having an affair, it would be to their advantage when it came to their respective divorce settlements. The sympathy and emotional support Bob and Gloria offered each other at their frequent meetings to discuss their situation soon blossomed into romance. They ended up marrying each other two days before Chris and Stephanie's wedding.

CHAPTER 4

Mission: Impossible

GEORGE WAS INTENTLY reviewing a file when his best friend, Dave, tapped on his office door. "Looks like you're busy," Dave said in an offhand way.

"Sure am. Isn't it great?" George and Dave were both mortgage loan officers, and the busier they were, the more money they made.

"If you're not doing anything tomorrow night, why don't you and Trish come over for dinner?" Dave asked.

"I'd like to," George answered, "but that might prove to be a problem."

"Oh, why is that?" Dave smiled, waiting for the punchline. George never could be serious, and he probably had some smart-ass comment ready.

"Trish moved out this past weekend," George responded without emotion.

"Oh, I'm sorry to hear that." George and Trish had been living together for almost a year. Dave had assumed George would marry her before much longer. She seemed so right for him.

"Well, things like that happen."

"Yeah, I guess they do," Dave responded, not knowing what else to say. George was Dave's best friend, but he was not all that surprised that George had not mentioned that he and Trish were having problems. George and Dave had worked together for almost four years, they played tennis together every weekend, and they had lunch together two or three times a week. But Dave still couldn't come close to understanding his friend. George had divorced his second wife shortly after coming to work at Dave's company, and before Trish he had lived with another woman for nearly a year. George seemed completely unfazed by the ending of all three of these relationships. Dave didn't even know if George had ended them or if the women had. And there was something about George that made Dave reluctant to ask.

Trish, however, was more than willing to talk about her relationship with George when she happened to run into Dave at the grocery store. Although her thirtieth birthday was less than a month away, her petite figure and her shoulder-length, dark brown hair made her appear younger. Seeing her again made Dave wonder how George could announce the end of his relationship with her without any trace of emotion. Dave invited her to have a cup of coffee, and she told him the following story: "After the first evening I spent with George, I couldn't believe how lucky I was to have met him. He was incredibly good-looking, which I didn't mind, but more importantly he seemed so together, so well adjusted. I married my first husband when we were both twenty, and he never did grow up. George seemed so mature, so sure of what he wanted that I just knew I could be happy with him.

"He told me that his first marriage didn't work out because his wife was so emotionally needy and dependent. According to George, she constantly demanded reassurance and finally, when he told her that it wasn't his responsibility to make her happy, she moved out. George told me the other women he had relationships with were similar to his wife and that he was hoping to find a woman with enough self-esteem that she wouldn't always be looking to him to satisfy her every emotional need. 'There are a lot of neurotic women out there,' he told me.

"I believed him because I've known women like that. He'd just been unlucky, I thought. I also knew that he wouldn't see me that way because I've always been a pretty independent person. Also, it had been five years since my divorce, so, if anything, I was worried about being too independent.

"I moved in with George four months after we met, and for the first month everything was great. I'd never been happier. But before long, I started to notice things that bothered me. He never seemed to want to talk things out when we had a disagreement. He would become very cold, very aloof, and just walk away when I would try to tell him why I was upset or angry. In fact, he wouldn't listen to anything that even hinted of problems. If I had a bad day at work and wanted to tell him about it, he would begin by making a joke out of it. But if I persisted, he would go into his ice-man act and say something like, 'You're a big girl. You don't need me to tell you how to solve your problems.'

"At first I thought he was overreacting to his marriage—that he was afraid I would become too dependent on him. Of course he denied it when I suggested this possibility, but I was sure it was true, so I decided to prove to him that he had nothing to worry about. I would teach him that it was possible for me to talk about problems without expecting him to solve them for me; that there was a difference between burdening someone and simply trying to get a little emotional support. But after almost a year, I had the feeling that I had gotten nowhere with him. He always reacted the same way—he would try to make a joke about what I was saying, and if I persisted, he would use that infuriatingly calm, ice-cold voice. It was obvious to everyone but George how angry he was when he went into that routine.

"I knew there was no chance for us when I told him that I was very unhappy and that I was thinking of moving out. He stiffened up and said in the coldest voice you can possibly imagine, 'If you think that's best, then you have to do it.' He never once asked me why I was so unhappy or offered to try to work things out. What's so amazing to me is that he seems to have no inkling of what an emotional cripple he is."

> "To See Oursels as Others See Us!"
> —Robert Burns

No one who responded to our survey admitted to having problems that precluded the possibility of their ever having a satisfying, lasting relationship. It takes more self-awareness than most of us are capable of to recognize when we, and not our partners, are responsible for our relationship problems. We did, however, hear from several people who, like George, complained about their string of bad luck; people who believed they had found the right person two, three, four, even five times, only to discover that once again they had been mistaken. These people, like George, seem incapable of understanding that they are suffering from more than bad luck, that perhaps it is something about them that results in their trail of failed relationships.

As Robert Burns suggested nearly two hundred years ago, it is extremely difficult to see ourselves as others see us, especially as one half of a marital relationship. Almost everyone enters a relationship wanting it to work; indeed, vowing to do everything possible to make it work. But once in the relationship, some people find that their old patterns and habits take over and undermine the bond they have with their spouse.

George saw himself as an even-tempered, easy-to-get-along-with man who never took anything too seriously. What he couldn't recognize was that he got mad just like everyone else and that he was virtually incapable of dealing with conflicts of any kind. Because it was so important to him to maintain his facade of being the ultimate nice guy, at the first sign of being threatened or angry, his unconscious kicked in and he fell into his cool, aloof mode. This allowed him to believe that he was above "such petty concerns," that he "wouldn't stoop so low as to exchange heated words with someone who was emotionally unbalanced." Unfortunately, George never learned that his style prevented him from having anything but the most superficial of relationships with women (and men, too, for that matter) and that he was unlikely to ever find a woman who would be able to tolerate his apparent indifference to her feelings.

Anyone can be unlucky in love once. Some people will get unlucky twice. And a handful may even be unlucky three times. But at some point those who have one bad experience after another have to stop and take a good look at themselves. It probably is more than their bad luck that is keeping them from having a satisfying long-term relationship, it is their own personal failings.

Because it is so difficult to acknowledge our own flaws, we must be sensitive to patterns. Do we hear the same complaints about us as we move from relationship to relationship? Do we eventually find the same flaws in our partner no matter how many times we believe we've found our "true love"? It takes courage to admit that we may be the cause of our failed relationships, but it is no harder than living a lonely, isolated existence because of our self-destructive patterns.

It also may be instructive to look for patterns in our interactions with acquaintances and business associates. Problems in relating to others are likely to be more pronounced and more obvious in intense, intimate relationships, but often such difficulties can become apparent in more casual relationships. George, for instance, was full of charm and humor, but only at the most superficial of levels. People who worked with him liked his company, as long as they did not have to work too closely with him. The office receptionist thought he was the funniest, sexiest man she knew, but then she only saw him a few times each day, and never longer than a couple of minutes. George's secretary, who often bore the brunt of his unreasonably high standards and his icy fury, had quite different feelings about him.

George is now in his mid-forties, and he recently accepted a similar position with another company—his sixth change of jobs in the past twenty years. Invariably, he is showered with invitations to lunch and dinner by his colleagues when he begins a new job, but within two to three years he is relatively isolated and he begins to tell the few acquaintances he has left how the company is filled with lazy, incompetent people. George is unusually competent himself, so his supervisors always have mixed feelings about his leaving the company. But there is always an audible sigh of relief when he finally does leave in search of "more congenial, more competent colleagues."

Despite the fact that the parallels between George's love life and his professional life are so obvious, he has made it to middle age with no more self-awareness than he had when his first marriage was disintegrating. Perhaps George is satisfied with his handful of casual acquaintances and his string of brief relationships with women. But it is more likely that, for whatever reason, it is too painful for him to take a close look at himself and how others react to him. It is important to him to retain his firm belief that everyone he meets is "too neurotic" to have a satisfying long-term relationship, rather than to explore his own potential for change.

George claims to be happy enough with his life, and some people who have known him ask why he would want to change. After all, he has been extremely successful in his career, so what does it matter if he has alienated a few secretaries and supervisors along the way? And he always seems to be dating one extraordinarily attractive woman after another, so why would he want to tie himself down? In many ways, George does seem to have it made.

Our response is that it is not George's lifestyle that is the problem, it is his complete lack of awareness as to why he does have the lifestyle he does. If George believed that he wanted to be successful at all costs and that the best way to achieve that success was to intimidate those he worked with, that would be one thing. It wouldn't make George a very nice guy, but at least he would be proceeding with his life in a planned way. But George sees himself as a tolerant, easygoing person, and it is only after he comes to believe he is surrounded by incompetent losers that his ability to charm others begins to fade. And George says he wants to have a stable relationship with a woman, that he is tired of his many years of casual dating. So once again, it is his self-deceit that is preventing him from achieving his goals.

Many people like George can make it through a good part of their lives none the worse for their own failings. If they are bright, charming, and attractive, as George is, they can fill their lives with their careers, casual acquaintances, and brief affairs to convince themselves that there is no need for self-examination. But the inability to connect with others usually catches up with such people. It may not be until their forties, fifties, or even later, but at some point they may experience despair over the emptiness of their lives. When looking back, people rarely focus on the money they made or the number of people they slept with. They value the times they spent with their spouse, their children, or their close friends. The tragedy of people like George, who cannot take a close look at themselves, is that they haven't had the deep, intimate relationships with others that give life meaning. They may end their days with a sense of emptiness and despair.

Two Common Problem Patterns

The factors that make a marriage successful are usually complex, yet often subtle. We have all known couples who seemed to have everything going for them, yet their marriage was a disaster. On the other hand, we've all known of cases where we were convinced that the bride and groom would never see their first anniversary, yet their marriage grows into a rock-solid partnership. Consequently, it is impossible to say with any certainty what sorts of people will never be able to have a stable relationship. Our knowledge of human behavior and marriage is not nearly to the point where such things can be predicted with any confidence. But enough research has been conducted by behavioral scientists to be able to identify the most frequent complaints that men and women have about their spouses. Let us take a look at two of the most common problematic personality types. We challenge you, the reader, to take a close look at the following descriptions, and if either of them sounds familiar, to summon the courage to alter the direction your life is taking.

The King of the House

The most common complaint women have about their husbands is that they are remote and distant, uninvolved in the relationship. Carla, for instance, was thirty-four before she married Ed. It was her first marriage and Ed's second. She had heard Ed talk endlessly about what a nag his first wife was, and she was sure they wouldn't have any of the problems Ed experienced in his first marriage. Carla had been on her own for more than fifteen years, and she had no more desire to control anyone else than she had for someone to control her.

Two months hadn't passed since their wedding day before Ed accused Carla of nagging him. She was astonished to discover how different his definition of nagging was from hers. As she tells it: "If I ask Ed to come to dinner before it gets cold, he'll accuse me of nagging. If I ask him to come out of his study and go for a walk with me, he'll accuse me of nagging. I can't think of a single request I can make of him that won't result in his accusing me of nagging him."

"I don't know how things could have become so bad so fast," Carla says in a weary tone. "Ed smokes and I'm allergic to it so he agreed that the only room he would smoke in is his study. The first month or two we were married he would go in there after dinner maybe three or four times in the evening for a cigarette and spend the rest of the time with me. But he started spending more and more time in there, until now (we've been married two years) he goes in there right after dinner and doesn't come out until it's time for bed. About half the time he'll fall asleep on his couch, so we don't even sleep together. I've tried to talk to him about how lonely it is for me to spend every evening by myself but as soon as I bring up the topic, he gets very angry and tells me I'm as big a nag as his first wife was."

We've heard from many other women who felt just as isolated and lonely as Carla even though their husbands did not have their own room to retreat to. Some men can spend five hours every night in front of the television and feel that five minutes of conversation is too much to be asked for. Others may go out every night with their buddies; still others spend every free moment on their hobbies. What they all have in common is an indifference, and in some cases an aversion, to intimacy with women.

We've seen several of these men in marital therapy when their wives have managed to drag them in, and what makes them especially interesting is that, almost without exception, they very much want to stay married. Ed, for example, seemed genuinely distraught when Carla brought up the possibility of divorce. He said that he loved her (although he never told her this when they were alone) and that he would work on changing so that she could be happy. He also was quick to point out that Carla could be very demanding and that they would get along much better if she would only allow him a little time to himself.

Ed and Carla worked out a compromise so that Ed could have time alone in his study and Carla could have the companionship she craved, and all was well—for about three weeks. Like so many men similar to him, Ed's good intentions could not be translated into sustained action. He spent about three hours with Carla the first three evenings, but on the fourth they had cross words about the monthly bills and Ed retreated to his study until the next morning. To his credit, he did apologize that morning and spent almost the entire evening with Carla that night. But he gradually increased his time alone until Carla could not longer control her frustration and anger. Carla's outburst provided all the justification Ed needed to hide away in his study. After all, she was a hopeless nag.

It is always dangerous to generalize, but men like Ed seem to fall into one of two broad categories. First, and Ed fell into this group, some men who distance themselves from their wives are unhappy with themselves. They may perceive themselves as failures (which may or may not be accurate), they may have regrets about the direction their lives have taken, or they may simply be bored with their routine. Ed, for example, had a small construction company that specialized in remodeling jobs. He was a good salesman and had no difficulty in generating business, but he was a poor manager and regularly lost money on his jobs. His remoteness from his wife was directly proportional to the amount of red ink on his books. Even though Carla was supportive and never chastised Ed for his shortcomings, he could not talk with her about his business prob lems. To do so would mean he would be admitting to his wife that he was a failure. Although he was in every bit as much pain as Carla, it was still easier for him to lock himself in his study than to share his feelings with Carla. Many men like Ed can easily share their successes and their triumphs with the woman in their life. When things are going well for these men, they may appear to be excep tionally capable of relating to women. But when their lives take an unwelcome turn, they retreat into themselves. For them, sharing their feelings with anyone, especially their wife, would be an open admission of their inadequacy. And their sense of their masculinity would never allow such a thing.

The second type of man who is prone to distance himself from his wife is one who tends to have rigid ideas regarding the appro priate roles for husbands and wives. He is likely to have come from a family where his father worked and his mother was a full-time homemaker. He learned firsthand that when the husband comes home from work, he plops down in his favorite chair with either a newspaper or the remote control for the television. His wife serves him dinner, and afterward, while his wife cleans up, he goes back to the television, or perhaps he goes out with his friends for the evening. He also learned that you don't talk to dad about your problems. Mom may have some good ideas about how to handle that older kid who's picking on you, or how to get that new girl's attention, but dad doesn't talk about things like that. He's the head of the household, and you don't bother the boss unless it's terribly important.

When boys who grew up in families like this become husbands and fathers themselves, they assume their role is to be the some what remote, self-indulgent, head of the household—the king of the castle. Wives are not equal partners in marriage—their role is to serve and pamper the man. Wives aren't for companionship, they have the television set for that. And these men couldn't imagine being close friends with their wives; they have their bowling or hunting buddies for that.

It's not that these men don't care about their wives—they are often devastated should their wives ask for a divorce. It is just that they have learned that husbands and wives have well-defined roles and these roles do not include emotional intimacy or, in extreme cases, even friendship. A generation or two ago, it was not all that difficult for such men to find women who had similar ideas about marriage. But times have changed. Now that women are more likely than not to be bringing home their share of the bacon, they are not interested (nor should they be) in coming home from work only to have to answer to another boss.

We've found this scenario to be especially common in somewhat older men and women who are contemplating a second marriage. A man in his fifties or sixties is looking for a second wife to provide him with the nurturing and household services he came to expect from his first wife. Never mind that his first wife may have found such expectations intolerable, it's no problem for him to dismiss her attitude as a symptom of her immaturity or selfishness. So our late-fifties man, who is a traditionalist at heart, sweeps his new love off her feet with his elaborate courtship and his gentlemanly ways. His bride-to-be most likely has been divorced herself for some time, so she has learned to take care of herself. She has come to value her independence but she is flattered by this man who seems so solicitous of her needs. But once she says "I do," he expects her to assume her proper role—that of serving him and not expecting too much in return. Needless to say, such marriages are in for some tough times.

The Queen of the House

The wife as the "ole ball and chain" is like most clichés—it contains a grain of truth. Most women have no desire to control their husband's every breath, just as most husbands are both capable of and interested in having a close, intimate relationship with their wives. There are, however, some women who have such rigid ideas about what it means to be married that their husbands soon get the feeling that they traded in their freedom for a very short leash.

Les, for example, was certain he found the woman he could be happy with for the rest of his life when he met Maureen in the office cafeteria. His first wife had died a year earlier, and Maureen was recovering from a vicious divorce; they spent hours talking about their hurt and comforting each other. After a few months of being sympathetic friends, their relationship began to move in more romantic directions. Although they were both in their mid-forties, they had a wilder, more passionate courtship than either had had in their first marriage. Often they would manage just a couple hours of sleep before their alarm clock announced the beginning of another workday.

Fourteen months after their chance meeting in the cafeteria, they were married. They took a month to travel through Europe for their honeymoon before settling back into their routine. But two weeks after they returned, Les experienced his first discomforting moment. As he remembers it: "It was the second weekend after we had returned from our honeymoon, and I got up early to play golf. I've been playing with the same foursome on Saturday mornings for about ten years, and it never entered my mind that Maureen would expect me to stop once we married. But she came into the kitchen while I was having breakfast and, in a rather harsh voice, asked, 'What are you doing?' She seemed shocked that I was about to leave the house without her. When I told her I was going to play golf, she said, 'You can't do that, I was planning on our getting some yard work done this morning.'

"It took us most of the week to get over that argument but then it started all over again the following Saturday when I left to play golf again. I might have been able to handle the golf issue, but that was just the tip of the iceberg. Maureen would get upset if I wanted to read instead of watch TV with her; she would be furious if I had a drink with some friends after work; she would even become irritated if I went to the hardware store without asking her to go along.

"The final straw came about six months after we were married. Every fall our foursome takes a trip to Pinehurst to play golf for four days. When I told Maureen about it, she said, 'I don't want you to go.' I was getting sick of her trying to control my every waking moment, so I probably wasn't as patient with her as I should have been, but I let her know I didn't care what she thought, I was going. One thing led to another, and she told me if I went on a vacation with my friends instead of her that she wouldn't be there when I got back. I said that was fine with me, and on the way home I was actually nervous that she wouldn't carry out her threat. It was like a ton of bricks had been lifted off my back when I got home and found that she had moved out."

Maureen's ideas about marriage weren't all that different from most people's. She thought that the marriage should come first once a man and woman tied the knot—not an unreasonable expectation. But she carried the concept of "forsaking all others" a bit further than most. She believed that her husband's desire to play golf with his friends meant that he cared more about "that stupid game" than he did about her. If Les wanted to read a book instead of watching TV with her, it mean that he found the book more interesting than her company. Maureen was constantly looking for evidence as to how much Les valued his marriage to her, and he could never do enough to convince her that he cared.

Obviously, it was Maureen's insecurities that caused her to have such unrealistically high expectations of the men in her life. She would often tell her friends, "I won't be second to anything or anybody," which in itself may not be all that bad. But she had such rigid ideas about what it meant to be first in someone's life that she invariably drove away the men who were initially attracted to her. Les, as well as her first husband, would try to appease her at first. They would give up time with friends and activities they enjoyed in order to spend it with her early in the relationship. But before long, her requests began to feel too confining, and when Les and Maureen's first husband began to rebel, her requests escalated into demands. Before long both men began to view Maureen as their jailer rather than as their wife.

Men and women who assume the "King" or "Queen" role in marriage almost always alienate their spouses. But the conflicts they have in their relationships are not all that different than the conflicts that many, perhaps even a majority, of men and women have. "Kings" and "Queens" are likely to have problems sustaining a relationship because they are extremes, not because their styles are unique.

Men and women do tend to view marriage differently, and they bring different needs and desires into the relationship. Some experts argue that men and women are fundamentally different, that evolutionary forces have shaped them to have slightly different makeups. A majority of behavioral scientists would argue that any differences between the sexes result from socialization; that is, in our society we expect little boys to grow up to be strong, independent men, and we expect little girls to develop into nurturing creatures who value relationships above all else. Whatever the source of the differences, however, virtually all experts would agree that men and women do tend to view marriage differently, and these differences can set the stage for conflicts.

Men value and want marriage; there is no doubt about that. Researchers have found that young men have a stronger desire than women to find someone to fall in love with so they can have a stable, long-term relationship. And should divorce occur, men are likely to remarry sooner than women. So, contrary to popular stereotypes, men are not trapped into marriage. They are not jealously guarding their freedom, careful to avoid anything that hints of commitment. They want to be married, and when they are not, they are usually unhappier about it than are single women.

Once they have "won" the heart of their true love, men tend to take the position that relationships are relatively maintenance-free. They are eager to get back to their premarriage routines, to spend time with their friends or hobbies that they neglected while they were caught up in the passion of courtship. They like being married, but don't feel it takes a special effort to do it successfully.

Women, on the other hand, tend to expect that the hours and hours they spent with their partner before marriage, each baring their soul to the other, will continue even after the honeymoon is over. Few are so unrealistic as to expect the intensity to remain as high as it was during the early stages of the relationship, but they don't expect the nature of the relationship to change. They assume that their new husbands will continue to want to take moonlit walks on the beach; they expect that their husbands will be eager to share their every thought with them just as they did when they were dating. Women tend to see dating and marriage as being on the same continuum, while men tend to view the marriage ceremony as marking a turning point in the relationship. So the woman wonders why her new husband isn't taking her out to dinner, and he wonders why she would want to waste the money now that they are married.

A second difference between the sexes is that women seem to have a greater need to talk about relationship issues than men do. If a woman feels that there are problems in the marriage, she is likely to want to discuss it with her husband—not an unreasonable expectation. Her husband, however, may view her desire to talk about "their problems" as little more than complaining or nagging. We've heard the following exchange more than once:

Wife: "He won't allow me to talk about my feelings, to tell him why I'm feeling unhappy."

Husband: "All she does is tell me about all my faults. If she would just tell me what she wants, I'd do it, but I don't want to have to listen to all those complaints."

We don't agree with those marital therapists and behavioral researchers who believe that men are afraid of intimacy, that they have been socialized to be strong and competent and this makes it difficult for them to share their innermost feelings with others. It seems more likely that men and women simply have different ideas about what it means to be emotionally intimate. Men tend to be more oriented toward problem solving. If they can't see a solution to an issue, they don't see the point of discussing it endlessly. Women, on the other hand, tend to place more value on simply expressing their feelings, regardless of whether they believe such talk will lead to a solution.

To illustrate, we know a couple who were having problems with their teenage daughter. The girl became involved with drugs, was failing her classes at high school, and frequently stayed out all night. The mother regularly spent hours talking about the situation with her own friends. She knew her friends didn't have the answers, but she found comfort in sharing her frustration and her despair with others. Her husband, on the other hand, had mentioned the problems he was having with his daughter to a couple of his close friends, and they had told him they were sorry to hear he was having trouble. None of these conversations lasted more than ten minutes. His wife couldn't believe how superficial these exchanges were, while he couldn't believe that she would want to spend so much time talking about something so depressing. The point is that they were both satisfied with their own style of emotional intimacy. It's not that one style is better than the other, but the difference can lead to frustration and anger when husbands and wives try to resolve their problems. The woman is convinced that if she can just explain her feelings clearly enough, all will be well. The man perceives her explanations not as a plea for understanding but as a litany of complaints. So the more she tries to tell him how she feels, the more he withdraws to avoid her "nagging."

Research has found that even when the relationship is more important to them, women are more likely to terminate it than men. Women tend to take the view that if the problems cannot be resolved, then it is better to end the relationship and try to find something better. Men, on the other hand, tend to be more passive about these things. They may see problems, but as long as things aren't "too bad" and there isn't anything more interesting on the horizon, they are willing to live with them. Perhaps because women are more active in evaluating their relationships, it has been found that they have, on the average, three times as many complaints about their marriages as do men. From the woman's point of view, they are more sensitive to problem areas and feel a greater need to resolve them. Men wonder why women can't leave well enough alone and simply accept that which cannot easily be changed.

Successful marriages are not completely free from these conflicts. Many couples have learned to accept and work with these differences, sometimes even to value them. The differences in style may serve to help them keep each other on an even keel, to be more effective in dealing with the challenges that life has to offer than they would be if they had to rely solely on their own coping strategies. But "Kings" and "Queens," the extreme forms of these masculine and feminine styles, can be extremely difficult to live with. They may find a partner who can tolerate their style, but more likely than not, they will leave behind a trail of failed relationships, all the time wondering how they could be so unlucky.

A final warning—beware of those who claim they have been unlucky in love or those who say they cannot find anyone well adjusted enough to sustain a relationship. These are the very people who themselves may be incapable of living with someone else.

We heard from a number of people who wished they had talked with their spouse's former husband or wife. While such a conversation could be illuminating, it seems unlikely that many former spouses would be capable of providing a dispassionate assessment. But at the very least, anyone who plans to marry someone who has been married before should listen carefully as to what he or she has to say about the first spouse. Perhaps everything you will hear is true, but it is also possible that what you hear will provide important clues about the personality of your prospective partner. And the possible pain from making a mistake makes it too risky to ignore such clues.

CHAPTER 5

Echoes of the Past

SANDY HAS BEEN MARRIED to Ben for less than a year, but she is already certain that she made a mistake. "My first husband, Doug, cheated on me the entire twelve years we were married, and I'm scared to death that Ben is doing the same thing," she says while trying to fight back the tears. "I was in love with Doug since the eighth grade, so when we were married a year after we finished high school, I thought life would be perfect. He had a steady, good-paying job with a cement contractor, and I was in training as a legal secretary, so our future looked bright.

"But three months after we were married I found out I was pregnant and everything changed. As soon as I started to show, Doug began getting home later and later from work and spending more evenings out 'with the boys.' After Chrissie was born, I quit my job to take care of her and Doug spent even more time away from home. What hurt the most is that he didn't seem to care if I knew he was spending time with other women. I would find scraps of paper with names and phone numbers in his pockets, and women would call for him frequently. He would tell me they were just friends but anyone would have to be a fool to believe that.

"I hated what was happening but I thought he was just having trouble adjusting to being a father at such a young age and that everything would be all right as soon as Chrissie was a little older. But six months after Chrissie was born, I found out I was pregnant again, and things only got worse. He wouldn't come home until midnight three or four nights a week, and every now and then, he would disappear for the entire weekend. When I told him I couldn't stand his constant affairs, he said that if I didn't like it, I could leave. But I couldn't. I had two babies and I was trapped.

"As soon as Melanie started the first grade, I went back to work. It took me two years to save enough money to get out on my own, but I was determined not to stay married to a man who would be unfaithful to me.

"The next four years were rough. Doug was always behind in his child support, and it was a constant struggle to make ends meet. I didn't have the time or the energy to get involved with anyone else. But then I met Ben. He was an office equipment salesman who regularly came by our office, and I liked him from the start. He was so different from other men. He was quiet for a salesman, almost shy, and after I hinted for a couple of months with no response, I finally had to ask him to lunch. We started dating immediately, and much of the time he would include my two daughters and his son from his previous marriage in our plans. He seemed too good to be true. While most of the men I had met were only interested in a good time, Ben really seemed to care about family. He was always telling me how much he wanted to settle down and have someone to come home to at night. I couldn't say yes fast enough when he asked me to marry him.

"But now I'm afraid I got myself in the same old mess. Everything was great for the first few months, but gradually Ben started getting home from work later and later. Sometimes I don't see him until eight or nine. I've tried to tell myself that he's working late but there have been lots of times when I've tried to reach him and he hasn't been where he said he would be. I want to trust him but I'm beginning to believe my friends when they tell me that all men are alike. They just aren't capable of being faithful."

Ben's perspective, as you might imagine, is considerably different. He doesn't understand what happened to the loving, sweet woman he married. "I was attracted to Sandy in the first place because she was so different from my first wife, Midge. Midge had the worst temper of anyone I've ever known. It didn't matter how small the issue was; Midge would yell and scream if she thought I had done something wrong. If I forgot to stop by the store on my way home from work, if I was twenty minutes late, or if I didn't guess correctly about what she wanted for her birthday—it didn't matter what it was, she would have a fit. For eight years I tried to do everything her way for the sake of our son, but finally I couldn't take it anymore. When I finally left, I swore I would never get married again.

"But Sandy was so different. She was reserved and dignified, but very friendly in a low-key sort of way, and I saw her handle all kinds of tense situations at her office without ever losing her temper. I was sure that I would never have the feeling of walking on eggshells if I married her.

"Boy, was I ever wrong! Sandy doesn't yell and scream the way Midge did, but she has her own way of letting me know how displeased she is when I don't toe the line. If I have to schedule an appointment in the early evening, by the time I get home, I can count on Sandy's not speaking to me. If we go out with friends, I know I'd better not say more than hello to another woman or she'll let me know I was being an obnoxious flirt. I've just about had it with her attempts to control my every waking moment. I almost liked it better when Midge would yell and scream. At least then I knew what she was mad about. But with Sandy, all I have is this vague feeling that I've let her down and I'm getting sick of it."

Sandy and Ben are both suffering as a result of the sins of their partner's ex-spouse. Sandy's first husband was an incurable womanizer, so Sandy suspects that all men—especially men who show an interest in her—are incapable of remaining faithful. And Ben's first wife used her temper to keep Ben on a short leash, so Ben is especially sensitive to any signs that his wife is trying to control him by expressing displeasure.

When a first marriage ends, whether it's with a sense of relief or loss, most people feel that at least they will get a fresh start with their next relationship. We all like to believe that we learn from our mistakes and that we are wise enough not to repeat them. We expect that given a second chance, we will build on our strengths, eliminate our shortcomings, and make the marriage a roaring success. What is difficult for most of us to imagine is that a failed first marriage, no matter how miserable it was, still creates certain expectations as to what marriage is all about—and what we are all about—and these expectations can hinder our adjustment to a second marriage.

In some ways, Sandy's situation is straightforward. Her first husband cheated on her openly and often, so it comes as no surprise to anyone that she would worry about her second husband's fidelity. She would try to tell herself that men were not all alike, that while some men could not resist even the mildest temptation for a little novel sex, there were others who placed much more value on family stability than sexual variety. But at another level, she wasn't so sure about this. It had happened to her once, it had happened to lots of her friends, so who was to say that it couldn't happen to her a second time. She wanted to believe that Ben was different, that he would never risk their marriage for a meaningless fling, but she couldn't be sure. As much as she hated herself for doing it, she couldn't help but make mental notes of his whereabouts, paying special attention to those occasions when he wasn't home on time or when he wasn't where he said he would be. She couldn't relax when they were with friends because she felt compelled to keep one eye on Ben, to make sure that he wasn't too attentive to any of the women in the group. She even became suspicious of some of her friends who seemed to like Ben "too much." Most people would agree that to a certain extent, it is only natural for Sandy to be sensitive to any signs pertaining to Ben's loyalty, given her experiences in her first marriage.

What is not so obvious is that her first marriage caused Sandy to formulate certain feelings about herself. Like so many people in her situation (both men and women), she began to wonder if it might be something about her that made her first husband jump into bed with every willing woman. Maybe she wasn't attractive enough, maybe she wasn't very good in bed, or maybe she wasn't interesting enough to hold a man's attention and interest. Sandy couldn't articulate these feelings on her own, but, nonetheless, they left their mark. Rather than serving as an opportunity to learn about relationships, her bad experience in her first marriage made it even more difficult for her to make a success of her second chance.

Those who find themselves in Sandy's situation and begin to wonder if they did something to drive their spouse into the arms of a stranger react in a variety of ways. Some women may go overboard in exercising or dieting in the futile belief that if only they are sexy enough, their husbands will not be tempted by other women. Others may become sexually demanding in the belief that if their husbands get more than they can handle at home, they will not have the energy to stray.

But other women, and Sandy was one of these, react in just the opposite way. When Sandy initially became convinced that her first husband was involved with other women, she began to gain weight, putting on forty pounds over a three-year period. She lost most of the excess weight after her divorce, but within six months of her marriage to Ben, she began to put on the extra pounds once again. Some psychotherapists argue that gaining weight can be a defense mechanism, that women like Sandy are trying to protect their self-esteem. If they are overweight, then their husband's affairs are not a rejection of them, but a reaction to a much more superficial issue—namely, the extra pounds. It is as if these women are saying to themselves, "It's not that he doesn't love me, he just doesn't find me very appealing since I've gained all this weight." In other words, it is less of a blow to one's self-esteem to think that one's partner is straying because of a few extra pounds than because of the possibility that he simply doesn't care.

Other theorists who place less stock in such Freudian explanations would argue that the extra weight could result from the stress and anxiety caused by worrying about the partner's fidelity. It is possible, if not likely, that Sandy used food the same way other people use tranquilizers or alcohol. When she began to worry that Ben was with another woman when he didn't arrive home on time, she would have a piece of cake or a couple of candy bars to calm her grinding stomach.

Sandy also reacted to her concerns about Ben's fidelity by losing much of her interest in sex. While they were dating, both Sandy and Ben marveled at how compatible they were sexually. Not only did pleasing each other seem to come naturally, they had fun during their sexual encounters, spending almost as much time laughing together as they did breathing heavily. But the first time Ben came home two hours late, Sandy found that she couldn't become aroused when Ben tried to make love to her that night. She couldn't get the mental image of Ben with another woman out of her mind. She wanted to make love to him, she wanted to show him that he could never match his experiences at home elsewhere, but instead, she found herself getting angrier and angrier as Ben caressed her body. Sandy's fears, fears that grew out of her failed first marriage, were causing her to react in ways that were undermining her second chance.

Although the issues were different for Ben, he reacted similarly to the pain of his first marriage as did Sandy. As Ben tells it: "I walked on eggshells for years with Midge until I realized at last that I could never please her, that she would always find something to get angry about. When it was finally over, I promised myself that if I ever did get married again, I would not allow my wife to make me feel guilty about every little transgression. I know I'm not perfect but I make a pretty damn good husband, and I have nothing to apologize for."

Ben was so determined not to repeat his "whipped puppy with his tail between his legs" role in his second marriage that he went out of his way to test Sandy. When he had to make an unscheduled stop to make emergency repairs on a recalcitrant copying or fax machine, he would purposely not call Sandy to let her know where he would be or that he would be late. He was not going to begin his second marriage by accounting for every minute of his time. Normally, a short call to let his wife know he would be an hour or two late would have been an act of simple consideration. But after having to account for his whereabouts minute by minute with Midge, the phone call was no longer a matter of etiquette, it had became a test of wills—whether or not he made the phone call would determine who was in control. He wasn't going to allow Sandy to make him feel as if he had to answer to her. So when she reacted negatively to his late arrivals, he began to experience the same old suffocating tightness that he experienced in his first marriage. He couldn't see that his determination to remain autonomous was making the situation worse. All he could think was that he had to maintain his independence no matter what the costs.

Our experience has been that while almost everyone who has had a failed marriage claims to have learned from their mistakes, they tend to learn only those lessons that are painfully obvious. Some people might learn that they cannot abuse alcohol and their spouse and expect their partner to remained committed to their marriage. Others may learn that they cannot run a dozen credit cards to the limit, accumulate such a burden of debt that buying groceries becomes a challenge, and assume their partner will cheerfully volunteer to find a second job at night. Yes, people may learn how their big mistakes caused a marriage to fail, but often they fail to understand how their more subtle, yet perhaps more important, behaviors contributed to the divorce.

For any marriage to succeed, people need to know how to communicate, how to resolve problems in a loving, effective manner. The best way to learn this is to grow up with parents who have these skills. We do know from research that divorce begets divorce. People whose parents divorced while they were living at home are more likely to get divorced themselves. It is interesting to note that young adults who come from broken homes are actually more committed to the stability of marriage than those men and women who come from intact families. So it is not the case that seeing divorce firsthand leads one to believe that divorce is a viable alternative to conflict. Such men and women have firsthand experience as to how painful and disruptive divorce can be, so they are likely to take the attitude that "I'll make my marriage work no matter what." Research has not progressed to the point where we can answer with certainty why such people who are so committed to the stability of marriage are more likely to divorce than those who come from intact families, but it does seem likely that it stems from their failure to learn, by example, how to be effective problem solvers.

Many of the people we heard from said that the failure of their first marriage had taught them the importance of communicating, but some still had little idea as to how to do it effectively. Ben and Sandy, for instance, learned about problem solving and communication in their first marriages, but unfortunately, they learned the wrong things. Sandy tried a variety of approaches with her first husband in her vain attempt to put a stop to his infidelities. She cried and told him how hurt she was; she screamed at him to let him know how angry she was; she pleaded with him and told him that their two daughters needed a father. But nothing worked, and Sandy learned that some problems could not be solved, that communication, no matter how effective, simply did not make any difference.

Ben learned a slightly different lesson in his first marriage, but one that proved to be just as damaging as Sandy's. When his first wife would become angry at Ben, he tried to talk with her, tried to communicate his perspective. But she was the sort of person who wasn't interested in understanding her husband's point of view. She only cared about making her point, about asserting her will. Ben was not forceful enough to get through to his first wife, and he learned that any time they had a verbal exchange, he lost. The only strategy that had any impact, he learned, was to walk away from her, to refuse to get into a discussion about whatever she was angry about at the moment. When Ben did this, it would give his wife a chance to calm down, and she would actually be pleasant when he returned. So Ben learned that the most effective way to deal with conflict was to walk away from it, to ignore it, to pretend it didn't exist. He learned that if he tried to talk things out, he would only end up with the short end of the stick. His first wife was so verbally facile and such a dominating woman that he was made to feel that he was always in the wrong. He had come to learn that he was dead the moment he opened his mouth.

It is significant to note that Sandy and Ben ended their first marriages in similar ways. Once Sandy had enough money saved to make a fresh start, she rented an apartment and moved her share of the furniture out while Doug was at work. She left a note for Doug informing him of her plans to seek a divorce. Ben had his attorney serve Midge divorce papers on the day he had to go out of town on a business trip. Both Sandy and Ben had learned their lessons well—that there was no point in talking about problems, that, in some cases, actions speak louder than words.

To anyone not emotionally involved, the solution to Ben's and Sandy's problems is painfully obvious. When Ben's arriving home from work late activated Sandy's fears regarding infidelity, all she had to do was to explain to Ben how she felt. Had she told him about the pain she experienced when she was home alone with her two babies while her first husband was out with another woman, surely Ben would have understood. Had Sandy said that she was terrified by the possibility that Ben was seeing someone else, Ben certainly would have been more considerate about calling to let Sandy know he would be late and where he was. And Ben certainly could have been more sensitive to Sandy's feelings. He had heard about Doug's other women countless times, and he knew how devastating this was for Sandy. Had he not been scarred by his first marriage, he might have allowed Sandy time to heal. He might have endured some feelings of being smothered so that Sandy would have time to develop a sense of trust in his loyalty to her.

But because of their painful first marriages, both Sandy and Ben could only think about protecting themselves. Rather than appear vulnerable by telling Ben about her fears when he came home late, Sandy would quiz him about his whereabouts and snap at him about trivial issues. And rather than understanding why Sandy was behaving as she was, Ben could only respond to the feelings of suffocation that developed in his first marriage. Part of him wanted to tell her that she had nothing to worry about, but old habits die hard. As soon as Sandy's words even hinted of an accusation, Ben would storm out of the room while informing Sandy that "you're not my mother and I won't answer to you!"

Perhaps one reason that marriages that are the first for one partner have a better chance of succeeding than marriages that are the second for both the husband and wife is that in the former at least one of the spouses does not have a history of unresolvable conflict. Had Sandy not been hurt by Doug's affairs, it would have been easy for her to understand Ben's fears of being dominated and controlled. And had Ben not spent years under the thumb of his first wife, he could have allowed Sandy the time she needed to develop confidence that he was as committed to their marriage as she was.

ELIMINATING THOSE ECHOES FROM THE PAST

What can one do to prevent echoes of the past from damaging a second chance? First, listen to your partner when he or she talks about the first marriage. Listen with the knowledge that it is not just history, that it is information that will probably influence your relationship. When Sandy told Ben about her first husband's affairs, she was in effect saying, "It will be difficult for me to trust you, so please be patient with me while I learn that marriage does not have to be the way it was with my first husband." Sandy, of course, did not realize that this is what she was communicating. She was in love, she was filled with optimism and hope. But anyone who took the time to take a close look at her situation would realize that she would have these feelings just below the surface waiting to come out at the first hint of trouble.

So, if your partner talks about alcohol abuse in the first marriage, expect him or her to be frightened the first time you have that extra drink at a party, no matter how responsible you are generally. If abuse was an issue in your partner's first marriage, then know that the first time you become angry, your partner will be unrealistically frightened. If your partner was married to a compulsive spender, don't be surprised when he or she becomes upset the first time you come home with some item that you bought impulsively, even if you are known for your fiscal conservativeness.

Remember that no matter how much your spouse insists that the first marriage is history, it will, nonetheless, affect your relationship. We may want to put past hurts and disappointments behind us, but few of us are so rational that we are able to do this. Our expectations of the future are inextricably tied to our experiences in the past, and when something happens in our current relationship that is similar to events in our previous marriage, no matter how slight the resemblance, our fears will be activated.

Once you have a grasp of the historical issues that may affect your second chance, be prepared to display the patience of Job. Fears that develop over many years will not disappear in a few weeks or even a few months. It could take a few years, depending on how long your spouse was married previously and the severity of the hurt.

You can hurry this process along by first being willing to bring the issue out into the open and, second, offering lots of reassurance. For instance, had Ben realized that it was her fears that were causing Sandy to demand "Where have you been?" when he arrived home from work a few hours late, he might have said, "Look, I know you're worried about my becoming involved with another woman after your experience with Doug, but you have nothing to worry about. I love you and I value our relationship too much to do anything to jeopardize it." Sandy may have denied that she had any such worries, but given her history and given her overreacting to Ben's lateness, it was as close to a sure bet as one can come that she did have such fears. And having her fears articulated can only serve to make them less terrifying.

He might have gone on to tell her, even if it was in a lighthearted way, how sexy she was and how any man would be a fool to look elsewhere when she was waiting at home. Even if Sandy knew he wasn't completely serious, simply acknowledging her fears and offering plenty of reassurance would gradually build up her trust and her self-esteem. Perhaps Ben would have to have conversations like this dozens of times before Sandy began to respond and, indeed, it can become trying to have to offer constant reassurance. But Ben must remember that should he respond with anger or irritation to Sandy's inquiries as to his whereabouts, he would be repeating the pattern she had with her first husband, Doug. When Ben would snap and tell Sandy, "Leave me alone, you're not my mother," or stubbornly refuse to call when he knew he would be late, it only served to convince Sandy that her first marriage was happening all over again.

Next, you can take a close look at your own first marriage and acknowledge that there will be some issues that will be impossible for you to be objective and rational about until you accumulate a little history with your second chance. For instance, had Sandy not tried so hard to close off the hurt and anger she experienced in her first marriage, she might have realized that she could expect to be overly sensitive to any sign, no matter how misleading, that Ben was fooling around. Had she done this when Ben arrived home late, she might have said, "I don't want you to have to account for every minute you're away from home but because of what happened in my first marriage, it really scares me when you're not home by five. Would you mind giving me a call when you're going to be late? I'm sure I'll get over this in a little while, but it would really help if you can do this for me."

Such an admission and request would be hard for many people to do. Most of us like to think of ourselves as strong, independent people, the kind of people who can put our bad experiences behind us. To admit to others, much less to ourselves, that we are still hurting from something that may have happened years earlier is to make ourselves vulnerable. But the best thing about a good marriage is that we do not have to be strong alone. We have someone to share our fears with, someone who can help to make things better. So if Sandy could share her fears with Ben, not only would he be likely to want to help her, the very act of doing so would bring them closer together.

Even those couples who cannot imagine how their first marriages could possibly harm their second should be sensitive to the possibility that there may be lingering issues that could rear their ugly heads at unexpected moments. Elaine, for instance, was happily married for almost twenty years when her first husband was killed in an automobile accident. Because her marriage was so deeply satisfying, she never considered the possibility that she would enter her second with fears that could be destructive. Her second husband, Will, also had no reason to expect that anything about his first marriage would affect his second chance with Elaine. He was a successful businessman who loved his first wife a great deal but because he was so committed to his business, he did not spend the time he should have in nurturing his relationship with her. She left him after twenty-two years of marriage when his frequent vows to spend more time with the family turned out to be nothing more than unfulfilled promissory notes. He accepted complete responsibility (or so he said) for the failure of his first marriage, claimed to feel no bitterness, and swore he would not let the same thing happen with Elaine.

All went well between Elaine and Will for the first eight months. Will was surprisingly successful in limiting himself to a fifty-hour workweek, and Elaine was as comfortable with her second marriage as she was with her first.

Their first blow-up happened on a snowy February day when Will told Elaine that he had to go out of town the following day to see an important client. It was a three-hundred-fifty-mile round-trip, and because it was a last-minute sort of thing, he wasn't able to get a plane reservation; he would be driving. When Elaine heard the news, she felt as though she had been kicked in the stomach. She didn't understand why she had such an intense reaction, but she angrily told him she did not want him to go. Will, who had been trying so hard not to allow his business to interfere with his marriage, blew up. The trip was extremely important, he told his wife, and he would not allow her to dictate when he could and when he could not leave town.

Over the next few weeks, Elaine felt herself withdraw from her husband. He had apologized for his outburst, had even brought her back an exquisite bracelet from his trip, but no matter how hard he tried to bridge the gap, Elaine maintained her polite distance.

It wasn't until Elaine sought the help of a therapist that she realized that she was scared that she would lose Will the same way she lost her first husband. She had become increasingly tense with every trip Will took out of town but had managed to keep her feeling to herself. The snowy day in February was too much for her, however, and she felt she had to keep Will from leaving. She couldn't articulate her feelings on her own, but should he drive three hundred and fifty miles under such bad conditions, he might leave her alone just as her first husband had.

Echoes from the past are not always tied to the unpleasant aspects of a former marriage. Almost all marriages, no matter how unsatisfying they were, have at least a few redeeming elements. Usually the couple is so focused on the unpleasant aspects that they don't stop to think about what was good about the marriage. But that doesn't mean the good part did not exist. When such men and women remarry, they vow to do something about the bad elements, but they typically do not think much about what was satisfying about the previous marriage; they simply assume that those aspects will not be a problem in the second marriage.

Don, for example, was quick to tell anyone who showed the slightest interest that his first marriage of twelve years was "pure living hell." He believes his first wife was "crazy," and indeed he presents a convincing argument for his case. According to Don, she had a drinking problem and was abusive with their two boys. He doesn't attribute their divorce to any one factor, but states that they never got along and that their homelife was in a constant turmoil.

Don remained a dedicated bachelor for a dozen years following his divorce, enjoying every day of it. He was a successful engineer, so he had plenty of money, he had no difficult meeting women, and he was good enough at his avocation of playing drums that his band found enough engagements to fill his weekends.

By the time he turned fifty, Don was ready to settle down. He thought it was time to find someone to spend the rest of his life with. His decision undoubtedly had something to do with his meeting Beth, a strikingly beautiful thirty-four-year-old woman, when his band played at the Christmas party for Beth's company. Beth was as taken with Don as he was with her, and within a year they were married.

Don was confident that his second marriage would be a roaring success. Not once in the year he had known Beth had he detected even the slightest sign of emotional instability—signs that he had become very sensitive to as a result of his first marriage. And Beth was doing very well in her job in advertising sales at a local radio station, so Don did not even have to worry about the extra costs associated with marriage.

Their first big fight occurred within two months of their wedding day. Beth had moved into Don's house, and she was eager to redecorate. She had always been amused at the casual—and inexpensive—way Don had furnished his expensive house, but she attributed it to his bachelorhood. He didn't spend that much time at home, so he didn't care that his black Naugahyde sofa didn't fit in a colonial house. The house badly needed a woman's touch.

Don had gone along with her plans, assuming that she was talking about buying a few pieces of furniture. He was stunned at first and then furious when he came home one day and found that the living room, dining room, kitchen, and master bedroom were completely different. Not a single piece of his furniture remained in those rooms; Beth had replaced them all, and with things that looked very expensive. Don explained to her, in a manner that was less than calm, that he was hoping to retire early in a few years to concentrate on his music and that they needed to invest money, not spend it on such foolishness. Beth was astounded. Hadn't she told him that she was willing to pay for the furniture? Hadn't Don agreed to let her be in charge of the redecorating? What business of his was it how much she spent?

Don was dumbfounded. His first wife worked, but she used her check to pay for a large portion of the household expenses. She would never think of spending more than $50 without consulting Don first. Don was responsible for their financial planning. Wasn't that the husband's role? After all, a secure future was worth a lot more than a bunch of stupid furniture.

Don managed to suppress his anger after convincing himself it was a one-time occurrence. Now that Beth had spent thousands of dollars so foolishly, it was over and nothing could be done about it. The house was now filled with her furniture, so there couldn't be any more big expenses.

But the furniture episode was just the beginning of Don's surprises. After six months he assumed they were both settling into married life when Beth blew up at him upon arriving home from work one evening. Don had been home for several hours, and he was getting hungry waiting for Beth to prepare dinner. When she walked in the door and Don asked, "What are we having tonight?" Beth couldn't take it anymore. Don doesn't remember exactly what she said but it was something to the effect that he almost always got home before she did and if he was so "goddamn hungry," he could fix dinner himself. Beth informed him that she was getting tired of being his slave and since they were both working, he had better start taking on his share of the household responsibilities.

Once again, Don did not know what to think. His first wife may have had her faults, but she did at least have dinner on the table and clean shirts in the closet. It was his job to cut the grass once a week, remove the leaves from the rain gutters every spring, and take the cars in for an oil change every six months. Why wasn't Beth being fair about this?

Beth moved out shortly after their first anniversary, convinced that Don was a relic from the past. How could he expect her to wait on him hand and foot when she worked longer hours than he did? Don wasn't sorry to see her go. He concluded that she simply wasn't mature enough to take on the responsibilities of marriage. His first wife had her faults, but at least she was competent at the nitty-gritty details of married life.

This clash of expectations seems to be especially common when older men marry younger women. Men like Don may have had problems in their first marriage, but they felt comfortable about the traditional roles they and their wives assumed. They simply accepted the idea that there is "women's work" and "men's work," and their first wives, who grew up in the same generation they did, went along with this scenario without complaint. But when these men marry women significantly younger than themselves, they often learn, quite painfully, that the younger generation of women has different ideas as to what marriage is all about.

Most everyone who is contemplating a second marriage will be more than willing to tell their prospective partner what they did not like about their first spouse—and this is important. But it can be almost as important to talk about what was satisfying about the first marriage. As Don learned, it is not safe to assume that one will retain what was good and find a way to eliminate the bad. Your prospective partner might have quite different ideas about what are appropriate expectations for married life.

CHAPTER 6

Any Frog Will Do

WHEN KATHY STARTED COLLEGE, she never considered the possibility that she might graduate. She was interested in one thing and one thing only—finding a man who would love her. It did not take her long. "I met Jimmy the second semester of my freshman year, and I knew he was the man I would marry after talking to him for twenty minutes. He was tall, blond, smart, funny, and on the basketball team. I was so proud that he wanted me. The last two months of that year were the best of my entire life.

"I almost died when he told me he had to go back home for the summer. I didn't know how I could make it for three months without seeing him. When school began in the fall, I vowed that we'd never be apart again. So when June came around, I convinced Jimmy that the time was right for us to get married. I was nineteen years old, and I was sure my life would be perfect."

It didn't take long for disillusionment to set in, however. Within six months of their marriage, Kathy was worried that she had made a mistake. "We agreed that I would work while Jimmy finished college, but he was only interested in having a good time. I was working as a waitress, and I didn't get home until ten or eleven, so Jimmy would go out drinking with his jock friends during the evening. At first he would be home when I got there, but by the end of the year he might not show up until one or two in the morning. I was sure things would be better when he finished school, so I was determined to stick it out. Well, Jimmy didn't graduate with his class, and because he lost his basketball scholarship, he had to get a job. I thought that might help him grow up, but nothing changed. He still stayed out with his friends and would come home drunk at one or two in the morning. I wanted to divorce him but I was afraid of being out on my own. My family had made it perfectly clear that I couldn't ask them for help.

"Then one night at the restaurant I met Pat. He was a naval officer and his wife had just left him. We got to talking about our troubles, and he asked me to have a drink with him after I finished work. I was so desperate for a little attention that I didn't have to think twice before saying yes. We spent a lot of time together for a few weeks, and before long we knew we were in love. One night he brought me a single red rose and asked me to marry him as soon as I could. I had never been so happy before. So I told Jimmy I wanted a divorce (he was as relieved about it as I was) and moved in with Pat. As soon as my divorce was final, we were married."

The first few years with Pat were happy ones for Kathy. Pat was ambitious and smart, and his career was moving ahead rapidly. He earned enough money so Kathy no longer had to work. She intended to finish college, but her heart wasn't in it, so when their daughter Tracy was born, it was a good time to drop out of school and concentrate her efforts on being the best wife and mother she could be.

Their problems started when Pat's first wife decided that she could not handle their son and asked Pat to take custody. As Kathy tells it: "Jeremy was a difficult child. He was very smart but he was doing terrible in school. He could be pleasant, but if anything happened that he did not like, he could become extremely ugly and just plain mean. One time he told me that if Tracy touched anything of his, he would kill her, and the look in his eye told me that it was more than a simple childhood threat.

"Well, Pat couldn't handle it. He felt guilty for leaving his son to begin with, so he was not an effective parent. He would let Jeremy get away with murder, and then Pat would explode and come very close to abusing the boy. About the same time, Pat began working for a man who was impossible to get along with. He drank more and more, and began to take his frustrations out on me. He never hit me, but he could say the cruelest things you could possibly imagine. I would vow to get out but the next day, Pat would bring me a dozen roses and beg me for my forgiveness. This went on for twelve years. I would tell Pat I wanted a divorce, and then he would turn on his incredible charm and I would agree to give him one more chance.

"When Tracy started school, I got my real estate license—partly for the extra money, but mostly to give me something to do. That's how I met George. He had been recently divorced and was looking for a townhouse. He was in his mid-forties, a successful business-man, and completely different from Pat. George was a quiet man, and he was willing to listen to me talk for hours. I had never met anyone who cared so much about what I thought or what I was feeling. About that time, Pat got orders for Washington, D.C., so the timing was perfect. I told Pat I would not be moving with him.

"Tracy and I stayed in our house until it was sold and then I moved in with George. That was the beginning of the end. Before I moved in with him, we were spending every evening together and it was exciting. We would go out dancing and then back to his place (the sex was great). But as soon as we were living together, all he wanted to do was watch television until he fell asleep on the couch. I'm not proud of it, but I started dating other men. Most of the time I would only go out with a man two or three times, but every now and then I would meet one that I would date for a few months. I never let anything get too serious. I just needed a little fun in my life, and George wasn't interested in giving it to me. What amazed me is that George never questioned me once when I told him I was working until midnight. I would have moved out, but by that time the real estate market was bad and I couldn't afford a place of my own."

Kathy's story is not over. For the past year Pat has been asking her to try a reconciliation. His son, Jeremy, is now at college, so a major source of stress has been removed. He also claims that his drinking is under control, so Kathy wouldn't have to worry about the psycho-logical abuse. Kathy is wary, however. She still thinks Pat is one of the most intelligent and charming men she has ever known, but she has too many bad memories to jump into a second marriage with him. So to give herself a chance to find out just how much Pat has changed, she is seeing him on weekends—while still living with George. Pat comes down from Washington about every other weekend, and they go out to dinner together and dancing afterward. Twice they have gone away together for the weekend, with Kathy leaving Tracy with George. Kathy realizes that her behavior is something less than honorable, but in her words, "I'm forty years old, I don't make enough money to support Tracy and myself, and I can't afford to give up the security of George until I'm sure things will work out with Pat."

Kathy has made it through four decades of life without once being self-sufficient. Her father picked up all her bills until she married Jimmy, and since then she has been able to find a man who was more than happy to support her—although Jimmy never did a very good job of it.

And it is not as if Kathy is incapable of leading an independent existence. She never went back to finish her college degree but she is intelligent and could do any number of things well. Photographs of her when she was in her early twenties show a strikingly attractive young woman, and she has not changed much in the intervening twenty years. She is tall, almost five-foot eight, has medium-length, dark-brown hair, and large, compelling brown eyes. She has had to struggle with her weight as she has grown older, but at her height, her one hundred forty pounds looks good. Kathy has an easy smile, an outgoing personality, and she has made the million dollar sales club twice—placing her in the top 10 percent of all real estate agents in her area. She has done this despite never taking her career seriously. For years her friends have told her that with even a little effort, she could be an exceptionally successful businesswoman.

But Kathy cannot see herself as others do. She enjoyed her good years in real estate, spending most of the money she earned on jewelry and clothes (her husband Pat would not allow her to contribute to the household expenses; it apparently threatened his masculinity to think that he was not the sole support of his family), and she has attributed her declining income of the past few years to a slow market rather than to her perfunctory efforts. She does not believe she could do any better even if she worked harder. But the simple truth is she finds it easier to find a man to take care of her than to step up her efforts in her profession.

There are at least two things going on with people like Kathy. First, and the more important factor in Kathy's case, is an intense need to feel loved by someone, and in some cases by anyone. This need usually has its origins in the childhood years. For instance, what Kathy remembers most from her childhood is feeling left out, of always being in the shadow of her older sister. "Brenda was obviously the favorite. She was two years older than I, and she was the family star. She got all A's in school, she was always winning some school office or another, and by the time she was in the ninth grade, boys were calling her constantly. The most painful thing I remember is the family get-togethers at Thanksgiving and Christmas when my mom and dad would talk endlessly about everything Brenda was doing and hardly even mention my name. I didn't really blame Brenda for being the center of attention, but I do remember having fantasies about being chosen homecoming queen or being so talented that people would ask me to sing at parties so my parents would love me as much as they loved Brenda."

So Kathy looked for the love she felt that she did not get from her parents in her relationships with men. She did not merely want it, she needed it and needed it just as badly as a junkie needs a fix.

Her strong need to feel loved not only caused her to move into a new relationship just as an old one was ending, it also influenced the type of men she was attracted to. It is not just a coincidence that the two men in her life who have held her attention the longest, Jimmy and Sam, have been, to put it kindly, somewhat unstable. Jimmy was the stereotypical jock, whose main goals in college were to party and be the star of the basketball team. He was taken with Kathy but agreed to marry her only because she seemed to enjoy the wild life as much as he did. But as far as Jimmy was concerned, just because Kathy had to work evenings after their marriage was no reason for him to give up booze, his friends, or other girls.

Kathy was attracted to Jimmy because he was such an intense fellow. After their first date, Jimmy convinced Kathy to sneak out of the dorm after checking in at one A.M. (those were the days when colleges were more paternalistic). He called her constantly, took her to parties four or five nights a week, and proudly introduced her to dozens of his friends. Kathy believed his intensity was a sign of how much he loved her.

Pat, although stable enough to be extremely successful in his career, was much the same way. Throughout their marriage, they would think nothing of spending hundreds of dollars every month going out drinking and dancing. Pat, like Jimmy, was unpredictable.

When he was happy, he would be exceptionally charming and romantic. He would come home early from work with a dozen roses and want to make love. It was more proof to Kathy that she was loved. But when Pat was in a bad mood (which was often triggered by his drinking too much), he could be unbelievably abusive. He would tell Kathy how stupid she was, how fat and ugly she was, and how no man would even want her if he were to walk out. In the early years of their marriage, these "black" periods were more than offset by the good times. Kathy was willing to endure them because at other times Pat made her feel so loved, so wanted. But as they became more frequent, and the good times became fewer and farther between, Kathy finally decided she could not tolerate the abuse.

It is also no coincidence that Kathy felt so unsatisfied with her relationship with George, even though a majority of women would have been more than happy to be married to a man like him. George was a kind, quiet man who never much cared for nightlife. He was relieved when Kathy moved in with him because he thought it would allow them to slow down. At the age of fifty, he was mostly interested in spending quiet evenings at home with someone he cared about and someone who cared about him. For George a perfect evening would be to watch a movie on television while sharing a bowl of popcorn with Kathy. But for Kathy, this was too reminiscent of her sense of being ignored while she was growing up. Sadly, Kathy received more emotional satisfaction from a one-night stand with a married man willing to put her on a pedestal for an evening in exchange for a little novel sex than she did from spending a quiet evening alone with a man who truly loved her. She needed the attention, she needed the excitement. For her, this was evidence that she was loved.

A second factor in the backgrounds of people who need to be in a relationship, any relationship, is a belief that they really cannot make it through life on their own. This pattern seems to be less common now that women are learning to value their intelligence and competence, but it is still found in women in their fifties and occasionally younger women. These women almost always grew up in very traditional families where the mother's role was to cook, clean house, and make sure that father's every need was met. Father was the one who brought home the paycheck, paid the bills, and decided if there was enough money to buy a new washing machine or if the old one should be repaired one more time. As little girls, these women learned by example that women are not competent to deal with the outside world, that they need a man to take care of them.

Ruth fit into this mold. She was in her early fifties when her husband died unexpectedly from a massive coronary. Her grief at being left alone in the world was mixed with sheer panic. Although her husband left enough insurance for her to live comfortably, she was certain that she would not survive. After all, she was quick to tell anyone who would listen, she had never so much as opened a checking account on her own.

Shortly after her husband's funeral, Ruth began to depend on a handful of men in her church, all friends of her husband, who offered to help. For the first several weeks, she would call one of them with an urgent problem, he would dutifully come over, and she would talk for hours about whether she should sell her house and move into a condo, if she should invest her insurance money in mutual funds or certificates of deposit, and the like. It did not take long before her husband's friends began to beg off when she called, and she was left with no one to help her.

So she began to invite the widowers in her church over for dinner. She was none too subtle in her hints about how much more satisfying life was when you could share it with someone. She finally found a taker in Winston, a man in his mid-sixties whose health was failing and who was as interested in finding someone to take care of him as Ruth was in finding someone to take care of her.

Ruth's story does have a happy ending, though (although not as far as Winston was concerned). The first few months of their marriage were satisfying for both. Winston took care of the monthly bills, and they did travel together using Ruth's insurance money. Then Winston suffered a stroke and was confined to a wheelchair. Ruth worked harder than she ever had in her life caring for Winston, who became more peevish as his health deteriorated. Ruth felt bitter about having to take care of a man she did not particularly like, much less love. But caring for Winston and being forced to deal with the nitty-gritty side of life did give her confidence in her ability to cope on her own. Winston died two years after their marriage and Ruth blossomed. She began to travel with various senior citizens groups, developed an active social life that included couples as well as the occasional widower, and vowed that she would not marry again until she found someone who "can sweep me off my feet."

MEN WILL SETTLE FOR FROGS, TOO

When we think about people who believe they must be in a relationship, most of us assume that this only applies to women. But in fact, it appears to be the case that men may be more likely to marry simply to avoid being alone than women are. Women are stereotyped as being the dependent, clinging sex, but men are the ones who often have the more difficult time being alone. A majority of women have enough sense to realize that it is better to suffer a little loneliness than a bad marriage.

Remember Les from Chapter 4? He became involved with Maureen almost immediately after his first wife died. It is not surprising that he jumped into a second marriage, since his first was exceptionally satisfying. He had no reason to think his second would be any different. But within a month of marrying Maureen, he learned that not all women were like his first wife. He kicked himself for jumping into marriage with so little thought, but once he escaped from his second wife, he swore to himself and to all his friends that he would never repeat his mistake.

After his divorce was final, Les reveled in his freedom for about eight months. He loved being able to come and go as he pleased, eat exactly what and when he wanted, and to play golf whenever the urge struck him. He dated a couple of women he met through friends, but he always volunteered (somewhat inappropriately) that he was never getting married again.

Then he met Becky. She was a friend of the wife of one of his golfing partners and had been divorced herself for several years. There was nothing special about their first date; Les thought she was attractive, but she was not beautiful by any means. He told Becky about his good first marriage and his disastrous second one and that he had no plans of repeating his mistake. Becky, unlike the other women he had gone out with, did not raise her eyebrows and stare at him with cold eyes, but rather she said, "I know what you mean. I would never give up my freedom to be with a man who expected me to be his maid and his mother." Les laughed and realized Becky was someone he would enjoy spending time with.

A month went by and Les saw Becky a dozen times, although she had turned down another half-dozen of his invitations. Les found himself spending more and more time thinking about Becky. He still didn't know that much about her, only that they clicked. He found it so easy to be with her. And it drove him crazy when he would call to suggest they have dinner together and she would say that she had other plans, or worse yet, that she wanted to spend the evening finishing a novel that she was engrossed in. Les wanted to be with her, and he couldn't understand why she didn't feel the same way.

You can guess the end of the story. Six months after he met Becky, Les asked her to marry him. After a few weeks of expressing her ambivalence, Becky finally agreed, and they were married less than two years after Les's divorce was final. They have been married for five years now and both are relatively satisfied with their relationship. Les still grumbles occasionally about having to account for his time, and Becky is often annoyed that Les doesn't take his responsibilities around the house more seriously, but they both feel they are happier together than they would be alone.

When asked why he remarried so soon after vowing he would remain single the rest of his days, Les is genuinely puzzled. "I really can't explain it," he says. "Sure I felt lonely at times after I divorced Maureen, but mostly I enjoyed myself. At my age (early fifties) there were plenty of available women, so it wasn't the case that I had trouble finding someone to spend time with. And I loved the freedom to come and go as I pleased without having to worry about a frosty reception when I got back. All I know is that it drove me crazy when I'd call Becky and she would be 'busy.' I came to hate that word. I just reached the point where I wanted to be with her all the time."

Becky is amused when asked how she managed to wrangle a proposal from someone who claimed to be a confirmed bachelor. "Men are all alike," she says with a smile. "I don't know how many times I've heard 'I'm never getting married again.' The first year after my husband left me, it would upset me when a man would tell me that on our first date. I wasn't thinking about marrying someone I had just met, so why did they feel compelled to tell me that? I finally realized that men are just like little boys who are telling their mommy, 'I won't take a bath.' If you try to argue with them, they get all the more blustery and determined. But if you just nod and smile and tell them, 'I wouldn't let you take a bath even if you begged me,' pretty soon they'll be on their knees pleading to get into the tub. Les isn't the first man who told me he was never getting married again and then later proposed, but he was the first man I was interested in marrying."

Becky's analysis of men is far from unique. We've heard from a number of women who say much the same thing—that men often announce on the first or second date that they intend to remain single, only to end up pleading for marriage a few months later.

Why are some men who have escaped one bad relationship so eager to jump into another? There doesn't appear to be any satisfactory answer to this question. Unlike women such as Kathy who often have a history of feeling neglected and unloved, men who will settle for "any frog" do not seem to have such common threads in their backgrounds. Les, for example, reports an uneventful childhood, and he cannot remember ever wondering about whether his parents loved him. Whatever quirks he may have, he appears to be a secure person.

But men in general seem to be more eager to enter a new relationship once an old one has ended. We know that after a divorce, the man will usually remarry before his ex-wife does. We know from psychologist Zick Ruebin's research that men are more likely than women to want to find someone they can fall in love with. And marriage seems to be good for men. We also know that, on the average, married men live longer than their single counterparts.

One possible explanation centers around the observation made by any number of social scientists that men find it difficult to be emotionally intimate with other men so they need a stable, ongoing relationship with a woman to be able to share their innermost thoughts, dreams, and fears. Women, on the other hand, find it easy to have this type of relationship with their female friends. So single men, no matter how footloose and fancy-free, tend to feel emotionally isolated. They crave a relationship with a woman in order to feel complete.

It is also true that men tend to be somewhat less practical about relationships than are women. As long as that "spark" is there, they often believe that the nitty-gritty issues will work themselves out no matter how troublesome they may be. So many men will not settle for just any frog, but they will take the first frog that comes along for whom they feel that special magic. Les, for instance, had dated several women after his divorce who did not inspire him to give up his bachelorhood, but as soon as Becky came along, he was eager to settle down even though he hadn't carefully considered how compatible they would be. He simply assumed that because they enjoyed each other's company so much, she could never object to his Saturday morning golf outings.

Becky, however, was much more calculating in her assessment of Les. As she tells it: "I thoroughly enjoyed being with Les, but I've been around long enough to know there's more to marriage than chemistry. I was careful to determine just what kind of a man Les was. I watched closely when we were at parties as to how much he drank. I had already gone through that once with my first husband. I listened when he talked about money—I wouldn't marry someone who wasn't responsible about it. And his relationship with his kids was important to me. They were all old enough to be out on their own, but I'd be suspicious of a man who did not get along with his own children. I only agreed to marry him after I was confident that he was a mature, responsible, kind, and decent man. He has his share of quirks, but I knew I could live with those, given all his good qualities."

In some ways, the problem of settling for any frog can be more troublesome for men than for women. Most women who tend to be overly dependent on men have at least some awareness of their tendencies. Kathy, for instance, realized that being without a man in her life was a frightening prospect. Periodically, she would tell herself that she needed to break the cycle, that she should try living on her own for a while. True, she wasn't able to do this, and when it came time to make a decision, she would always find plenty of ways to rationalize jumping from one relationship to another, but at least she had some idea about what she was doing.

Many men, however, can't see their behavior for what it is. Because they pay lip service to their independence and their determination to not have to answer to anyone, they often do not realize that they are jumping into a relationship for the wrong reasons. Les was lucky the second time, but he married Becky for almost all the same reasons he married Maureen. In neither case did he carefully consider how compatible his expectations were with his fiancée's. He only knew that he was in love and that he had found the woman he wanted to spend the rest of his life with. He was fortunate that his second frog turned out to be a princess.

HOW TO PASS UP THOSE FROGS

Changing any long-standing pattern of behavior that goes back to one's childhood is extremely difficult, and ridding oneself of dependence on relationships is no exception. We have known many people who have struggled with this issue for years—often with the help of a therapist—and still find themselves prone to jumping into the first relationship that comes along. It is extremely difficult to be a self-sufficient person when you have been trained over a lifetime to be dependent on others.

Like so many other behavioral patterns, dependency is a pattern that is likely to be passed down from generation to generation. Kathy, for instance, was so involved in satisfying her own dependency needs that she neglected her daughter, Tracy. Tracy was a quiet, compliant child, so she never objected when Kathy would stay out until three or four in the morning with George. Kathy's intentions were good, but her idea of being a mother was taking her daughter to Burger King for dinner and renting her a couple of videos before going out for the evening.

It surprised no one but Kathy that by the time her daughter was a sophomore in high school, she was sexually active and not very selective about it. Clearly, she was trying to find the love she did not get at home. So dependent people owe it not only to themselves but also to their children to do something about their lifestyle.

The best advice for people like Kathy comes from the old cliché that suggests you can't be happy with someone else until you're happy with yourself. Until people like Kathy can feel comfortable, even enjoy, leading an independent existence, the chances are they will jump into the next relationship for all the wrong reasons.

We've known a few people who have managed to do this on their own. Sheila's first husband left her for another woman after fourteen years of marriage. She was devastated by her divorce and convinced that she would never be happy again. As could be expected when one is dumped for another woman, Sheila had doubts about her own desirability as a woman. She craved attention from men, any men, and she married the first person who showed any interest.

Her second marriage was a disaster, but Sheila did have the strength to put an end to it quickly. When she found herself having the same intense desires to find another man that she had after her first marriage, she decided that she had to do something to change the course of her life. "I could feel myself drawn to any man who paid the slightest attention to me no matter what a bum he may have been, and it scared me. I did not want a repeat of my second marriage. I decided that I wouldn't go out again until I felt stronger.

"I was severely depressed for about six months. I would burst into tears every time I saw a couple that seemed happy, since I was sure I would never feel like that again. But I was determined. I started seeing a therapist, I concentrated on being the best mom I could be, and I tried to find a hobby that would get me through those Friday and Saturday evenings when my kids were out with their friends.

I knew I had turned the corner about eight months after my second divorce. It was a Saturday morning, I was eating breakfast with the kids, and Darlene was talking about some silly thing one of her friends had done the night before—I don't even remember what it was. But for the first time in months I laughed, I really laughed. I felt sad and lonely again that night, but from that moment on I had more and more days when I felt happy to be alive.

About four months after that something happened that helped me to know I was getting better. A man I had met at work asked me to have dinner with him and, as I had done reflexively for the past year and a half, I said no. But then I realized I had said no because I didn't relish the prospect of spending time with him and that was a first. Before, I wanted to say yes to almost anyone just to avoid being alone. That marked the point where I began to trust myself enough to believe that I would say yes for the right reasons." Sheila began to date again shortly after this revelation, and while her social life never became frenetic, she has enjoyed the company of several men over the past several years. She says that she will remarry one day, but she still hasn't met a man she wants to spend the rest of her life with.

What makes Sheila's accomplishment so remarkable is that most of us cannot endure long periods of sadness and depression with only a vague hope that someday, maybe, things will be better. Kathy, for instance, would have periods where she resolved to change, but after feeling down for a week or so, she would become desperate to have contact with any man. Sheila was wise enough to realize (and we like to think her sessions with her therapist helped her along these lines) that if she was ever to reach the point where she could choose to have a relationship because she wanted it and not because she needed it, she would have to experience some difficult times.

The most important lesson Sheila learned was that there were other ways of achieving emotional satisfaction, that she did not have to be with a man in order to be happy. She learned that her children were interesting people. For the first time in her life, she learned that she could enjoy talking with them, listening to what they had to say rather than simply being their disciplinarian. She learned that with just a little effort she could find other women who were as interested in having a friend as she was, and she learned that these friendships were much more satisfying in the long run than a bad relationship with a man. And perhaps most important of all, she learned that she could be content with her own company. She began to read books that she had always meant to get around to but never could seem to find the time to read before. She began to take pride in her garden and became something of an expert in the care of azaleas. And she realized there were many things she was interested in but knew nothing about, so she began to take classes through the adult education division of the local university. In short, Sheila became a complete person, rather than a woman whose very existence depended upon the love and acceptance of a man.

If you suspect that you have much in common with Kathy or the old Sheila, please keep in mind that the discomfort you will have to go through should you decide to change will be well worth it in the end. Being self-sufficient and independent is a much more comfortable way to live than relying on someone else for happiness. As Sheila describes it: "Before, my sense of well-being always depended on the actions of someone else. Even in the early years of my first marriage, I was always worried about what my husband was thinking, whether or not he really loved me. I wasn't at peace unless he was paying lots of attention to me. But now that I'm comfortable with myself, my life is a lot more even-keeled. If I haven't had a date for a month or so, I don't worry about it; I have plenty of things to occupy my time. And if I'm in a relationship and we've had a fight, it isn't the end of the world. I know I'll survive no matter how it turns out. That year when I was trying to change was the hardest time of my life, but it was a small price to pay for the contentment I feel now. No, things aren't perfect. I still feel lonely at times, and I would rather be married than single, but I know I'll have a good life regardless of whether or not there is a man in my life."

CHAPTER 7

The Root of All Evil

WOODY PULLED HIS Ford Bronco into the driveway in front of his townhouse. He had just finished a long twelve hours at his job as shipping supervisor for a cement company. When a shipload of cement came in, he had to report to work no matter what time of day or night it might be, and he couldn't leave until the ship was unloaded. It was a killer schedule, but he made good money, and besides, he liked not being tied down by regular hours.

Woody stopped to look down the street before going into his house on this unusually warm January afternoon. He never could predict his reaction when he thought about his situation too hard. On one hand, he was proud of his new home. It was an all-brick three-bedroom townhouse with a good-sized family room complete with a masonry fireplace. He knew he was lucky to have it. With his child support payments, he just squeezed through in qualifying for the loan. It was a good place for his one-year-old son to grow up. The development was filled with young couples, so his boy would have plenty of playmates as he got a little older. On the other hand, he sometimes felt depressed when he looked down the street and couldn't see a single blade of grass. Parking was always at a premium in townhouse developments so the front yards were solid driveways. It was such a contrast to the house he lived in a few years ago—a sprawling single-family ranch on nearly a third of an acre. But, he told himself, a somewhat more modest lifestyle was a

89

small price to pay to be able to look forward to coming home to his new family. During the last several years of his first marriage, he couldn't face his wife without stopping off to have a few drinks first.

As Woody walked into the foyer, his son, Nick, broke into a big smile and toddled over to greet him. Woody picked up Nick, gave him a big hug, and walked into the kitchen to give his wife, Emily, a kiss on the cheek. "Hi. What's for dinner?" he asked.

"Alice just left with Jeremy a few minutes ago." Emily baby-sat for the children of two working mothers who lived on their street. "I was hoping you'd bring home a pizza."

"I thought about it, but I was just too beat to do anything but come straight home. I left the house at three-thirty this morning." Actually, Woody thought about it and rejected the idea because he still had a week to go before he was paid. He hated the idea of not having enough money in his pocket to buy a lousy pizza. It was one thing to have to pinch pennies when you were twenty, but it was humiliating to have to live that way when you were forty years old.

"That's all right," Emily said. "I'll take some hamburger out of the freezer. It will only take a few minutes to thaw it out in the microwave."

Woody carried Nick into the family room and set him down in his playpen. He plopped down in his reclining chair, flipped on the television with the remote control, leaned back in his chair, and closed his eyes. Perhaps if he could take a ten-minute nap he would feel better.

Just as he was about to doze off, Emily came into the room and handed him a letter. "Probably more bad news." she stood over him, waiting for him to open the letter.

Woody felt his stomach knot up as soon as he saw the envelope. It was from Gail, his first wife, and Emily was right. Gail's letters never contained good news. He read the letter in silence, then crumpled it into a tight ball and threw it across the room in the general direction of the waste basket. He closed his eyes once again.

"What is it this time?" Emily asked with a mixture of anger and concern in her voice.

"Josh had an ear infection and she wants $55 for the doctor and the prescription." Josh was the younger of Woody's two sons from his first marriage. Woody's voice was flat, tired.

Emily's mouth tightened into a frown. "We'll never get ahead," she said as she stomped back into the kitchen.

Woody tried to let his stomach relax. He couldn't stand it. He made $40,000 a year, more than anyone else he knew with only two years of college. But by the time he made the house and car payments, paid a half dozen other bills, and sent Gail $700 for child support, he had only a little more than $100 a week to live on. He simply couldn't absorb an extra $55 for an ear infection.

Yes, it was still worth it, he reminded himself. He loved Emily, and after three years of marriage, they could still talk to each other for hours—something he couldn't do with Gail on their honeymoon. He just wished it wasn't so damn hard. He wished that his wife didn't have to take in the neighborhood kids so they could make it. He wished that he could live as comfortably as he did when he was thirty years old.

Yes, money problems are a major source of stress in second marriages. Fully 40 percent of the men and women who responded to our survey indicated that financial obligations to a former spouse affected their current lifestyle. And those who said they were having money problems were significantly more likely to have frequent quarrels and less likely to predict that their marriage would last forever.

But this certainly does not make second marriages unique. After all, money problems are near the top of the list of problems that couples in first marriages struggle with. Any time two people have a finite pool of resources and different ideas about how those resources should be allocated, there are bound to be conflicts. No, the simple fact that there is not enough money to make it to the end of the month does not set second marriages apart.

Second marriages, which are complicated enough to begin with, do add additional dimensions to money issues. One of the first of these has to do with one's frame of reference. Many men and women who enter their second marriages with such high hopes for happiness are surprised to discover that their standard of living is uncomfortably lower than it was in their first marriage.

Woody, who protested often that "money is not the most important thing in life," nonetheless talked to us at length about the difference between his lifestyle in his first marriage and in his second. "My first wife, Gail, was a dental hygienist, and she made almost as much money as I did. We had more than our share of problems, but one thing we rarely argued about was money. We lived in the same house for more than ten years, so our payments were next to nothing, and we could pretty much buy what we wanted. I never had to give it a second thought if I wanted to stop after work to buy a few drinks for my friends or to take the family out to dinner.

"But now, even though I'm making 25 percent more than I was before my promotion, it's a constant struggle to make ends meet. If Emily wants to buy a simple knickknack for the house, we have to check our budget to see if there's an extra twenty bucks. We never go out to eat; in fact it's a real treat if I bring home a pizza. Before, I rarely used credit cards, now our monthly balance is creeping higher and higher on four of the damn things. I thought I had everything figured out before Emily and I married, but it all fell apart in a matter of months."

Perhaps Woody was somewhat naïve when he tried to predict his finances in his second marriage, but he did give it a lot of thought. Shortly after he left Gail, he did receive a promotion which meant an additional $10,000 a year, so he figured that would easily cover his child-support payments. Indeed, he would be ahead since, because his wife had custody of his two boys, he would not have the expense of their day-to-day maintenance. He knew Emily did not have the training to earn as much as his first wife did, but she could get some kind of job, so they should do almost as well financially as he and Gail did. Sure, he would have to cut back a little, but it would be a small price to pay for happiness.

But there were several things Woody did not consider. First, his promotion required him to move from his small hometown in Pennsylvania to Virginia Beach, where housing prices were at least one third higher than he was used to. Secondly, Emily wanted to have a child of her own. At almost forty, Woody thought he was too old for more babies, but Emily was ten years younger than he and she did not have any children in her first marriage. Because it was so important to her, Woody agreed, but it meant that Emily would not be working for several years. So $15,000 a year that he was counting on to help finance his second chance vanished in a heartbeat.

Woody also failed to anticipate the extra expenses associated with his obligation to his sons. His divorce settlement called for him to pay their medical expenses in addition to his child-support payments. He had a good health insurance policy at work, so he thought this would be, at most, a minor expense. But he discovered his former wife was much quicker to take the boys to a doctor than she had been when they were married (Woody insists she does it to hurt him). In addition, his younger son needed braces, which were not covered by insurance, so that was an additional $2,500.

Woody also accepted responsibility for the travel expenses for his boys when they came to visit him. When he moved to Virginia Beach this was no big deal. It was only a six-hour drive to Pennsylvania, so he could drive up there, pick them up, and be back home in one day. But less than a year after he moved, Gail remarried and moved to Miami. So now, rather than a day's drive three times a year, it is $400 worth of plane tickets every Christmas, spring vacation, and summer. He rarely has his loan from the credit union paid off before it's time to buy more tickets.

As Woody tells his story, he makes frequent references to the relative unimportance of money, but he also adds, with bitterness in his voice, that in addition to the $700 he is paying for child support every month, he is paying an additional $250 each month for the unanticipated expenses. Since Emily is not working, this places an unbearable strain on their budget. It is not merely a coincidence that the worst argument he and Emily have had in their three-year marriage was over an $8 discrepancy in their bill for cable television. Money has become a constant source of strain for Woody. He hates feeling poorer at the age of forty than he did when he was nineteen.

Interestingly, Emily does not experience their financial straits in the same way as Woody. Her first husband was a construction worker in an economically depressed town, and to make matters worse, he was prone to missing work when it was available because of frequent hangovers. Emily worked as a waitress in a deli, so between the two of them it was a struggle to pay the rent on their one-bedroom furnished apartment. Emily has never lived in a house as nice as the one she has now, and she has never been in the position of spending money without having to think hard about it. So while she appreciates the fact that money is tight, she feels that she is better off than she ever has been.

But Emily can still become very angry over what she perceives as the unfairness of Woody's divorce settlement. Woody's first wife married a successful businessman, so she has experienced a dramatic increase in her standard of living. Gail lives in a large waterfront house complete with swimming pool and a twenty-eight-foot boat moored at the dock. Not only does she have everything she could want, she is able to buy her two sons everything they want as well. As Emily tells it: "I can't help but get very upset when Woody's boys come to visit and I see them in designer jeans while I have to buy clothes for my baby at garage sales. It drives me crazy to think how hard we have to sacrifice to send that money to Florida every month when I know she's (Gail) probably using it to pay her maid to wash her windows or her gardener to trim her bushes. It's just unfair!"

Emily knows how much Woody loves his sons and how proud he is of them, so she is careful never to say anything that could possibly be taken as negative about them. But when talking with friends, she does admit to feeling somewhat resentful about them. "They're nice kids," she concedes, "but I don't like having to spend $1,200 a year for plane tickets for them when Woody and I haven't had a vacation in more than two years. They're used to doing all kinds of things at home, so when they're here, Woody takes them out to the movies and to eat several times a week. I understand that he wants them to enjoy their visits, but I can't help but resent the fact that we spend more on entertainment the six weeks they are with us than we do the rest of the year." Emily has managed to keep her feelings about Woody's boys to herself, but one cannot help but wonder how her simmering resentments will affect her marriage.

The one word we heard more than any other when talking with people about their financial obligations incurred by a first marriage was "unfair." Like Emily, many people felt that changing circumstances coupled with the relative inflexibility of divorce settlements made their situations unfair. What makes these situations so difficult is that "fairness" is clearly a matter of perspective. We did not talk to Gail, Woody's first wife, but we talked to enough people like her to be able to guess with confidence what she might say in response to the charge that the amount of money she received for child support was unfair. First of all, she would probably point out that she was not the one who wanted the divorce, that Woody left her for a younger woman. Secondly, she might argue that Woody's obligation to his children has nothing to do with how much money her second husband earns. Woody fathered the boys, so he has a moral as well as a legal obligation to contribute to their support until they are eighteen. Just because her second husband can afford to provide her with a comfortable lifestyle does not relieve Woody of his responsibilities.

It is easy to sympathize with Woody and Emily's frustration at having to struggle so hard to honor Woody's obligations to his ex-wife when the money means relatively little to her, but that does not mean the situation is necessarily unfair. For every woman in Gail's situation there are probably ten ex-wives who were not lucky enough to marry money the second time around. These women learn in short order that child-support payments do not go very far when trying to keep a single-parent family afloat.

As tight as Woody's finances are as a result of his obligations from his first marriage, they could be a lot worse. We heard from many people who were driven to the point of bankruptcy as a result of their ex-spouse's legal maneuvering. Arnold, for instance, divorced his wife of sixteen years because his "marriage was dead" and he wanted to have a second chance with Laura, a woman eleven years younger than himself who worked in his office. As important as his decision was to his happiness, Arnold felt guilty about leaving his first wife, who had not worked during their marriage, so he was generous to a fault in their divorce settlement. He wanted his children to be comfortable, and he did not want Jenny to suffer. Besides, he was a successful man and he could afford it.

As his second wife, Laura, tells their story: "I thought from the beginning that Arnold gave too much away. His ex-wife was living in the same house she always had, and she didn't have to work to be able to do it. We bought a similar house, but with Arnold's alimony and child support, I had to continue working in order for us to be able to afford it. But the real problems didn't start until about six months after Arnold and I were married. His ex-wife filed suit to cut back Arnold's visitation rights with the children, claiming that I was a bad influence on them. It was absurd, and she didn't get anywhere with it, but it cost us $2,000 in legal fees. For the past two years, she has dragged Arnold into court about every four months. Every time they have a disagreement about the kids, she wants to go to court.

Every time she has to call a repairman, she goes to court to get the money from Arnold. She's told Arnold that she's going to make him pay for leaving her, and she's doing a pretty good job of it. Not only are the legal costs killing us, but Arnold's company has begun to let him know they're not happy about all the time he's missing from work to appear in court. I hate to say it, but I don't know how much more of this I can take. His ex-wife might just get what she wants— to break up our marriage."

Laura's situation is not unusual. Often financial obligations to an ex-spouse serve to aggravate other stresses that are associated with second marriages. We heard from several women in their first marriage who married men with an ex-wife and children. They reported that they were surprised at how much they resented their husband's alimony and child-support payments, but with a little reflection, it became clear that money was not the primary issue.

Karen is representative of these women. At the age of twenty-eight, she married Kyle, who had been divorced for four years but was still supporting his three children. It was her first marriage, and her biggest concern was how she would get along with Kyle's children. She wasn't sure that she was ready for instant motherhood, but Kyle assured her that everything would be fine, that they would only have the kids every other weekend and for a month during the summer. No one was expecting her to assume the role of their mother, she could be more like a friend to them.

We talked with Karen after she had been married to Kyle for six years, and the first thing she mentioned was money. In her words, "Trying to make a stepfamily work is much harder than I ever thought it would be. I dread the weekends when Kyle has the kids. They still haven't accepted me, and they seem to go out of their way to hurt me. Kyle is so concerned with keeping their visits on an even keel, he refuses to discipline them when they're rude to me. By the time they leave on Sunday night, I'm furious with Kyle and just as I'm getting over it, it's time for them to come again. The worst part of all this is that it takes almost my entire take-home pay to make Kyle's child-support payments. So when I'm paying the bills and I write out a check to his ex, I always think to myself, 'And I'm working full-time to be able to afford to be this miserable!' "

Kyle and Karen had frequent arguments about money. She resented his spending money on his hobbies while she had to do without some small luxuries, which she could afford when she was single, in order to make the child-support payments. She believed she should be able to spend her paychecks as she wanted and Kyle should be the one to make all the sacrifices. After all, they were his children, not hers.

It does not take a great deal of insight to recognize that their fights over money were just a smokescreen for other, more troublesome issues. Kyle felt guilty about the effect his divorce was having on his children, so he was reluctant to discipline them during their brief visits. He was all too aware how badly his children were treating his new wife, but his own conflicts made him ultrasensitive to any suggestions from Karen. If she would ask him to do something about the kids' ugly comments to her, he would only become angry and tell her that they needed time to adjust. So Karen learned to let these episodes pass but her resentment remained. She found it easier to focus her feelings on the more concrete issue of their finances.

All of the couples we've discussed so far had one important plus going for them, despite the severe strain they were under as a result of financial obligations to an ex-spouse—they were honest with each other about their finances to begin with. This is not always the case. While most people do tell their prospective spouse the truth about their finances, we found that 9 percent of our respondents reported that they were deceived. Needless to say, lies are not a very good foundation upon which to build a marriage.

The most common complaint we heard along these lines concerned a spouse bringing a pile of unpaid bills into the second marriage. Scott, for example, said that he went out of his way to tell Georgia everything about his financial situation before they were married. "I told her exactly how much money I made, that I had three more years to pay alimony and nine more years of child support, I even showed her my stack of bills at the end of one month to make sure she knew exactly what she was getting into. I wanted her to realize that while we could be comfortable, she would have to continue working until my youngest child was through college and my obligations to my family were over.

"Now I know I should have realized something was wrong by her reaction. The only thing she ever said when we talked about money was, 'I know we'll be fine, you don't have to worry about telling me about every last penny you owe.' But to tell you the truth, I never thought about it. She had never been married, she made pretty good money as a teacher, and she had a six-year-old car and a modest apartment. I was sure she was responsible about money. As soon as we got back from our honeymoon, I learned that she had thousands of dollars' worth of debts and several judgments against her. She owes almost $4,000 on credit cards, $2,000 to her dentist, and another $1,000 to a former landlord. We can't even buy a house until she gets her bills paid off, which could be years from now. When I asked her why she didn't tell me about her debts, she said that it wasn't any of my business, that she would pay them off with the money she earns. What she doesn't seem to realize is that the budget I had worked out for us is based on the assumption—which she allowed me to have—that she was debt-free."

Perhaps we can give Georgia the benefit of the doubt. Perhaps she did not intend to be dishonest, that she really believed that her unpaid bills were her concern and not her new husband's. As angry as Scott was when he learned the truth, he was able to forgive her and try to work within their new constraints. But Georgia did place her marriage in jeopardy by not telling her husband the whole truth. She is lucky that Scott cares enough about her to try to work things out. Other people who behaved similarly have not been so fortunate.

We heard from other people for whom it is impossible to give their spouse the benefit of the doubt. Remember Jan and Robert from Chapter 2? Jan is the woman who sold her house in Washington, D.C., and gave up a very comfortable lifestyle to move to Virginia Beach to marry Robert. Looking back at their courtship, Jan realizes that the warning signs were obvious enough, she simply chose to ignore them. "Robert told me about his financial problems, but he claimed they all resulted from his messy divorce from his first wife. For instance, before we were married he asked me to put his car on my insurance policy because his wife had wrecked her car so many times. I let him use my credit card for gas because he had to close his account so his wife couldn't run up his bill. The list went on and on, and none of it was true. He just wasn't paying his bills. Even after we were married, I had to use the money I got for selling my house in D.C. to make the down payment on our new house. He said he would pay me back as soon as everything was settled from his divorce.

"It didn't take me long before I had to face the fact that he had lied to me about everything. It was true that his divorce had caused him problems, but his wife had divorced him in the first place because he was a compulsive spender and completely irresponsible about money. Shortly after we were married, back in the middle 1970s, we would regularly have our phone, gas, and electricity turned off because Robert hadn't paid the bills—despite the fact that he was making more than $50,000 a year! It wasn't unusual for us to have a couple of hundred dollars of returned check charges in a single month. I would be worried about buying food, and Robert would come home with two pairs of $80 shoes for himself because they were on sale. It was a nightmare."

Jan's nightmare has only become worse in the fifteen years following her marriage. Robert recently left her again, with three children under the age of eight, after their third attempt at a reconciliation. He accepted a job in another state for $96,000 per year and in the divorce settlement, agreed to continue making Jan's house payment and to provide $800 per month in child support. Despite his high salary, his obligations are so low as a result of the mountain of debt he has accumulated. Jan, who did not work during their marriage at Robert's insistence, has gone back to school to be certified to teach. In the meantime, Robert is three months behind in the house payments, and the bank is threatening foreclosure; he is two months behind in his child support, and Jan cannot afford to pay her heating bills. Jan is not the type of woman who dwells on the past, but she does have times when she hates herself for ignoring the warning signs. "If I had insisted that Robert provide me with all the details of his financial situation, I would have never married him. And I would have saved myself fifteen years of heart-ache."

AN OUNCE OF PREVENTION

It's difficult to think of a situation where the old cliché "An ounce of prevention is worth a pound of cure" fits better than when it comes to money issues and second marriages. Many of the couples we talked with who were having severe money problems could have prevented much of the anger and hurt that resulted if they had only been completely honest and realistic with their partner—and with themselves—before beginning their second chance.

On the positive side of the ledger, it seems that generally men and women marrying for the second time tend to be more realistic and practical when it comes to money than young couples marrying for the first time. Part of the reason for this is that older couples have more to lose. They usually earn more money, have accumulated some assets, even if it is only equity in a house, and have obligations to children from a first marriage. This places them in quite a different situation than a young couple just starting out who bring nothing more into the marriage than the furniture they accumulated from secondhand stores while they were in college.

As evidence of this practicality, men and women entering second marriages are much more likely to have a prenuptial agreement than are couples entering a first marriage. Such agreements may spell out the financial obligations of each partner, and how their estate will be divided should the marriage not work out. Some people would argue that such agreements are planning for failure; that a couple who come to a prenuptial agreement cannot be very serious about their marriage vows. But others would make the argument that prenuptial agreements are like fire insurance on your house. Just because people take out an insurance policy does not mean that they will be careless with matches or intentionally leave the gas on before they go on vacation. Prenuptial agreements make good sense in an age where second marriages have less than a fifty-fifty chance of survival and when considerable assets are involved.

Jan certainly wishes she had worked out such an agreement with Robert before marrying him. "First of all," Jan says, "had we worked out a prenuptial agreement, I probably would have had a clear picture of his irresponsibility and I wouldn't have married him in the first place. But at the very least, I might have been able to protect the money I brought into the marriage. I put $50,000 down on our house, but even though it's doubled in value, I wouldn't get anything out of it if I sold it. Robert refinanced it several times to pay off debts. I had a nice house and a good job when I met Robert. Now I'm forty-four years old, I have virtually nothing except my ten-year-old station wagon that breaks down every other month, and it will be another year before I can get a job that pays me enough to support myself and my kids." Jan paid a heavy price for not taking her ounce of prevention.

We received several practical, albeit unromantic, suggestions from men and women who wished they had followed their own advice before entering a second marriage. One thirty-one-year-old woman said, "If I every marry again, I will insist on seeing his tax returns for the previous three years. A bank would insist on seeing them if he wanted a loan, so why shouldn't I since I'm making a much more important decision." This woman was bitter that her husband, who was in sales, had grossly exaggerated his income.

Ned, aged forty-four, wishes he would have asked to see his second wife's canceled checks for the previous six months. "Caroline told me how hard it was for a single mother to make it when I first met her, and I believed her. After all, I knew the problems both my ex-wife and I were having. But it didn't take long before I realized why Caroline was having such a hard time—she couldn't resist a sale, any sale. I probably would have married her anyway even had I known how much she was paying to department stores every month, but it sure would have saved us a lot of grief as well as sleepless nights had I had a clear idea of how she was spending her money to begin with."

Of course, the real problem for many of these couples is that they were not completely honest with each other to begin with. In some cases, the dishonesty was deliberate. A few men and women feared that their partner might back out of the marriage if the full truth was made known. But in many other cases, the failure to reveal the full truth seemed to result from a reluctance to openly discuss money issues. As one woman put it, "I'm sure Jack would have told me the truth about his financial situation had I insisted, but somehow it seemed too personal. It's strange, but somehow money seems more private than even sex. I didn't have any trouble asking him how many women he had been to bed with, but I felt embarrassed about asking him exactly how much money he made or how much he owed." It's too bad she felt this way, because in the long run fiscal compatibility is probably as important, if not more so, than sexual compatibility.

After one has done everything possible to ensure that he or she has a clear sense of the partner's financial health before marriage, it is important to recognize that conflicts about money often are symptomatic of other emotional issues. Karen, for instance, should have been honest with herself as to why she resented Kyle's child-support payments so much. And Kyle, of course, should have realized that money wasn't really the issue when Karen complained to him about the monthly checks. After all, he had been honest with her about his obligations before they were married. Had they been able to recognize the underlying conflict, it might have been possible for them to do something to alleviate the strains in their marriage. It is possible to do something about resentful step-children. It is much more difficult to do something about money problems when income and expenses are relatively fixed.

We heard from several people who were especially sensitive to their partner's conflicts that, on the surface, appeared to center on money and who were effective in dealing with them. Our favorite example came from Nancy, a thirty-six-year-old woman whose second husband had three children from his first marriage. According to Nancy, "Bill's first marriage was a disaster, and he really hates his first wife for what she did to him in court and for trying to turn the children against him. The first year we were married, he would go into a rage first, and then a deep depression, every time he had to write the alimony check or every time his ex called about some problem with the kids. I tried to talk to him about it, but he had a real blind spot when it came to her. He couldn't be rational about it. So to preserve our marriage, I decided I would take over some of his responsibilities. I write his alimony check now, and when his ex-wife calls with some money problem, he tells her that I'm in charge of the finances and hands the phone over to me. I don't like doing it, but it has removed a major source of stress in our marriage so it's well worth it."

Not everyone can be as perceptive as Nancy, or as willing to take on the dirty business, but it is wise to remember that even if it is your spouse's obligations that are causing your money problems, your partner probably has as many bad feelings about it as you do. Nancy was smart enough to know this. She realized that it would do her no good to join in with her husband and complain about all the money going out every month to his ex-wife. She realized that if her marriage was to remain stable, she would have to help her husband through his very difficult time. And after all, isn't that what marriage is all about?

As destructive as money problems can be, we did hear from couples who were quite effective in dealing with very serious situations. Perhaps the most dramatic example concerns Stephanie and Chris, the couple we introduced to you in Chapter 3. They were the ones who fell in love with each other while still married to their first spouses, pursued an affair, and finally left their spouses with the intention of marrying each other. Their ex's got together to share the cost of a private detective, fell in love themselves, and ended up marrying each other two days before Stephanie and Chris married.

Because of the circumstances of their divorces, both Stephanie and Chris left their first marriages with virtually nothing. Each of their ex-spouses got the house, Chris was saddled with heavy alimony and child support, and Stephanie (an adulteress in the eyes of the court) did not get custody of the children, hence she received no alimony or child support.

Both Chris and Stephanie recall vividly how tight things were during the early years of their marriage. They both went from living in large houses in the suburbs to a cramped, two-bedroom apartment. It was adequate for themselves, but on weekends when the children visited, Chris and Stephanie slept on a foldout bed in the family room so the boys and girls could have separate bedrooms. The most extravagant entertaining they did for several years was to grill hot dogs and hamburgers out by the apartment's swimming pool.

But now, eight years later, they are back on their feet. They have their own house again, and while they haven't finished furnishing it, they are satisfied to do it a piece at a time. They acknowledge they will never have as much as their ex-spouses until the children are finished with their education, but they have never regretted their decision. They have never blamed each other for their difficult times, and both have been willing to work hard to make the most of their second chance.

Chris and Stephanie are the best argument we know of to support the proposition that it is not how much or how little money a couple has, but rather how they deal with what they do have that matters. Money problems may undermine many a second change, but the couple that is committed to the marriage and is willing to face issues squarely has a good chance of making a go of their relationship.

CHAPTER 8

It Doesn't Really Matter, but. . .

DAVE FELT HIS TEMPLES pounding as he checked his watch again. It was seven-thirty in the morning and he had only thirty minutes to shave, shower, get dressed, and get to his office. He had an extremely important appointment with a potential client, and if he could land this account, he would be a shoo-in for a partnership in his accounting firm next year. He couldn't afford to keep the man waiting. Dave had to get in that bathroom and get in there now.

He banged on the bathroom door for the third time. "Caroline, for Christ's sake! I have an important meeting this morning!"

"I'll be right out." At least the shower was turned off. His wife couldn't be that much longer. As he leaned against the hallway wall, trying to calm is racing pulse, he saw his stepdaughter emerge from her bedroom, dressed in her nightgown. She was carrying her hair dryer and her huge bag of cosmetics.

"I gotta go next, Dave. I barely have time to get ready for school."

Dave felt his self-control eroding rapidly. "The hell you do! I told you last night I have an important meeting at eight o'clock this morning!"

"I overslept." Sheila's voice was sullen and resentful. "I hardly slept all night. I kept hearing you snore through the walls."

"Well, you can wash up in the kitchen if you have to. I have to meet with a prospective client this morning, and I can't shower in the kitchen."

Sheila stared at her stepfather in disbelief. "You think I can wash my hair and shave my legs in the kitchen sink?"

"So go without for one day. You and your boyfriends will survive." Thank God! The door was finally opening. Caroline emerged, her hair in a towel.

Dave quickly escaped into the bathroom, but he couldn't shut out the heated voices on the other side of the door. "Mom, I'm getting sick of living like this. I have to go to school looking like a hag just because Dave is too selfish to let me go first!"

"Now, Sheila, he told you last night he had to be in the bathroom early this morning. Now that we live in a house with only one bathroom, we have to stick to a schedule and be considerate."

"That sucks! You didn't have to move in here, anyway! You just wanted to be in the social-climbing neighborhood!"

Dave turned on the shower to drown out the noise. Sheila was a selfish little adolescent, and he knew he should just ignore her tantrums, but he found it impossible to remain calm during these constant altercations. He seethed with all the things he'd like to say to Sheila. What was more important, his job or her preening herself for a bunch of teenage delinquents? Where did she think the money was going to come from to put her through college, to pay for all her clothes and makeup and shoes, and for all of the other things she just had to have? Not her father, that's for sure. He hadn't paid child support in more than five years.

Dave shaved with manic haste (cutting himself twice), showered, and rushed into his bedroom. Dressing took rather longer than usual, because in his hurry and tension, he buttoned his shirt wrong and couldn't get his tie right. All the time he kept thinking about the incident with his stepdaughter, and the more he thought about it, the angrier he got. At his age, he shouldn't have to fight for the bathroom in the morning! He knew it was just a trivial, unimportant thing, but he couldn't help feeling outraged. Sheila had behaved badly, but she was a teenager, and she probably couldn't help it.

As an adult, better behavior was to be expected from him. Why couldn't he just ignore these little irritations? What was the matter with him?

As petty as they seem, it is precisely these little things that can do a lot to sabotage a marriage. The results of our survey showed a strong link between everyday annoyances and serious problems in marriages. For instance, those respondents who had arguments about the housework also were more likely to have frequent, serious quarrels and were less likely to think their marriage would last forever. Respondents who had too little privacy were also less likely to think that their marriage would last forever. Respondents who answered "false" to "My partner and I agree about most things" were much less likely to answer "true" to "I would marry my present spouse again if I had to do it over"; they, too, were also much more likely to have frequent, serious quarrels.

The men and women who responded to our survey provided us with a number of examples of how petty irritations could grow into serious marriage problems. Carl, a fifty-four-year-old man who was in the process of ending his second marriage, wrote, "I moved into my wife's house and sold mine. For the next thirteen years I felt like I was paying rent as she constantly referred to it as 'my house.'. . . We are now separated and our divorce will be final in a couple of months." It seems unlikely that his wife's references to "my house" was solely responsible for the divorce, but it certainly played a large role in Carl's mind.

Julia, a thirty-nine-year-old woman with no children from her previous marriage, also found it difficult to overlook what she called the "small issue" of the inconveniences associated with the weekend visits of her stepchildren. "The children and I get along well enough, but I don't have any feeling of deep, abiding love for them. Every other weekend they come to stay with us, and in my mind, they disrupt the calm, quiet life that I like to lead. Twelve days out of fourteen, my husband and I fix meals we enjoy, we walk around in our underwear, we play quiet music now and then on the stereo, we come and go as we please into any room of the house. Two days out of fourteen, we have to buy and fix foods his kids like, we have to remember to close the bedroom door to change clothes, we have to ask permission to go into one of the kids' rooms, and his kids prefer hard rock music. Because I see this as an intrusion, I feel some animosity towards his kids." This woman's sentiments may not be admirable, but they are very human and are shared by many other people. Let's take a look at some of the troublesome "trivial issues" that our respondents told us about.

TRIVIAL THINGS THAT CAN DRIVE YOU CRAZY

Everyone's had the experience of "It doesn't really matter, but . . ." They're stupid little things that you feel almost ashamed to mention, but which grate horribly on your nerves. It can be confusing and upsetting. When you love someone enough to marry him or her, you should be able to overlook such things or at least work them out. Right? But it's not always that easy. And there is such an unlimited potential number of irritating things.

Housework is one example. It seems to be a bone of contention for an awful lot of people. Two people often have very different standards about how clean the house should be. One partner may feel anxious and uneasy if each ornament in the house is not in its precise position; the other spouse may feel it's quite all right to let the dust and garbage accumulate a few inches, as long as there's a clear path to the door. You don't have to be as extreme as Oscar Madison and Felix Unger for this to be a problem. The issue could simply be that one spouse wants to have just a little more time for fun, to have a few occasions when standards are relaxed a little, but the other thinks that work should always come before play. Unfortunately, like so many other of the "little things" that people fight about, arguments sometimes grow way out of proportion to the original cause.

Another "housework" issue involves keeping your side of the bargain. In stepfamilies where both partners work, the chores are often shared by both spouses. When one spouse has faithfully done the cooking, laundry, vacuuming, and dusting, it can be maddening to watch the dishes pile up in the sink and the bathtub become black with scum. This is not to say that it is earthshakingly important to do these things on an exact schedule, but if you are the one who has done your share of the work faithfully, you can start to be resentful. "If you really loved me, you'd do what you promised" is the way many people feel. The unfairness also grates on some people's nerves: "We had a bargain and you're breaking it."

It can be hard to know what to do about this kind of problem. To walk around seething with unspoken rage is not one of the better options, but it can be hard to express your feelings about these things without sounding like a nag or a whiner. If you just give up and do the work yourself, you probably become even more angry.

Another potential disagreement over housework is about specific ways of doing things. For instance, one woman told us how irritated she was that her husband never learned the habit of screwing the tops of jars on tightly. If that seems just too trivial, think how our respondent felt when she picked up a full jar of mayonnaise by the lid, only to have the jar come crashing down on the floor, covering the immediate area with gobs of mayonnaise and chunks of glass. She could have trained herself to pick up containers by the bottom, but, as she asked, "Why should I have to completely change my habits just because my husband is such a slob?"

Or take a more disgusting refrigerator example. People vary widely in just how long they will allow leftovers and other perishable food items to remain in the fridge. Some people monitor this regularly; others wait until the zucchini has dissolved into yellow mush and green mold is growing on the sides of Tupperware containers. It's not just a question of cleanliness—it can be a case of thrift versus health. Some feel they're wasting valuable resources if they throw away food that is in anything but a state of moldering decay, while others become nauseated when they see a tiny spot of mold on a piece of bread. If you get a thrift-conscious and a health-conscious person in the same household, managing the contents of the refrigerator can turn into quite a problem.

These aren't the only food issues. What kind of food to eat can be just as worrisome. Someone who loves meat, butter, and starch can get really sick of eating tofu, broccoli, and bran cereal. So what if it's good for you? They'd rather die young and enjoy themselves while they're still alive. On the other hand, people who have starved themselves and painfully forced themselves to exercise every day for the last two years, and have finally got down to their ideal weight, are probably not going to enjoy sitting down to a T-bone steak and a baked potato smothered in sour cream every night. Oh, they might enjoy it at the time, but the ensuing regrets and anxieties may qualify their pleasure considerably.

Such admittedly trivial concerns can also become a problem when deciding what television show to watch. There may be a second, or a third TV, and then there's the VCR to play back later what you can't watch now. But what kind of togetherness is that? So you sit and watch the Monday Night Movie, switching to the Bears and Eagles game on every commercial. You miss all the important plays that way, but so what, if it makes your spouse happy? Or maybe you sit and watch every single one of the major league baseball games, on all the cable channels, all summer long. You don't understand the first thing about the game—but your spouse enjoys it, so let's play ball! However, over time you may find that your unselfishness and tolerance become thin.

As many of our respondents told us, pets can be another source of friction. If you're not a cat lover, it can be hard to understand the almost frantic adoration some cat worshipers feel for their feline companions. If you are allergic to the furry creatures, you could have a real problem on your hands. Perpetual sneezing, itching, watery eyes, and headache are not much fun. But to your partner, the idea of getting rid of their precious pet may be unthinkable. He or she would sooner consider getting rid of you. Dogs can create problems, too. They have to be walked, fed, groomed, played with, and their hair gets all over your clothing. Dogs take a lot of work, and you may end up being the one who does that work.

Even holidays can create difficulties. People can have very, very different ideas of how to celebrate them. One spouse may think that the birthday ritual should include a special dinner, cake, presents, and a card with a loving or sexy note. Another may think that the card alone may suffice. Or if they give a present, a Whitman's Sampler or maybe a Dust-Buster would be appropriate.

Christmas can be a particular source of friction. One spouse may feel that the festivities of the holiday season are incomplete without decorations in every room, homemade candies and cookies, lights in every window, Christmas cards sent to every relative, friend, and acquaintance, an enormous Christmas dinner, a lavishly decorated tree, and mounds of presents. The other spouse may be appalled by the sheer work all this entails. Bringing all the boxes down from the attic, unpacking (and packing) the dozens of ornaments, setting up the lights, signing and addressing and stamping the cards, buying the food, decorating the tree, selecting, buying, and wrapping all the presents—is it really worth it? Especially when the Christmas cheer is dimmed by universal grouchiness resulting from little sleep and unceasing hard work.

Yet another sore spot can be recreational choices. One spouse may think the perfect vacation is to go to Disney World; the other may dream of attending performances at Covent Garden. One may gladly spend every spare moment playing golf; the other may be irresistibly attracted to antique auctions. One may truly enjoy spending time with out-of-town relatives, while the other dreads it like the plague. One may enjoy fine dining at expensive restaurants; the other may be never happier than when in front of a big-screen TV in a sports pub, eating the taco special and cheering on the Flames.

What other trivial things may cause problems for couples? It's almost scary how many there are. For instance, who gets up early on weekends has been known to create difficulties. Some couples have an agreement that they will take turns getting up with the kids on Saturday and Sunday. But what if it's your turn to sleep late, and the children have been up and squealing for the last thirty minutes, and every time you try to get your spouse up, you get the "Just a minute" routine? The choices then seem to narrow to having a fit of screaming hysterics or getting up yourself (you're wide awake by this time, anyway). Either way, you won't be at all pleased about it.

Household repairs can cause marital stress as well. Some men and women are handy around the house. They are good with their hands, and they enjoy repairing ripped screens or fixing the plumbing. When this is true of one or both partners in a marriage, fixing things is rarely a source of stress. But when both spouses are all thumbs, it can be a source of irritation. Not everyone has the money to pay professionals to do this work, and it can be very annoying to go week after week with a broken window in your bedroom.

What other trivial things do loving couples fight about? The list could go on forever and still not include a couple of things you might think to add after reading it. Whose friends to spend time with, who does the shopping, how much money is spent, what kind of music to listen to, snoring, how warm or cool to keep the house, leaving hairs on the walls of the shower, leaving the toilet seat up, differences in personal hygiene standards, tying up the phone too long, even personal mannerisms (like the way you laugh).

These "little" problems exist in any family, of course. But in a stepfamily the potential for trivial irritations is greater than usual for two reasons. First, frequently both spouses and children are old enough to have very definite ideas about how they want to do things. The parents have been running their own households for years and they like things to be done a certain way, and the children are past the malleable age of infancy when their tastes and habits are just being formed. Second, there are often many people involved in a stepfamily. There are frequently a number of children in the picture, and these children may not even be regular members of the household. They have less time to get used to the routine, and as a result they may have complaints about the way things are done. Also, children in second marriages usually have problems adjusting emotionally because they've been through the stress of a divorce. Because of these special problems, it's especially important for people living in stepfamilies to understand why these trivial things can become such an untrivial issue, and to discover what they can do to minimize the problem.

WHY TRIVIAL THINGS DRIVE YOU CRAZY

There are a number of reasons why small, seemingly unimportant things can irritate way out of proportion to the original cause. The first possibility is something we call the "honeymoon syndrome." Early in a romantic relationship, most couples are highly motivated to please each other. When you are falling in love, you often actually enjoy doing things for your loved one, even if it means putting your own wishes aside. To you, he or she is the center of the universe, the most important person on the planet. What he or she wants or feels carries the weight of a moral imperative.

Most people feel somewhat insecure in the beginning of a relationship. They want to make a good impression, and they are on their best behavior. They are afraid that if they are too demanding or picky, the other person will reject them. Also, the newness of the relationship prevents the trivial things from becoming a hassle. You are still adjusting to the other person, learning his or her ways and preferences. The things that later annoy you unendurably at first seem cute and appealing.

So what happens? Why does the person you love so much begin to irritate you? In terms of the honeymoon syndrome, it's mainly because you cannot keep up your best behavior forever. Best behavior is only for company, for special occasions. When you are with someone every day, day in and day out, your own natural ways are going to emerge. There's nothing wrong with that. True intimacy is based largely on honesty; on sharing your real feelings, real habits, and real thoughts.

The trouble comes when the "best behavior" natural to the honeymoon phase of the relationship becomes the standard for later phases. Both partners sometimes try to maintain the same standard of politeness, consideration, and unselfishness that was established in the first flush of new love, only to feel their resentment and annoyance grow behind their polite words and actions. To express their real feelings and needs seems to these people selfish and unloving, and they feel ashamed and guilty that they want more out of the relationship. They may also feel angry and hurt that their spouse does not intuitively understand their needs. They may interpret this as a sign that their spouse does not love them anymore.

Even worse, some people insist on a kind of double standard for their marriage. They feel free to insist on their own ways of doing things, but are hurt if their spouse tries to express his or her own needs and feelings as well. What they seem to feel is, "If you really loved me, you would want the same things I want."

One thing that probably contributes to these unrealistic expectations about the way married men and women should behave is the powerful mystique of romantic love, which was discussed in Chapter 2. People in our society are exposed to many idealistic notions about living happily ever after. They may feel like failures or fear that they are falling out of love when their own marriage doesn't fit the idealistic stereotypes portrayed in books, movies, and television. But if they force themselves to act the part of the fantasy lover, or try to hold on to standards of behavior developed early in their relationships, they will run into trouble. They are likely to become disillusioned with their marriage, thinking that if they really were in love, the magic would have lasted forever.

The honeymoon syndrome is not the only reason that marriage partners may drive each other crazy over the trivial problems. Even people who have realistic expectations for each other after the honeymoon may find themselves at each other's throats over bewilderingly unimportant incidents. The reason for this may be that there are underlying issues in the marriage that have not been recognized, and these trivial problems have somehow become the focus for all the unpleasant feelings connected with those issues. For example, Andy, a thirty-one-year-old man married for the second time, found himself experiencing overpowering annoyance every time his wife was late coming home. He could not stop himself from verbally attacking her even when she was only five minutes late, or when she had a legitimate excuse for not arriving on time. What made his behavior worse was that his wife was only late once in a while; it was not a common practice. Andy knew his behavior was out of proportion to the cause, and he felt ashamed of himself for treating his wife so abusively for something so trivial.

What Andy didn't recognize was that there was more to the situation than met the eye. He had a deep fear of his wife being unfaithful to him, because his first wife had left him for another man. He also had low self-esteem, which made it hard for him to believe anyone could love him enough to be faithful to him. Deep down, he couldn't help suspecting when his wife was late that she had been seeing another man and was lying to him. He couldn't admit this fear to himself because it was too painful, and because he was too afraid of finding out he was right. He just couldn't bring himself to face his fear and to tell his wife about his real concerns. The hurt from the past was too strong for him.

In order to find an outlet for his fear and rage, Andy focused on the external sign of his wife's supposed infidelity—her tardiness. Unfortunately, all that accomplished was to make his wife angry with him and to create distance between them. If he had talked to her about his real feelings, she might have been able to reassure him. This is true for too many couples. It is often hard to admit or even to recognize your own real feelings about the important emotional issues. It can sometimes feel very risky to admit to such feelings about your primary relationship. But it's rarely possible to ignore such feelings altogether. They will find a way of expressing themselves somehow, and often that way will be through the trivial things that really shouldn't matter.

An additional reason why stepfamilies may drive each other crazy over little things is "knee-jerk reactions." Colin, a forty-one-year-old man with a sixteen-year-old stepdaughter, had problems with this. He flew off the handle every time he found his stepdaughter talking on the phone. His stepdaughter was like many other teenagers; she liked to talk on the phone. If left undisturbed, she could do so by the hour; however, she was quick to end her phone conversations when someone else needed to use the phone. Colin's reaction was based on his own problems with a sister when he was growing up. This sister was not as accommodating as his stepdaughter. She would blandly ignore her brother's requests and threats and continue with her conversation, apparently oblivious to his frantic attempts to get her to hang up.

Colin had suffered extreme frustration at times over his sister's lack of consideration (on one occasion, he missed an expected phone call from his girlfriend, who had a flat tire and was calling from a phone booth), and seeing his stepdaughter on the telephone reminded him of all the frustration and aggravation of his youth. Colin didn't realize that those memories were having this effect on him; he reacted without thinking, and then wondered what was the matter with him.

Many people have had this experience. They learned early in life to make a connection between certain experiences and a strong emotion; whenever they encounter similar experiences in later life, the same feelings come back, whether or not they are appropriate to the current situation. It is possible to unlearn such connections, but they must first be recognized.

A fourth reason why people in stepfamilies may find themselves tied up in knots over small, seemingly trivial things is that they have very different value systems. After living together for some time, they may come to find that they really don't have very much in common with each other. As we've emphasized repeatedly throughout this book, similar tastes, interests, and feelings are crucial if a marriage is to survive.

Being in love does not guarantee that you have similar values. In the glow of romantic love and sexual desire, little things like how you like to spend your free time and how clean you like to keep the kitchen sometimes seem unimportant. In fact, the saying that "opposites attract" is probably based at least partly on the fact that the appeal of someone very dissimilar can be all the stronger because he or she is so different. He or she may seem exotic, exciting, mysterious. But those very things that make your loved one so enticing in the beginning may become a source of irritation when you are trying to get along in everyday life. You may wake up someday and feel that you're married to a stranger, someone with whom you have no sympathy, someone whose entire outlook on life is alien to you.

The final reason why stepfamilies may have difficulty dealing with the little things is probably the most difficult to face. That is the problem of fundamental character flaws. Some people have ingrained personality problems that are very hard to change, and can be extremely difficult to live with. Jan, who we discussed in the first chapter, found herself married to such a man. Robert was chronically unfaithful, chronically irresponsible about money matters, physically and verbally abusive, and consistently blamed Jan for everything that went wrong in their mutual lives. The operative words here are "consistent" and "chronic." Everyone can have a bad day occasionally, but people with character problems do the same unpleasant things over and over. They don't take responsibility for their actions and see no reason to change. Everyone else has problems, but not them.

These people can be hard to recognize at first, because it takes time to see the underlying pattern. It can be so easy to accept their rationalizations the first few times something goes seriously wrong. Even long after the pattern should have become clear, many people begin to believe their spouse's accusations and explanations and blame themselves for everything that goes wrong.

We want to make it clear the Jan's situation was an extreme one. Many people with character problems are not as openly exploitive and abusive as Robert was. They may "only" be extremely possessive, controlling, or distant. If you find yourself continually at odds with your partner about things that really shouldn't matter and can't seem to improve the situation no matter how hard you try, you may have to consider the possibility of serious character flaws. Your spouse may be a person who no one could get along with (or, you may be one of those people!).

How to Keep Trivial Things From Driving You Crazy

The solution really depends on the definition of the problem. You need to determine what is causing all the aggravation in your particular situation; it may be a combination of causes. You need to look honestly at your marriage and your family and see if any or all of the above descriptions fit your case. If you have friends, relatives, or even a therapist with whom you feel comfortable talking about these things, listen to what they say for an objective opinion. It can be very hard to see these things clearly when you're in the heat of battle.

If you decide that the main problem is the "honeymoon syndrome," you will have to (slowly, gently) begin expressing more of your real feelings and needs, and encourage your spouse to do likewise. Remember, you don't have to accommodate each other 100 percent of the time. It's okay to have some differences and to do some things separately. You can even express some dissatisfaction occasionally, as long as you do it in a respectful way.

We don't want to encourage you to indulge every whim and fancy at the expense of the other, or to give vent to every negative feeling without restraint. You still need to respect your partner and to treat him or her as someone worthy of consideration and esteem. But you need to respect yourself too, and to make sure that you're getting enough of your needs met to be comfortable in your daily life. No matter how much your spouse and children love you, they cannot foresee your every need. You have to take some responsibility for making sure you are satisfied. This is not a denial of true love; it is just the reality of everyday life.

If your problem is that there are underlying issues which keep cropping up, you need to take a deep breath and face them head-on. Even for you (or for your spouse) to admit your real feelings may clear the air significantly. It may seem like a scary thing to have to do, but once you've got these things out in the open, you have a chance of solving them. If you keep them hidden, the tension will just continue to build, and that can, in time, erode all the good feelings of your marriage.

If you, your spouse, or the children in your household are experiencing "knee-jerk reactions," you can work at weakening the association between the past and present. If you are the one who is having the problem, counter your feelings of irritation by distracting yourself with something you really like. Have a snack, read an interesting book, go for a walk, or pet your dog. Take deep breaths, and remind yourself that the past is not the present. Learn relaxation techniques to rid your mind and body of excess tension. The more you can do these things, the more your irrational irritation will dim, and you will feel satisfaction in being able to control your own emotions.

If your spouse or child is the one having these reactions, you can try to talk to him or her about what is going on, and encourage him or her to learn self-distraction and to unlearn that connection from the past. You can also have a more direct influence. You can go out of your way to be nice to your spouse or child, and do something you know he or she will like when you see that annoyance is starting to build. If you come in after problems have already started, try to avoid getting involved in a negative way. Don't respond to attempts to get your sympathy; don't support his or her continued association of past annoyances with the present.

If you are the object of your spouse's knee-jerk reaction, the best strategy is to react as little as possible, and to change the subject as quickly as you can. When the storm has blown over, you can discuss the problem at an appropriate time. You should also remind yourself that it is not your fault this is happening, and that you are just an innocent bystander caught in stray gunfire.

If you decide that you do not have very much in common, your problem is more serious. You have several options open. One is to accept that your relationship is a limited one; you and your partner will not be able to share as many things as you had once hoped. In that case, you can cut down on all the petty irritations by doing more things apart, by living more separate lives. In some cases, where the various parties involved are comfortable with a relatively low level of intimacy, that may work. Not everyone has the same need for closeness, and as long as a compromise can be reached that is acceptable to all members of the family, commitment and contentment may be maintained.

Another option is to make an effort to adjust to each other's ways and to become more like each other. Whether this is possible depends largely on how flexible and adaptable the people involved are. It's also highly advisable that all members of the family change to some degree, instead of requiring just one to make all the adjustments. Not to do so could lead to resentment on the part of the person who is doing all the adjusting. Besides, this is potentially an opportunity to grow and to learn new things. It could be an extremely enriching experience.

Now we come to the final option. It is important to realize that there are situations that are hopeless. Sometimes two people are just too different ever to have a satisfying mutual life. One of the classic examples is Sam and Diane on the television show *Cheers*. That sort of thing is amusing on a television program, but it's not so funny when it happens in real life. Sometimes the only solution, painful though it may be, is to admit that you've made a mistake and to start over again.

If your family includes a person with character problems, you may have two options. You can put up with their behavior or you can leave. They are unlikely to change, because they will not admit that they even have a problem. If they make you feel sorry enough for them, you may feel compelled to stick around and be their human punching bag, just so they don't have to face the consequences of their own chronic problems. In that case, you'll be doing a kind of volunteer social work; you won't have a real relationship. And you may find, over time, that those "little things," joined with the larger issues of lack of trust, intimacy, and sympathy, may become impossible to bear.

Finally, if you are stuck in an unsatisfying relationship that you feel will never change, you must consider the possibility that the reason you stay is because you have so little belief in yourself. You may think that no one else will love you if you leave this marriage, or that you deserve everything your spouse dishes out. If that is the case, you should consider counseling. You have serious problems with self-esteem and self-worth that no book can fix.

CHAPTER 9

Bridges That Cannot Be Burned

"OH, NO," Pam thought as the phone rang. "Not again." They were just sitting down to dinner, and somehow her husband's ex-wife always managed to call just at that time. She had to be doing it on purpose! Out loud Pam said, "I bet I know who that is." Her husband Eric gave her an annoyed look as she got up and went to the phone in the kitchen. "Hello?"

"Hello, Pam?" The saccharin sweetness of the hated voice set Pam's teeth on edge. "Is Eric there? I'm *so* sorry to interrupt, but I just *have* to talk to him."

"Yeah, just a minute." Pam dropped the phone. Damn it! She tried, she really tried to be just as phony as Sue, to conceal how angry and upset every conversation with Eric's ex-wife made her, but she didn't have the self-control. And Pam knew that Sue loved nothing better than to get under her skin.

Back at the dinner table, she tried to concentrate on feeding her eighteen-month-old son, but she couldn't help overhearing the conversation in the kitchen. "I understand. . . . No, it's no problem. . . . Sure, I'll be over in a little while." Now she was really getting upset. He was always going over there! You'd think they were still married.

Eric came back to the table, trying to ignore the resentful glares of his wife. But he was not allowed to escape. "What is it this time?" Pam asked in a carefully neutral voice.

"Stephanie needs help with her math homework. Sue's no good at math, so I have to help her. I know you wanted me home tonight, but I can't let Steph get behind in math again, like she was last year."

Pam sat fuming silently. Of course Eric should spend time with his ten-year-old daughter, but that really wasn't the issue. Sue was just using Stephanie to get Eric over there. Just like always, he'd spend about five minutes with Stephanie, and then two hours with Sue, listening to all her stupid problems. But Pam was afraid to say anything, because Eric was so sick of her "jealousy." Pam wasn't jealous—she trusted her husband—but it made her mad to see Sue manipulate him like that.

Pam and Eric had been married for almost three years. They had met when Eric was still married to Sue. Eric told Pam right from the beginning that as far as he was concerned, his marriage with Sue had been emotionally dead for a long time. For years Sue had been cold and uncaring to Eric, and Eric had felt sure that his wife was as disenchanted with their marriage as he was. When he told her about Pam, however, Sue had acted as though the thought of divorce was a major tragedy.

However, Pam didn't believe that Sue really cared much for Eric—she just didn't want anyone else to have him. Sue tried every trick in the book to keep Eric with her: asking him to stay for Stephanie's sake, marriage counseling, flirting with other men, pretending to be cool and indifferent, begging, tears, hysterics, even threatening suicide. Pam was sure it was all an act, just the behavior of a spoiled child who wanted to get her way. Sue just could not let it go.

The thing that really irritated Pam was the way Eric treated Sue now, three years later. He was so ridiculously nice to her. Sometimes Pam wondered if he still had feelings for Sue, though she realized that that was impossible. But when he came back home from Sue's house, he was often in a good mood, and even told little stories about what Sue had said, and about how well Sue and Stephanie got along. Big deal, so she was nice to her own daughter! Pam trusted Eric, she knew Eric loved her, but it was hard to live with the fact that he was seeing so much of a woman he had once been married to.

Pam had never been married before, but she felt that if she had, she wouldn't enjoy having her ex-husband around all the time. She didn't even like seeing her old boyfriends; it was impossible to have a casual relationship with either of them. Every time she saw one of them, she would be troubled by memories and emotions she would much rather forget. Whether good or bad, these memories brought back a past that was no part of the present. It was unsettling and distressing. If she could feel that much for a former boyfriend, how much might Eric feel for his former wife? Eric claimed that he felt absolutely nothing for Sue now. But he went over to her house so often; he spent so much time on the phone with her. And he seemed to enjoy it. Was all this time and effort just for his daughter? Or was it for Sue, too?

Ex-Spouses: Dangerous Legacy From the Past

Pam's problems with her husband's ex-wife have the potential to damage her marriage. Her trust in her husband is faltering, her resentment over the time he spends with his ex-wife is causing tension between her and her husband, and her fear of appearing jealous is preventing her from expressing her real needs and feelings. She can't be truly intimate with her husband because she is never completely open and honest with him. Unless one of the two families moves to another city, Eric's contact with his ex-wife is likely to continue until Stephanie is grown up. If Pam does not figure out a better way of coping with the situation, the problems in her marriage may just get worse.

This is not the only problem that ex-spouses can cause in a stepfamily. Almost 60 percent of the people who responded to our survey had serious problems with an ex-spouse. Some of them said that their major problem was ex-spouses who hated each other. While this eliminates the problem of jealousy, it creates other problems. Some ex-spouses can be remarkably vindictive. They may carry grudges for years; they may take every opportunity they can find to express their anger and resentment over what happened in the past. They may poison every conversation with subtle innuendos, or they may openly express their contempt. They may try to turn the children against their ex-spouse. They may have endless criticisms about how the children are treated while with their ex-spouse; they may complain about the food the children eat, the time they go to bed, the television shows they're allowed to watch, the neighborhood children they play with, the way the children are disciplined. They may refuse to compromise on any scheduling conflicts with the children, no matter how much it inconveniences their ex-spouse. They may not allow their ex-spouse any contact with the children outside of the times specified in the custody agreement (for instance, they may refuse to allow their ex-spouse to attend their son's Little League game, because that's not the ex-spouse's weekend to have the child).

It is not difficult to imagine the effect this kind of behavior can have on a stepfamily when it continues for a long time. Even the most stable stepfamily is going to experience some stress as a result of this treatment; every contact with the ex-spouse is likely to cause a little more irritation. And constant irritation will make it even harder to blend two families into a happy stepfamily.

Another ex-spouse problem experienced by the people in our survey was unfair child-support settlements. This was a common problem; almost 40 percent of our respondents said they suffered serious financial problems because of a previous marriage. Very often the mother was awarded custody and received substantial child-support payments from her ex-husband. However, this equitable arrangement seemed less than fair to our respondents when the mother subsequently married a man with a large income. If the ex-husband married again and started a new family, he was in the unenviable position of having to deprive the children from his second family in order to finance luxuries for his first family.

One woman in our survey, Deborah, was the current wife of a man in this situation. Despite the overall happiness of her marriage, Deborah had a hard time dealing with the anger that this situation caused her. "You would have to be a saint to just smile and keep on going. The children aren't always the problem; it's the adults around them. Mom buys them everything under the sun (with Dad's money) to 'help' them through the change. The children have grown up with every material item they could possibly want. They live in a large house complete with inground swimming pool. Their stepfather has bought a boat and has given them skis and knee boards to go with it. It's wonderful to be able to give all these things to your children, but I can't help wondering if this is what our child-support money is going for. We find it so hard to get from paycheck to paycheck, and there are so many things my two-year-old son needs that he has to go without. It makes me mad to see my stepsons come here with designer jeans when my son needs new shoes and we can't afford them."

Some of the people in our survey were also troubled with the "ghosts" of ex-spouses. Even though many of them had minimal contact with their ex-spouse, they were so embittered by the experiences of their previous marriage that they were still carrying around all kinds of "old garbage" or "unfinished business" (as our respondents called it). They had extremely negative expectations of their new spouse, because they had come to believe that all married people insulted, rejected, or controlled each other. Sometimes it seemed almost as if they were reliving the past in the present.

Diane, a thirty-nine-year-old woman who married a man with three adolescent children, became well acquainted with the "ghost" of her husband's ex-wife. She wrote, "Quite often when we argue, I can tell that some of his anger is not directed at me specifically, but at women in general. It is as though he is projecting his ex-wife's qualities on to all women, and because she would have felt this way or that way, he thinks I and all women feel that same way. How often have I heard, 'You women always . . .' or 'You women never . . .' Or sometimes I will say something perfectly innocent, but it will bring up an old wound and it sets him off. I know there are some topics that aren't safe for discussion, not because of anything happening in our marriage, but because of something that happened in his previous marriage." In this way, an absent ex-spouse can create almost as much tension as one who is angrily conducting constant guerilla warfare.

A final ex-spouse problem experienced by the men and women in our survey was that of being compared unfavorably with the ex-husband or ex-wife. Surprisingly, this can happen even when the earlier marriage was quite unhappy. It is rare to find a marriage that had no good points; usually some memories remain that can evoke lost happiness, however brief it might have been. Perhaps the ex-husband always took the trouble to give her a backrub after she had a hard day. Perhaps his ex-wife always got up early on Sunday and made him a delicious coffee cake.

Such things grew naturally out of a relationship that is over, and the last thing you want to do is to try to recreate your spouse's old marriage. You want to develop special traditions of your own. When you spouse says things like "My ex-wife always did it this way" or "My ex-husband knew how to fix it," it is easy to think that your husband or wife misses his or her ex-spouse. It is easy to think that in your spouse's mind you do not measure up to the ex-spouse. Even if your spouse does not put it that way, that is the way it can sound.

It is natural to think these things, but they may not be very accurate. People react according to their own frame of reference, based on all the experiences of their lives, including their own past relationships, their parents' marriage, and stories that they have heard from friends. The problem lies in the fact that two marriage partners often have very different frames of reference. They have had different past relationships, different parents, and different friends; they have different past marriages. That is why it is so risky to make assumptions about your partner's feelings about an ex-spouse. Their past marriage very likely means something very, very different to him or her than it does to you, no matter how much you have discussed it.

Sometimes it is hard to realize that this difference in perspective exists, because most people who are in love and get married feel they understand each other well. That is because the experience of being in love breaks down so many barriers all at once; you feel as though the two of you understand each other in a unique and extremely intimate way. But you can't quite see everything through each other's eyes, no matter how much you feel that you do. Too much is invested in the relationship for that to be possible. Not only do you have a different framework of experiences, but the person that you are in love with is extremely precious to you, almost a part of you. Your own needs and feelings are too closely intertwined with theirs for you to be completely impartial. No matter how unselfish and generous you are, if you love someone, you have a strong desire to have your own needs met. Because of this, there are going to be times when you misread between the lines; you will sometimes misinterpret what each other says and does because your own needs are getting in the way.

When this happens about trivial things, it is not necessarily a serious problem. Your marriage will not be in trouble just because you assume your spouse didn't eat the rice pudding because he or she didn't like it, when the real reason was lack of hunger. Unfortunately, most ex-spouse issues tend to carry much more emotional weight than rice pudding issues.

COPING WITH THE EX-SPOUSE LEGACY

Step One: Understanding Your Spouse

How can you ease the stress caused by an ex-spouse? First, make a real effort to develop a better understanding of your spouse's frame of reference. Don't be discouraging when he or she talks about the past marriage; listen carefully and try to learn all that you can. If you start to feel threatened and upset, stop and consider why you are reacting that way. Is your spouse really expressing lingering affection for the ex-spouse? Or is it upsetting for you to think of your spouse being that intimate with someone else?

You must also listen carefully to anything your spouse may tell you about other past relationships, and about what things were like in his or her family when they were growing up. Think of yourself as collecting all the pieces to a puzzle as you get the various bits of information. How many relationships has your spouse had? How did they end? What initially attracted your spouse to the people he or she was previously involved with? What kinds of things did your spouse do for fun in each relationship? Did your spouse change much to suit past relationships? The more you learn, the more you will understand the kind of relationship your spouse really has with his or her ex-spouse. And, as a side benefit, you will probably strengthen your friendship with your spouse, which is one of the best things you can do for your marriage.

Step Two: Understanding Your Problem

Once you have put together some of the pieces of this puzzle, you will have a better idea of what kind of problem you're facing. All of the situations we described earlier in this chapter can be seen as stemming from one (or both) of two causes:

1. Highly annoying but basically inconsequential events.
2. Unresolved feelings between your spouse and his or her ex-spouse.

The first cause can be irritating, stressful, and unpleasant, but it need not be a major threat to your marriage. The second, however, could mean the eventual end of your marriage. It is very important to determine which one you are dealing with. If you mistake the first for the second, you could be making too much of trivial things. Such things are not really important in the long run, but they could become important if you are constantly worrying about them and talking about them. If you mistake the second for the first, you could be rationalizing a serious situation that needs to be faced and resolved.

It is not all that easy to tell the two causes apart sometimes. For example, Pam and Eric's situation could be seen in two ways. The first was Pam had to deal with a lot of petty irritations caused by Eric's contact with Sue. Her best course of action would be to fight her own feelings of insecurity and jealousy so they wouldn't continue to cause problems between her and Eric. She would have to learn to express her feelings honestly to Eric so he would understand that she was hurting and needed reassurance. Once she was more secure in the marriage, she would have to be more tolerant of the time he spent with Stephanie and Sue, and not make him feel guilty about it. At the same time, Pam would need to develop the ability to put her foot down when she feels that she and her child are being neglected for the sake of Sue and Stephanie. This is relatively easy to do in the context of an honest and trusting relationship. However, when one or both partners are putting on an act because they're afraid of being rejected or hurt, honesty may be difficult or impossible.

The second possibility is that Eric may still have feelings for Sue that he is not acknowledging. The fear of this can be especially haunting when you've already been rejected for somebody else, as Pam had been by one of her old boyfriends. Pam could try to resolve this question by confronting her husband, but confrontation doesn't always provide a solution. Eric might respond with anger to such a question: "You really don't trust me, do you?" Or he might seem to enjoy Pam's jealousy and drop little innuendos that just add fuel to her fire of insecurity. "No, I don't think about Sue *much* [big sigh]." Or he might resolutely change the subject, refusing to discuss it. Or he might read all kinds of deep psychological meanings into her questions. "I know what this is all about. It's because your father left your mother when you were fourteen. Now you can't trust any man." Or, possibly the worst of all, Eric may strongly deny that he feels anything for Sue, but deny it in such a way that Pam doesn't believe him.

The reason that these things are so complicated is because everyone has his or her own agenda. The fact that everyone has different experiences means that everyone has a different way of interpreting conversations, actions, relationships, reality itself. Because of this, Eric may be interpreting Pam's worries about his relationship with Sue in any number of ways. He may be angry because he thinks she is trying to control him and run his life. He may enjoy her jealousy, because he feels secure when his partner is worried and upset. He may feel guilty and uncomfortable when he sees she is upset, and may feel that the best way to handle it is to ignore the problem in the hope that it will go away. He may be horrified by jealousy, because he's seen jealous people do ugly things; he may feel that jealousy is a sure sign of psychological problems. He may be a man who is so unused to examining his feelings that he really does not understand what his own emotions are. Or he may be lying. Almost nobody is going to admit to their current spouse that they still care for their ex-spouse, unless they're considering another divorce.

Pam and Eric have to create their own shared language, in which they can talk about these things and really understand what each other means, without all the intervening layers of experiences and assumptions clouding the issue. The best way to do this is to set time aside to discuss the basics of how they feel and how they see things. In these conversations, they should not assume that they understand what each other is saying. They should be very careful to explain their own feelings and attitudes in simple but specific terms, which are not liable to be misinterpreted easily.

For instance, when Pam talks to Eric about how it makes her feel when he goes over to Sue's house, she should not say: "I get really upset when you go over there." That's too vague. "Upset" can mean practically anything. Instead, she should say something like "When you go over there so much, it makes me think you care too much for her, and then I feel scared and afraid I'm going to lose you someday." To say that does take a great deal of courage and the willingness to be vulnerable, but those are two of the major requirements for true intimacy.

There is a potential pitfall here. Not everyone is equally willing to engage in extensive talks about his or her romantic relationship. Some people feel that talking about a relationship is unnecessary and boring. More men than women feel this way, probably as a result of socialization. Such people may make it very hard to conduct the kind of conversations we have described. However, no matter how averse such people are to "just talking," they will respond if their spouse makes it clear he or she is unhappy and has serious issues to discuss. However, it is important that this discussion not be an argument or a series of accusations. You have to be willing to reveal your true feelings and to be prepared for your spouse to do the same.

There are men and women who have never really learned to express their feelings easily. In a way, that can be an advantage. People who are extremely articulate about their feelings often have a hard time confining themselves to the emotional basics. They want to deduce, infer, elaborate, and conclude. Their imaginations play too big a role in the discussion. Someone who is naturally more reticent is liable to stick closely to the emotional facts of the case, because it is an effort just to find words for his or her feelings. Such people, if they can be brought to talk about these things, are less likely to contribute to marital misunderstandings. But they do need much patience and encouragement to talk in the first place.

Even if a couple does learn to have the courage and vulnerability for honest communication, the outcome is still uncertain. There are no guarantees. Even if Pam does learn about Eric's past, and tries to communicate with him honestly and openly, that does not mean that her marriage will automatically become a union of bliss and harmony. There are other barriers that may stand in the way. He may be unwilling to invest a lot of energy in a relationship and may be satisfied with what is for Pam a superficial and uncommitted marriage. She may have emotional issues which are too powerful or too complex for Eric to understand without the help of a professional. Her value system may be so different from Eric's that they may never be able to agree on what's important. He may be so involved with Sue that he can't let Pam get any closer.

All they can do is try to find out what the real situation is. At the worst, they will have learned how to be emotionally honest; they also will have learned what kind of person they *don't* want to be with. This is not particularly comforting knowledge, but for those of us who prefer to look life in the face and to grow and learn even from unpleasant experiences, it is knowledge that just might be useful in the next relationship. At the best, they will have laid the groundwork for a solid, lifelong love that is based on trust, understanding, and true friendship.

When the problem is two ex-spouses who hate each other, the first thing is to determine if all the unpleasantness is due to petty irritations or to unresolved feelings. If your spouse gets into a shouting match every time he or she has something to do with his or her ex-spouse, what is really going on? Is it the actual circumstances of their contact? Is the ex-spouse habitually late picking the children up? Does he or she return them dirty and exhausted and full of forbidden foods? Is he or she chronically late with the child-support payments? These kinds of things are annoying, but there are ways to handle them (see Chapter 8).

On the other hand, your spouse may still have rage and resentment bottled up inside over the way his or her first marriage ended. Perhaps the name of the ex-spouse seems to lash your spouse into a fury, and he or she often talks angrily about things that happened in his or her previous marriage. If so, your spouse may have unresolved feelings about the ex-spouse that he or she needs to confront and resolve. You are the best person for your spouse to talk to, for two reasons. First, his or her self-esteem may have taken such a beating in the divorce that he or she is obsessed with self-doubts; every contact with the ex-spouse may be a reminder of his or her own inadequacy. In that case, you can provide the reassurance and support that will help your spouse recover from that experience. Second, you will gain more understanding of your partner's feelings. You will find out if these feelings limit your spouse's commitment to you in any way. It is possible that your spouse is still so emotionally involved (positively or negatively) with the ex-spouse that he or she is unable to commit himself or herself fully to you.

Problems with child-support settlements can be viewed similarly. At first glance, this might seem to be a straightforward case. Either you are paying an unfair amount of money or you aren't. But the money itself is not necessarily the real problem (though it doesn't help to be financially strapped). It comes down to the same two causes. On the one hand, the real problem could just be the petty irritations adding up. It's annoying to be short of money, but most of us have learned over the years to adjust to it when it is unavoidable. You have to do without some things, you may have to change your lifestyle, but after a while you get used to it and stop thinking about it so much.

On the other hand, the real problem could be continued resentment and anger because of intense feelings between the ex-spouses, or between the first and second wife (or husband). For instance, Deborah, who was angry that her stepsons had designer jeans and an inground swimming pool, had had a complicated relationship with her husband's ex-wife. She had started dating her husband while he was still living with his first wife and two sons. Deborah saw this first wife, Carol, as a clinging harpy who did not have the sense to know when to let go. When Carol reacted with shock and depression to the news that her husband wanted to leave her for another woman, Deborah was disgusted. How could Carol not have seen what was going on? She was just playing dumb, trying to make her husband feel sorry for her. Deborah saw everything Carol did either as a manipulative ploy aimed at getting her husband back or as an act of revenge. When Carol married a wealthy man shortly after her divorce was final, Deborah was sure she had final proof that Carol had never cared for her first husband, anyway.

Every contact with Carol and her sons made Deborah more and more angry. After Deborah's own son was born, and she began to feel the squeeze of the child-support payments, she became more angry than ever. Deborah never stopped to consider just what was making her so angry. She never realized that she, not Carol, was the one who did not know when to let go. She was still caught up in a romantic triangle; she was still dealing with the emotions of being the Other Woman.

As the other woman, Deborah had to despise Carol in order to maintain her own self-respect, because nobody wants to see themselves as an unprincipled homewrecker. Consciously, she took the attitude of "If he didn't want to leave, he wouldn't have left, so it's not my fault." But underneath, she was tortured with feelings of guilt and fear. Guilt because she had caused a whole family to suffer, at least for a while; fear because she was married to a man who had already left one wife for another woman. Instead of confronting these feelings, she tried to believe that her marriage was a match made in heaven, her husband was a misunderstood hero, and his ex-wife was a witch. It was much easier for Deborah to hate Carol and to blame her for everything than it was to face her own guilt and fear.

Deborah was not doing herself a favor in the long run. Though she told herself that she and her husband were perfect for each other, she was haunted by jealousy and by self-doubt. She was not pretty enough or thin enough. A wonderful man like her husband might lose interest in her. She starved herself down to anorexic thinness and devoted her life to pleasing her husband. But no matter how hard she tried, she could not hide her resentment when her stepsons came to visit. She could not restrain little sarcastic comments about their mother. Her husband loved his two sons from his first marriage very much, and he began to dislike Deborah's constant remarks about Carol. Deborah also found that her preoccupation with Carol's sins made her irritable and grouchy, even though it was all-important to her to be unfailingly pleasing and charming.

Deborah made the mistake of failing to acknowledge the real emotional issues at work in her relationship with her husband's ex-wife. By doing so, she missed the chance to deepen the trust and intimacy in her marriage. If she had been honest with her husband about her feelings of fear and guilt, he would have had a chance to reassure her, to tell her what he really wanted and needed, and to learn how he could please her. Unfortunately, it is impossible to be completely honest with others when you are lying to yourself.

Deborah continued to struggle to maintain the fiction of a perfect marriage, while all the time she was drained by her own feelings of doubt and insecurity.

It is important to look beneath the surface of even so mundane a thing as child-support payments. There may be more going on than appears on the surface. However, it is possible to overinterpret your problems as well. Sometimes it can be very hard to tell the difference between when things are pretty much as they appear and when you have to look deeper for a solution.

People in our survey who had to deal with the "ghosts" of ex-spouses found this out. At first glance, this problem would appear to be caused by psychological conflicts over the ended marriage. For instance, when Libby met Ed, she was struck by all the bitterness and pessimism he was carrying around as a result (she thought) of his divorce five years earlier. After hearing the grim story of his nightmarish marriage with Alice, she had nothing but sympathy for him. Of course he was bitter! Libby knew something of psychology, and she could well understand how the treatment he had received had hurt him deeply and wounded his self-esteem. He needed to be validated by someone who really loved him, by someone who would support him and console him for his sufferings.

After six years of being married to Ed, Libby had a different picture of her husband. Ed was a bottomless pit who took all of her affection and support and gave back nothing. He was still talking about his evil ex-wife and spent countless hours working himself up into a frenzy by brooding over her many transgressions. Worse, his pessimistic attitude was having a bad effect on Libby's children from her own first marriage. Libby wrote: "He's a real 'wet blanket' person, and seems to relish criticizing and mocking others' dreams. He uses ridicule as a disciplinary tool, which I strongly dislike. His poor self-image often causes discipline flare-ups if the children 'look at me like I'm an idiot, or something!' . . . I think I made the right decision at the time, but even though it beats going back on welfare, I can see how his negative personality has affected my kids. All three of them are much less carefree and happy than they were, and approach life with more apprehension than they used to. The youngest, especially, has become a sadder person, while as an infant she was very happy-go-lucky. I feel his negative comments, his criticism of her childish joys, have had a permanent effect on her joy of life."

Libby was mistaken in attributing Ed's pessimism and cynicism to deep psychological conflicts about his marriage. His negativeness was not just the temporary effect of a traumatic experience, it was a enduring personality characteristic. This personality characteristic may have been the result of unpleasant childhood experiences, but such things are not easily changed. In Libby's case, the ghost of Ed's ex-wife was just the tip of the iceberg. Had she realized that, Libby would have run fast and far in the opposite direction; but she saw the iceberg tip as just a stray patch of bad weather.

These ghosts do not have to mean the eventual shipwreck of a committed relationship. Sometimes they can be just a passing storm. The case of Kevin and Lisa is an example of this. Lisa's husband left her for another woman, and subsequently she was badly treated by two other men before her best friend introduced her to Kevin. Because of these experiences, she expected rejection. At the beginning of their relationship, she read all kinds of meanings into Kevin's every action, interpreting his every word and deed as evidence that he didn't really care for her. If he forgot to call her, she assumed he did it on purpose to show her that he wasn't really committed to her. If he was late, she imagined that he was with another woman. If he wanted a night out with his friends, she thought it was because he was hoping to meet someone new to date.

At first, Kevin didn't understand what was going on. All he knew was that Lisa seemed to get mad over little things. He put up with it because he liked her, and because to him there were a lot of nice things about Lisa. Later in the relationship, she began to tell him what she was thinking, and to explain why she got so angry at times. At first, he thought she was joking—to him, it was crazy to think he would be looking for someone else when he already had Lisa.

Gradually, Kevin realized that because of what Lisa had gone through in her previous relationships, she needed extra reassurance. Over time, he found that the more he was able to provide that reassurance, the more Lisa forgot about her ghosts from the past. Today they are married, have two children, and seem to be very happy.

Lisa had some advantages in this situation, First, she had devoted a lot of time and energy to understanding the end of her marriage and her other relationships. She had spent some time in psychotherapy as part of this process. She had confronted her own problems, had taken responsibility for what she had done wrong in previous relationships, and had learned from her mistakes. When she met Kevin, she was enough in touch with her own feelings to be able to talk to him honestly, instead of playing games or acting out old traumas. She had resolved her feelings about the men in her past, and she worked hard at developing a relationship with Kevin.

Second, her problems were the result not of chronic personality tendencies but of acute stress in her personal life. Once the stress was removed, and once she understood that Kevin was not going to treat her as the other men in her life had, she was able to leave the past behind and become a much happier person. Had Kevin assumed that her behavior early in the relationship was typical for her, and not the result of stressful experiences, he may not have persevered in the relationship no matter how much he cared for her. It is vitally important to be able to tell the difference between chronic and situational problems, but it can be very difficult to do so. That is one of the many reasons that it is best to know your partner for a long time before you marry; chronic problems often do become obvious over time, if you have the courage to acknowledge them.

Being compared with an ex-wife or ex-husband is yet another ex-spouse problem that can be interpreted two ways. Such a comparison may mean that your spouse is still inappropriately connected with his or her ex-spouse, or it may be a casual comment. It is very easy to read too much into such comments. Your spouse may simply be used to a certain way of doing things. For instance, the comment "My ex-wife always made roast chicken on Sunday" could be an observation, or perhaps a suggestion, about a basically mundane matter. A wife who hears this need not assume that her husband is finding her inadequate compared to his ex-spouse. That is why it is so important that the two partners in a marriage spend time learning how to communicate clearly and honestly; they must develop the relationship skills that will enable them to discuss and resolve such issues.

Step Three: Putting It All Together

In each problem situation that can occur, there are three ways to look at what is going on: The cause may be external factors, irritations, and annoyances that are being blown up into major crises; there may be underlying emotional problems or issues that are being ignored or rationalized; or there may be a combination of the two at work. Your job is to figure out which is happening in your situation. There is no easy way to do that. Every set of circumstances is complicated, and there is no pat answer that works for everyone. Everyone sees the world differently, and your own understanding of your own situation is unique and important. You must rely on your own instincts, insight, commitment, and hard work. You have the power to resolve your problems and to shape your relationship in the way best for you.

Take a careful look at what assumptions you have made about your relationship and your partner. Is there another explanation for the facts? Are you listening carefully to what your partner is saying about the ex-spouse, without filling in the blanks with assumptions of your own? Do you overreact to any kind of contact with the ex-spouse and then wonder why? Be as honest as you can be with yourself and listen to your own heart. Then, when you sit down to talk to your spouse about all of this, you'll have somewhere to begin.

SOME STRATEGIES TO REDUCE EX-SPOUSE STRESS

Once you and your spouse have come to a mutual understanding of your ex-spouse situation, you still have to decide what to do about it. Once you have established true confidence and trust in your marriage, these problems will already seem less important and less stressful. There are some ways you can reduce ex-spouse trouble still more.

First, deal with the practical side of things. You need to realize that you have control over the everyday details that contribute to your ex-spouse problem. If your spouse is spending too much time with an ex-spouse, as in the case of Eric and Pam, decide on some specific rules based on your needs and feelings. This will be much easier to stick to if you choose rules that are fair to your spouse's children from the previous marriage. For instance, it would be quite all right for Pam to tell Eric that she needed to have him home a certain number of nights a week. Stephanie's homework is important, but not important enough to jeopardize Pam and Eric's marriage. Pam, as Eric's current wife, should be able to take control of the situation when she needs to.

If your problem is ex-spouses who hate each other, minimize the contact all you can. If an ex-spouse is calling up and picking fights with your partner, get an answering machine and screen your calls. Do not encourage your spouse to dwell on the situation by excessive discussion and analysis of the ex-spouse's character and behavior; just tactfully change the subject. Avoid places where you know the ex-spouse might be. When the ex-spouse returns your stepchildren after having them for a weekend, answer the door yourself.

If unfair child-support settlements are getting you down, work at putting it out of your mind. If there is really nothing you can do about it, you need to make a realistic budget and stick to it, and avoid aggravating comparisons of what your children have and what the stepchildren have. Don't complain to your friends about it, don't write to your sister about it, don't harass your spouse about it; that will only make you think about it even more and fan the flames of resentment. And if you find it impossible to stop thinking about it, you'd better start considering whether the problem is really just financial. Maybe there are emotional issues at work here that you need to explore.

As for the "ghosts," you have to determine what problems they represent and why they are still around. Did you or your spouse experience a rejection that made you really question your own worth, your own desirability? Do you or your spouse feel that your ex-spouse had something you just cannot forget, even though he or she treated you badly? You may find that there are serious emotional issues you need to work through before you can really commit yourself wholeheartedly to your marriage.

Being compared to your husband's or wife's ex-spouse is definitely an annoyance. Tell your spouse up front how it makes you feel. Be careful to concentrate on your own feelings (e.g., "It makes me feel second-best when you're always talking about him"), not on assumptions you have made about your partner's feelings (e.g., "You seem to care more about him than me"). Explain what you are feeling and help your spouse see your point of view. If, after time, that doesn't have an effect, something may be wrong. Reminiscences about the first spouse should not be more important than feelings for the current one. You need to let your spouse know that he or she is endangering your chances of a successful second chance.

Aside from these practical strategies, there's another thing you can do to improve your ex-spouse situation; you can try to develop some sympathy for the ex-spouse. In a lot of cases that may be difficult to do, but it can reap rich rewards. After all, the ex-spouse is probably finding it very hard to see someone who was once their husband or wife in somebody else's arms. No matter how unhappy the marriage was, most people tend to feel that way. After all, he or she once loved your spouse enough to promise, before all the world, to love, honor, and cherish forever. He or she probably had hopes and dreams of the relationship similar to those which you treasure now. Those dreams are over now, and only pain remains, the soreness of the end of love.

Many people try to hide from the pain of rejection or failure by hatred. You can be bigger than that. You can refuse to be limited by petty jealousies and inconsequential irritations, and be generous to the ones who have lost. For whatever the circumstances behind your marriage, the ex-spouse will almost certainly feel that in some way you have won. You can reduce his or her anger and resentment simply by being kind; by not putting them in the position of being a heartless harpy or a relentless nag; by not holding it against them that they too once were your spouse's husband or wife. It takes a certain security and strength to do this, but if you have or can develop that strength, you may find that your ex-spouse problems quickly fade away.

Several of the people who responded to our survey were able to do this. Linda, a forty-year-old woman who acquired two stepsons when she married Stephen, was fortunate in this regard. She wrote, "I encourage my stepsons to talk about their mother. I am lucky to have been able to establish an excellent relationship with her. . . . Their mother has told me that I am the only other person in the world she would want her sons to be with if anything ever happened to her—the ultimate compliment. I have worked very hard at establishing her trust in me—and she does trust me! We respect the roles we play. I am the number one wife and woman in his new life and she is the mother of their children."

Michelle and John, whom we discussed in earlier chapters, also had this experience. Michelle decided from the first that since John disliked talking to his first wife, she would be the one to discuss the arrangements for John's son with his ex-wife. Michelle felt sorry for Anne and went out of her way to sympathize with her, and to understand her emotional and financial problems. Soon Anne was calling her up, not just to discuss her son, but to have someone sympathetic to talk to. Not everyone is capable of this degree of generosity and empathy, but even a great deal less would ease the problems of the ex-spouse.

Finally, if all attempts to increase the trust and honesty in your marriage fail, and if no matter how hard you try to communicate honestly and clearly with your spouse, you always end up miscommunicating, you may have a serious problem. The problem may be that your spouse is still too involved with the previous marriage to be fully committed to the present one. The problem may be that the two of you have unusual barriers, of one kind or another, to trusting each other. In either case, you should consider some kind of marriage counseling to help you understand and resolve your problems. You must put your marriage first, even for your stepfamily's sake. If the marriage is solid, the difficulties of blending two families into one will be very much lessened.

CHAPTER 10

Love for Sale: Loyalties in the Second Marriage

BEN FELT THE PAINFUL, familiar thumping of his heart as his mother drove her car up to his father's house. He was supposed to spend the weekend with his father and his stepmother. He didn't want to go. He didn't mind seeing his father, even though Dad had changed so much since he married *her*. But Ben didn't like leaving his mother. Ever since his mother had left his father two years ago, when Ben was five, Ben felt scared when he was away from her. Maybe something would happen to her while he was away, maybe he would never see her again. Or maybe she would think Ben wanted to live with his father all the time; maybe she'd never come to get him.

And it was yucky at his Dad's house now. *She* was always there. She wouldn't leave him alone. She was always trying to give him things, make him special food, saying she loved him. It was gross. She tried to act like she was his mother. She even wanted him to call her Mom. How stupid could she be! A kid could only have one Mom, she ought to know that. She was trying to make him forget his real mom, she was trying to trick him into staying there. Even Dad didn't understand. He was always saying he hoped Ben could love his stepmother.

The car pulled up in front of his father's house. Ben felt his eyes fill with tears, even though it made him mad and embarrassed to cry. His mother hugged him. "I hope you're going to have a good time this weekend, sweetie. Remember, we all love you, me and your dad and Marsha. Just be a good boy the way you are at home and everything will be fine." Why did Mom look so worried? Did she know how much he really didn't want to go?

Dad came out of the house. He must have been watching for them. He took Ben's suitcase out of the backseat and chatted with Mom for a minute. They were always so polite to each other, but their words didn't really mean anything. Ben listened to them, hoping to hear some sign that they still loved each other, that they might get back together so the three of them could be a family again. But their faces were cold and their talk was soon over. It was time for him to go into the house. He waved good-bye to his mother with a dead feeling in his chest.

As they walked together up to the house, his dad said, "We're real glad to see you Ben. Me and Marsha. You're going to try harder to be nice to her, aren't you?" His father's voice was worried and kind of sad.

"I guess," Ben said softly, avoiding his father's eyes. No, Dad didn't understand at all.

Marsha was waiting right in the vestibule. She couldn't even let him be alone with Dad for a minute when he first came. "Hello, Ben!" She was trying to sound friendly and excited, but Ben could tell that something was bothering her. Something was always bothering her. "We made your favorite supper for tonight, hamburgers and french fries and creamed corn! And I made a chocolate cake for dessert!"

Ben could feel his father's eyes on him. "Thank you," he mumbled uncomfortably.

Marsha went on, "And we're going to go to the movies tomorrow! We'll go to whichever one you want." She paused for a moment, then reached down to hug him. Ben stood very still, feeling like a boy made out of marble. He had seen marble statues in the museum, when his mother took him to see all the art. The thought of his mother made his eyes tear up again. He turned away his head and pulled away from Marsha slightly. Why couldn't she just act normal?

Marsha stood up, her eyes glittering strangely. Ben noticed that Dad had a funny look on his face, a sad look. He looked like he felt sorry for somebody. "Well!" Marsha said, straightening up. "Why don't I just—" Without finishing her sentence, she turned and walked out of the room.

Ben and his dad looked at each other. "Ben, I think we'd better have another little talk," his dad said.

In the kitchen, Marsha struggled to control her emotions. Why, why, why was Ben so cold to her? Hadn't she done everything she could to make him love her? She'd pampered him, bought him toys, tried to talk to him and to play with him. But even after a whole year of these visits, he still acted like she was some kind of monster. Marsha knew for a fact that her husband, Peter, had several times talked to Ben about the way he treated her; why, even Ben's mother had talked to Ben about it. None of it seemed to have done any good.

Marsha had hoped for a real relationship with Ben. Though she had wanted children ever since she was a little girl, she knew now that she would never have any of her own. Accepting that reality had been very hard, but her sense of emptiness had been lessened when she met Peter and Ben. Ben was still young enough to be adaptable and to need the care of a mother. She had assumed that he would eventually accept her as a stepmother. The fact that he hadn't after all this time could mean only one thing: She wasn't good with kids, there was something unlovable about her.

Marsha was quite wrong in her assumption that she was at fault because her relationship with Ben wasn't all that she had hoped for. But her underlying expectations were also unrealistic. She seriously underestimated how difficult it would be for Ben to accept her even as "just" a friend; she didn't know that it was virtually impossible for him to accept her as a mother. Marsha was confusing her own needs with the needs of the child.

THE STEPCHILD'S LOYALTY DILEMMA

Ben was confused about loyalties; he instinctively felt that to be nice to Marsha would be a betrayal of his mother. Many children who are part of a stepfamily have feelings similar to Ben's. In fact, 57 percent of the people who responded to our survey said that the children in their families seemed confused about where they should place their loyalties.

Ben felt that Marsha was trying to take his mother's place. His feelings of loyalty to his mother made it very hard for him to feel positively about Marsha; to him, affection for his stepmother was a betrayal of his mother. These feelings were intensified by the fact that Ben was afraid of losing his mother altogether. His parents' divorce had made the world seem a frightening and uncertain place to Ben.

Parents are the only security a young child has, and when something is wrong with the child's parents, it seems to the child that the whole world is falling apart. Aside from the death of a parent, divorce can be one of the most terrifying events in a child's life. No matter how much strain and turmoil there has been in the home in the past, divorce causes even more emotional upheaval, at least temporarily. The child is separated from one of his or her parents, or is shuttled back and forth between them. He or she feels uprooted, confused, insecure, and vulnerable. Those of us who have been divorced can identify with those feelings. But for the child, there is another dimension—helplessness. Children have a very limited ability to control events. They are totally dependent on their parents, and the same feelings that to us would be disturbing are to them overwhelming, because they have no means of escaping or changing things.

Ben was unable to control or tolerate the feelings of fear, anger, and confusion caused by his parents' divorce the way an adult might. Instead, he clung even tighter to the one person who had always been there for him—his mother. Because she was now his world, she was sacred to him. To think of someone taking her place, even just on the weekends, seemed like sacrilege. Also, Marsha's presence was a denial of Ben's secret hope that one day his mother and father would get back together.

HELPING YOUR STEPCHILD ADJUST: SETTING THE STAGE

How should Marsha handle this situation? Our respondents had much advice to give to people in circumstances similar to Marsha's. Some stepparents focused on what should be done before the marriage takes place. Most stressed the importance of getting to know your stepchildren well before the wedding. A lot of heartache can be saved if you develop relationships with your future stepchildren before the wedding takes place, though it's never too late. One stepparent who gave this kind of advice was Cynthia, who, at thirty-one, married a man with three children from his first marriage. She wrote, "I would advise prospective stepparents to spend time together as a unit *before* getting married. I would tell them to listen to their children and to allow them to express their feelings. I would also encourage them to reassure the children of their place in their natural parents' lives." Cynthia was wise enough to recognize the need her stepchildren had to know that they would never lose the love of their natural parents; she was also secure enough in herself and her relationship with her husband to be able to provide that reassurance without feeling threatened.

Rosemary, whose stepfamily included her son, Allen, from a previous marriage and the three children of her present husband, gave similar advice. "It's important to spend time alone with the children before you get married. My stepchildren spent weekends with my child and myself several times. This gave us a chance to see each other as ourselves without feeling like Dad was watching. . . . There have been times when my husband's children have wanted help with problems. I've tried to listen as a friend and to let them talk themselves out without agreeing or disagreeing. A few of these talks have concerned matters that were very important to them, and I've been proud that they love and respect me enough to share not only their happy times but also their hardships." Rosemary's ability to be a friend to her stepchildren obviously reaped rich rewards.

Lenna, a thirty-six-year-old woman with a son and daughter from a previous marriage and two stepsons from her current marriage, commented that getting to know your stepchildren doesn't mean constantly entertaining them. She wrote, "Spend time together, not just time going places, but also time where you just hang around the house. They need to know that while you can have fun, life is not always a continuous party." It's not your duty to provide constant treats and excitement for your stepchildren; if you do, they may not really get to know you if you always act like you're on your best behavior. Further, you may also be creating false expectations. No matter how much you want to please them and make them like you, you will regret providing a "continuous party" if the end result is resentment and disillusionment from the children when the flow of goodies stop.

The importance of getting to know your stepchildren, and of trying to be their friend rather than a substitute parent, was emphasized by Helen, who got married for the first time at twenty-nine, and acquired a five-year-old stepson. She wrote, "Be sure you meet and get to know your stepchildren. I made the mistake of assuming I could get along with any child because I loved children. I did not meet my stepson prior to marriage. . . . It's important to try to develop friendships with the children, realizing you are not their natural parent and never will be." Helen was able to understand that a stepparent can never really replace the natural parent in a child's heart; she was able nevertheless to develop a healthy and beneficial relationship with her stepson.

Sarah became the stepmother of five children from three different marriages when she married Burt. Like Helen, she learned it was important not to try to replace the children's natural mother. She wrote, "The stepmother must find a way of explaining to her prospective stepchildren that she is *not* replacing their mother. In my experience, I find that boys and girls alike can handle having a stepfather much better than [having] a stepmother. Children are consistently closer to their mother. Explain that you would like to be their friend, and let them come to you in their own time for 'mothering.' I have not pushed myself on my stepchildren. . . . I have allowed them to choose what to call me. Two call me Mom, and the other three call me by my name."

If these women, who have also been through the experience of trying to blend a stepfamily, could give advice to Marsha, they would probably tell her not to work so hard at being a stepmother, and not to expect so much from Ben. The fact that Marsha wanted children of her own but couldn't have them makes it likely that she has strong emotional needs which are not being fulfilled. Though these needs must be addressed, it is not appropriate for her to try to fulfill them through her relationship with Ben. He already has a mother. Marsha must try to understand Ben's point of view; she must offer him only what he can accept.

There are other needs that can cloud the issue between stepparents and stepchildren. Sometimes stepparents may feel threatened by their spouse's relationship with their natural children. They may try to make their spouse love them more by attempting to win over the children. Another problem is when the stepparent feels threatened by their spouse's ex-wife or ex-husband, and tries to compete by being "super-stepmom" or "super-stepdad." In either case, they may ignore the children's real needs because they are trying too hard to get their own needs met. They're setting themselves up for failure, because unless the children's needs happen to coincide exactly with their own (an unlikely occurrence), the stepparents may end up feeling just as frustrated and rejected as Marsha did.

HOW TO BE SENSITIVE TO YOUR STEPCHILDREN'S NEEDS

How can you distinguish between your own needs and the needs of your stepchildren? Children are just like adults in that they communicate through subtle signals which can be read by a sensitive person. If a child doesn't want you to hug him or her or receive presents from you, you will be able to tell if you pay close attention. It's important to try not to feel rejected, hurt, or offended if you perceive that your stepchildren don't want what you're trying to give them. You can't force your affection on them—the relationship between a stepchild and a stepparent is a two-way street, and the child's needs must be considered as well as the adult's. Sharon, who had a six-year-old stepdaughter from her husband's previous marriage, had to learn the hard way that she couldn't become an instant mother to her stepchild. She wrote, "The biggest obstacle has been a stepdaughter who has serious emotional problems, centering around her nonacceptance of the divorce and remarriages of her natural parents to others. . . . The biggest mistake I made, and that most people make in this situation, is trying too hard to be a mother and to be accepted."

Many people may feel hurt or resentful when their stepchildren are aloof or rejecting. If you find yourself in this kind of situation, you must try not to take your stepchildren's reactions personally. Try to see the children's point of view; try to understand that they're confused and hurt themselves and that they're trying to make sense out of their lives. They may be struggling to comprehend just what role their natural parents play in their lives, or they may be trying hard to grasp what it means to be a son or daughter. It may take much time for them to accept you.

The best way for you to proceed is to approach them on a person-to-person level. What qualities do you admire in other people? Consideration, loyalty, integrity, honesty, fairness, kindness, generosity? That's the point from which you should start. Make sure the children learn to respect you and trust you as a person; that's the seed from which all healthy relationships grow.

Corinne and Daniel each had two children from a previous marriage, and in the process of blending their two families into one, they realized that respect was extremely important. Corinne wrote, "The advice I would give a friend who was planning to marry someone with children is to differentiate between love and respect with stepchildren. Remember they are only innocent victims of a marriage that did not work. It's natural to hope that one's stepchildren will love you, but it's not fair to *expect* them to love you. You must first earn their respect, and I do mean *earn*. It's not really even fair to demand respect until you've earned it, and after there is an even keel of respect achieved, you can only be thankful for the love that will most probably follow from stepchildren. Children are naturally full of love, but I feel that after divorce they sometimes are afraid of openly loving a new stepparent for fear that the natural parent will see it as a disloyalty."

If you make it clear to your stepchildren that you are not going to force them to renounce their natural parent, if you allow them to define the relationship in their own way, and give them time to accept it and to learn to trust you, you will have a good chance of building a loving relationship with your stepchildren. It won't be a quick or easy process. Don't beat yourself or tell yourself, as Marsha did, that there must be something wrong with you if the relationship doesn't blossom as quickly as you'd hoped. Keep your expectations reasonable, or you may come to feel like a failure.

Above all, patience is extremely important. As Corinne wrote, "It's important to be sure there is acceptance on both sides and to move slowly. Time does heal all wounds and with time, patience, and love, the relationship will grow and prosper. . . . Actions do speak louder than words."

STEPPARENTS CAN BE CONFUSED, TOO

You may have noticed that Ben's story was a kind of best-case scenario. His natural parents got along with each other (at least superficially), his mother was supportive of Marsha, and Marsha herself was eager for Ben to like her and had no children of her own to cause problems. However, not all stepfamilies are this harmonious.

Sometimes the stepparent has loyalty issues, especially if he or she is the noncustodial parent of his or her own children. Elise and Fred were faced with this problem. Elise had two young daughters and a twelve-year-old son from a previous marriage, and Fred also had a twelve-year-old son, who lived with Fred's ex-wife. Elise wrote, "When my husband and I were first married, he felt a tremendous amount of guilt because my son lived with us and his son of the same age lived with his mother. I think the constant reminder that my son was here and his was not caused a lot of stress in our relationship. My husband would not give my children any attention or affection after we were married because he felt like a traitor to his own son. This was difficult for both the children and me. I was very naïve going into this marriage and truly believed we were destined to be the next Brady Bunch. I had no idea that my husband would have such a difficult time both giving and *receiving* affection from my children initially (even to the extreme that he would not allow them to call him Dad)."

There is no easy solution to this kind of problem. There may be perfectly legitimate reasons for parents to feel guilt toward their children. First, they may feel guilty because they have put their children through a divorce. In a divorce children often suffer because they see their parents in serious conflict. Sometimes the stress and unhappiness caused by the end of a marriage can even cause parents temporarily to become cold or overly punitive to their children. The memories of what the children went through in this time may haunt the parents. Second, a parent may feel guilt for having allowed the other parent to have custody. Third, those who leave their spouse for another person with children may feel that the divorce was their fault.

Whatever the reason, if guilt toward your natural children is affecting your relationship with your stepchildren, you need to confront your feelings directly. Neglecting or ignoring your step-children is not a solution. Counseling is one possibility, and it may even be advisable to include the entire stepfamily in the counseling process, depending on the age of the children.

Don't allow yourself or your spouse to be pressured by the children, no matter how emotionally needy they are. Explain the problem to them in language they can understand. You might say that you or your spouse miss the children from the other family, and that you feel a little sad. They'll understand that because they've had to face a similar kind of sadness over separation from part of their family as well. Treat them as a friend or as a niece or nephew if you can't feel like a parent to them. Treat them with as much respect, consideration, honesty, and empathy as you can. Try to find things that you both would enjoy doing together. Imagine how you would like your own children treated by a stepparent, and behave accordingly. Don't try to bracket or limit the relationship in your mind. Let it develop naturally, and give whatever you can bring yourself to give at the time. Don't forget that no matter what the situation is, your stepchildren didn't cause your problems, and you shouldn't take your pain and guilt out on them.

A different kind of mistake that stepparents sometimes make when both partners have children from previous marriages is to believe that they can and/or should feel the same way about their stepchildren as they do about their own children. In most cases, people who believe this are fooling themselves. They may have the best possible intentions, but they are simply not in touch with the reality of their feelings. They are like the people who claim that the color of a person's skin means nothing to them. This is certainly not to say that it is impossible to have a close, loving relationship with either a stepchild or a person of another race. But to ignore the differences in such a situation is to be willfully blind, and probably will lead to a shallow, superficial relationship. (The one possible exception is when the stepparent enters the family when the child is still an infant; in that case a bond similar to that between a natural parent and child may be formed.) Another important point is that you may not necessarily *like* your own child better than your stepchild. Your stepchild could be the more agreeable, pleasant person. But for most people, there is an intensity of feeling, a deeper kind of loyalty, an almost instinctive attachment that they feel for their own children. And if it comes down to a choice between your own child and your stepchild, you may become extremely confused if you've been deceiving yourself about your feelings.

Chris, whose family we discussed in several previous chapters, came to realize how true that was. He was part of a stepfamily that included both his own and his wife's children from previous marriages, and he had this to say about the difference between his feelings for his own children and for his stepchildren: "I have to laugh when I hear people saying they love their stepchildren as much as their own children. That's totally unrealistic! And I'm saying it as someone who does care about my stepchildren. But what do you think you'd do if you saw that both your own child and your stepchild were being attacked by rabid dogs and you could only save one of them? You wouldn't hesitate; you'd save your own child. That's what it comes down to, and I don't care how heartless it sounds, it's the truth."

If you find yourself asserting that there is no difference in your feelings between your natural children and your stepchildren, you'd better take some time to examine your feelings more closely. You should realize that it's not a moral imperative that you love both sets of children equally. What *is* necessary is that you treat both sets of children with fairness. If you or your spouse feel some of the children in your stepfamily are receiving better treatment than others, you are not alone. Though most of the people who answered our survey said that all the children in their stepfamily were treated alike, 22 percent admitted that they were concerned about this issue. It's all the more important that you handle this problem properly, because it is highly likely that the children themselves may be adding fuel to the fire. Fifty-eight percent of our respondents said that there was jealousy and rivalry between the children in their stepfamilies.

How can you ensure that all the children in your stepfamily receive fair treatment? You don't have to pretend you feel the same way toward all the children, but you should make sure that all the children in your stepfamily receive similar amounts of attention, similar privileges, gifts, and so forth. If you play favorites, even unintentionally, you will probably have a new set of problems on your hands—you will have marital problems. Nowhere can loyalties cause more turmoil than when each spouse is zealously defending the rights of his or her children and denying those of his or her stepchildren.

A related loyalty issue can arise when the stepfamily includes children both from a previous marriage and from the current marriage. Adrienne, an articulate and educated woman who married a man with a ten-year-old son, wrote: "The birth of my son created such intense feelings and attachments that I found myself stepping back from my stepson, assuming that he would understand. Neither myself, my husband, nor my stepson were able to (or chose to) deal with the resultant changes until the following year. But then, small problems had become large, all-encompassing ones. I think my husband and I were totally unprepared for the changes my motherhood would bring, and we both developed resentment toward each other because he/she was unsympathetic to the other spouse's perspective and needs. . . . My husband and I finally went into counseling when our son was two and a half and I was pregnant with our twins. We realized we needed techniques in order to communicate and make decisions, as we had lost those skills when we struggled with the roles and responsibilities of parent/stepparent after our son was born. We realized that additional children would only exacerbate the problems, which we had never handled in the first place."

Some of the preceding situations are reminiscent of a familiar fairy tale: Cinderella. As everyone knows, Cinderella's father, a widower, married a woman who turned out to be a Wicked Stepmother. She had two daughters, but whether they were the result of a previous marriage or were the natural children of Cinderella's father is unclear. Either way, the end result was the same: Cinderella was a despised outsider, who was made to do the most menial chores and was denied the opportunity of going to the Royal Ball.

Her stepmother seemed to see Cinderella as inferior to her own children; she gave Cinderella crusts of bread to eat and made her sleep in the hearth. In real life, of course, these loyalty issues are much more complex and subtle, and few stepchildren are going to be forced to sleep in front of the fireplace. But all the same, loyalty conflicts need to be addressed, whether you're planning to have your own family, are currently pregnant, or whether you're already part of a family that includes both children from one previous marriage and children from the current marriage. Differential treatment of children in a stepfamily can become a terrible marital problem, and can cause serious problems in the children's emotional development.

The story of Jan and Robert, which has been described in other chapters, is a good example of marital problems exacerbated by loyalty conflicts. As you may recall, Robert and Jan both had one son from a previous marriage; the other three children had been born after Robert and Jan were married. Early in the relationship, Jan became convinced that Robert was showing extreme favoritism toward Todd, and was neglecting his other children. She saw everything Robert did for Todd as unreasonable, unfair, and discriminatory; she was convinced that his attachment to Todd was a form of bizarre, pathological identification, and that he was obsessed with his son. She told us that he was constantly afraid that someone was mistreating his son, and that he wouldn't allow Jan to discipline her stepson. According to Jan, Robert was lavishly generous when it came to the things Todd wanted. On the other hand, Robert's mother accused Jan of buying more things for her own children than she did for Todd, which gives a different side of the picture. Maybe Robert really did have reasons to protect his oldest son from neglect.

Who was right? Unfortunately, in a situation like this, nobody is. Jan and Robert's marriage could not be taken as a model by anyone, but they provide a good example of how such things can snowball. It may have started with some relatively insignificant rivalry between Jan and Robert as to whether Todd or one of the other children was going to get new shoes, or go to camp for the summer, or whether Todd would have friends over on a night when one of the other children was sick. With Jan defending her children and

Robert defending Todd, the parents' opinions could quickly become polarized, each becoming more and more extreme in their views in order to make their position seem like the right one. Such polarization can create resentments and animosity that could permanently damage the marriage, as the parents become adversaries rather than partners.

This is the worst-case scenario, and is likely to occur only when, as in the case of Jan and Robert, both spouses have serious personality problems and the marriage is already shaky. However, even in a fundamentally good marriage, if the parents have different sets of loyalties to different children, there is obviously fertile ground for conflict. It is extremely hard for loving parents to look on and say nothing when their child is being slighted or neglected, and it is easy to become angry and resentful in such a situation.

What should you do if you think you have this kind of problem? First of all, be willing to consider that you yourself might be somewhat prejudiced in favor of your own children. If you can make that admission, it is likely that your spouse will be able to as well. Then, each of you should sit down and list your grievances on paper. Concentrate on what should be done for your own children, rather than what *shouldn't* be done for your stepchildren (the latter is far more likely to lead to unpleasantness). Then, each of you should pick one thing from the other's list that you can do for each child you've been accused of neglecting (by the way, it's far better to concentrate on activities with the children, than on things you can buy for them).

Notice that we recommend you concentrate your efforts on improving your relationships with the children you have the poorest relationship with, rather than defending the children you think are not getting their fair share of the pie. Listen to your spouse, and get the other's point of view. Remember that you're a family, that you need to pull together as much as possible, not take sides and defend your positions. If the problems in your stepfamily are severe enough, you may need to consult a family therapist to have an impersonal forum in which to discuss these things in a civilized way. But remember, treating some children in the stepfamily better or worse than others can have a very negative impact on the whole family.

THE PROBLEM OF CHOOSING SIDES

One loyalty problem we haven't discussed yet involves the ex-spouse. Sometimes children's loyalties are confused and even twisted by the attitudes the two ex-spouses have toward each other; the children may be drawn into the bitterness still echoing from a former failed marriage. One way this may happen is if the children are asked by one parent to function as spies during their visits to the other parent. In this situation, the children are often asked, directly or indirectly, to choose between their parents; such a choice is, of course, quite contrary to the children's best interests.

Bobby Marks is a good example of this. He and his brother, Tim, visited his father every summer. Their natural parents had been divorced for eight years, and his father had remarried several years ago. But even though so much time had passed, his father still seemed to be preoccupied, even obsessed, with Bobby's mother. Every visit to his father began with a cross-examination. How was his mother doing? Who was she dating? Did she still drink like a fish? Had she gained any more weight? Was she still fighting with all her relatives? Did she still have a nasty temper? Was her cooking just as lousy as it used to be? And on and on.

Bobby felt like a traitor answering all of these questions, but he didn't know how to tell his father how he felt. Even though he tried not to say anything bad about his mother, somehow his father would make her sound like an evil person. But that wasn't all. After the interrogation, his father talked about the things that happened in the old days, when Bobby's father and mother were still married to each other. Some of these memories were nice, but mostly they were mean and awful. And the strange part was, Bobby had heard his mother talk about a lot of the same things, but her version of the same events was totally different. Once he told his dad that, and Dad had just laughed and said his mother always had been a little liar.

Bobby hated these conversations. They made him feel so bad! It was like he had two nice new cars, and someone told him to crash one car into the other. But Dad couldn't be wrong. He was so generous, always giving him things, and being so affectionate to him. He was a good person, even if he did lose control of his temper sometimes. Mom must be telling lies after all; she must be not a good person. After all, she was cold and mean sometimes. She wouldn't let him go out with his friends when he wanted to, she was so critical of his grades, and she had done so many mean things to Dad.

And so, over the course of a summer, Bobby's attitude toward his mother underwent a change. Bobby wasn't able to evaluate his father's distortions and manipulations, and because he wanted so badly to be accepted by his father, he began to believe what his father said. When he returned home to his mother, he was hostile, rebellious, and defiant. She in turn became exasperated with him and compared him to his father. Bobby wanted to live with his father all the time, but his stepmother, being pregnant with their second child, wasn't willing to agree to that. So Bobby was forced for nine months of every year to live with a parent whom he had been taught to despise and with whom he had a continually deteriorating relationship. It should come as no surprise that Bobby's later emotional adjustment was extremely problematic.

Children should not be forced to choose between their parents. Even if the noncustodial parent has been abusive or neglectful, children should be encouraged to admire and emulate whatever praiseworthy qualities that parent does have (*everyone* has some). Children should be told that the other parent does love them, that he or she is doing what they can to be a good parent. Don't forget that even though you are able to divorce a spouse when things don't work out, children can't divorce their parents. Even if they never see one of their parents again, they will always know that parent is part of them. If they are taught to despise that parent, they will also learn to despise part of themselves. If you use their sense of loyalty to you to force them to make a choice between parents, you will probably succeed; but the cost will be the children's sense of wholeness and self-respect as the children of *both* their parents. There is also the possibility that you may be wrong, that your ex-spouse is not a hideous monster, and that you are exaggerating merely human flaws into diabolical traits because of your own bitterness and unresolved conflicts concerning your divorce. In that case, you may be depriving your children of a beneficial and valuable relationship because of your own problems.

Caroline, a thirty-one-year-old woman who married a man with three children, wrote movingly on this subject. "My stepchildren had been given so much misinformation about my husband (their father) and myself, we were not given a chance to be accepted by them. To this day, my husband's three children do not accept me, nor will they ever, and they have no contact with their father at all. . . . My fondest wish is that sometime in the future my present husband's children come to realize that their father is a wonderful man. They are all missing so much. He has tried contact with them only to be rebuffed. There have been no Father's Day cards, Christmas cards, nor any other day remembered, such as a birthday. My own father has been dead now for fifteen years; how easily we all forget how precious our parents are to us. If only we had time to do some things over again. I hope my stepchildren will come to their senses and call their father, just to say hello, and not to give him a bad time."

In all the loyalty issues that can come up in a stepfamily, it is wise to remember that how the loyalty needs of children are met (or not met) can have an impact on both their own development and on the adjustment and happiness of the stepfamily as a whole. You may not fully understand the feelings of your stepchildren, but try to be sensitive to them anyway. Don't assume that you're being personally rejected if it takes time for your stepchildren to warm up to you. You should keep your expectations low for the short term, but don't be afraid to hope that with patience and perseverance, the future of your stepfamily can be very bright.

CHAPTER 11

The Wicked Stepmother?

"GIRLS! GIRLS, I want you to listen to me!" Terri's head was starting to pound again. She had heard the giggles coming from the living room and had gone to investigate. Against her express orders, her stepdaughters were jumping up and down on the new sofa. Not only were they ruining the springs, they were coming dangerously close to some very valuable ornaments Terri had inherited from her mother. "Do you hear me? Patty, stop that right now, young lady! I mean it! NOW!!"

Nine-year-old Patty didn't even miss a jump as she turned to look at her stepmother. She stuck out her tongue. "We don't have to listen to you, so there!" she cried. "Daddy says so!"

Terri clenched her fists involuntarily. The trouble was, Daddy probably *had* said so. Despite all his promises to the contrary, Ed had been unforgivably soft with his daughters. Whenever Terri tried to establish decent rules in this house, the girls could always get around her by running to their father and complaining about their mean stepmother.

Katie, the younger one, was starting to climb down. "Hey, Patty. Why don't we . . ." she began. Patty grabbed her by the arm.

"Hey, don't let her boss you around, you dope!" Patti whispered audibly. "What are you, some kind of wimp?"

"I want you both to go to your rooms right now!" Terri almost shouted. "And you're both on restriction for a week for not doing what I asked!"

Patty stopped her jumping and stared at Terri with disturbingly adult eyes. "You can't put us on restriction," she said calmly. "You're not our mother, and we don't have to listen to you. Daddy would never punish us for jumping. He used to let us do it all the time. Besides, Daddy never puts us on restriction; he just makes us go without dessert."

"I don't care what your father does! I am the one in charge right now, because Daddy's not home! And I want you to get off that couch and go to your room this minute!"

Patty and Katie looked at each other for a moment. "I'm tired of jumping," Patty said with a yawn. "Let's go outside and play, Katie."

Terri followed them all the way to the front door, her voice beginning to sound a little hysterical. "You listen to me! I told you to go to your room! You can't go out there! I'm going to tell your father and then you'll be sorry!" As the front door slammed after the girls, she leaned against the wall, feeling suddenly weak. She was disgusted, exasperated, and furious. She didn't believe in spanking, and anyway, her husband had told her that was the one thing he absolutely would not tolerate. But how else could she get these little hellions under control? When Ed wasn't around, they were frequently defiant, destructive, and irresponsible. Around him, of course, they behaved liked little angels, so he didn't believe it when Terri told him about the mayhem the two girls caused almost every day.

Even when he did believe her, he was infuriating. He had promised, before they got married, that he would back her up in whatever disciplinary measures she thought necessary for the girls (always excluding spanking). He had admitted that he himself wasn't much of a disciplinarian. He was so easygoing, he could tolerate anything. He had let his children run wild in the years since his divorce. Now Ed admitted that the girls needed a firm and steady hand at the helm; they needed to learn respect, proper manners. He was confident that Terri, as a former schoolteacher, would be able to discipline them effectively, even if she had never been a mother herself.

That last part was certainly true. She knew how to discipline, but she wasn't being allowed to use what she knew. The girls were always going to their father, and he had absolutely no backbone. When it came right down to it, he just didn't have the heart to take away privileges. This dessert thing was all he would stick to, and that was no punishment, since the girls would be sure to sneak into the kitchen later and take some of the Twinkies, Hostess Cupcakes, or cookies Ed always kept in the house for his sweet tooth. He would always defend them, saying, "They were hungry! They're growing girls; they need their nourishment! Isn't it enough they couldn't have any of the peach pie you made?" Everything Terri knew about disciplining children told her one thing: Until these kids knew there would be consistent consequences for their misbehavior, they would keep right on misbehaving. They seemed to even enjoy it. It was fun to defy an adult and get away with it. Terri shook her head, feeling defeated. How could she convince Ed to back her up? And just how long could she tolerate this infuriating situation without going crazy or having to leave her husband?

Terri is certainly not alone in this problem. Many of our respondents also experienced disciplinary difficulties with their stepchildren. Thirty percent of the people who responded to our survey said that their stepchildren did not accept discipline from them easily, and this problem appeared to have wider ramifications. When the children in a stepfamily did not accept discipline easily from their stepparent, one or both parents were likely to feel doubtful about the strength of their marriage. Disapproval of the way their spouse disciplined the children was also a serious source of discord. However, if both parents felt free to discipline the children, they were also much more likely to feel positively about their marriage, and about the family's future together.

Many of our respondents also mentioned disciplinary matters in their letters. Some of them, like Ed, found participation in any kind of disciplinary techniques difficult. Walter, who had two children from a previous marriage, wrote, "Our most difficult obstacle has been to get me to be the disciplinarian of my daughters. I have had a lot of trouble motivating the girls and getting them to accept responsibility."

Others had trouble agreeing on what disciplinary method should be used. Valerie, a twenty-three-year-old woman with three stepchildren and two young children from her first marriage, had trouble agreeing with her husband about disciplinary techniques. "Our biggest problem has been the difference between his view of child-rearing and mine. I believe in spankings; he doesn't. He believes talking out a situation will solve it, but I believe that after three times or so a spanking is sometimes necessary."

Meg, whose stepfamily included three children from her first marriage and two from her husband's previous marriage, couldn't resist the urge to get involved when her husband tried to discipline the children: "There was a difference in how we wanted to discipline the children. Not that we wanted to use different methods, but we both felt a need to watch out for our own natural children when the other was correcting. I know I have spoken up too much when he was doing the correcting, and I've tried to curb this, but it is a maternal instinct for a mother. I do it for all our children."

For some respondents, disciplinary problems became an issue which caused serious disruption in the stepfamily. Judy, a young woman in her first marriage, found that her initial optimism about her stepfamily faded as discipline became an issue. "I believed that I could make 'everything okay' by taking in my two stepdaughters when we first married. I had finally found the perfect mate and wanted to be one big happy family. . . . I wanted to be 'all' to everyone. The girls and I got along fine while their dad and I dated; we even took them on our honeymoon. I was sure everything would work out perfectly. Was I naïve! It became too much for me. . . . Everyone was unhappy with disciplinary techniques. . . . In my immaturity, I made the girls hate me."

How can stepparents be involved in disciplining their stepchildren without causing stress and turmoil in the family? What are the pitfalls? What are some potential solutions? Is it possible to discipline your stepchildren and still avoid becoming the Wicked Stepmother (or Stepfather)?

SHOULD THE STEPPARENT DISCIPLINE?

Some people may wonder whether it is really necessary for the stepparent to discipline the children at all. Why can't the natural parent take over that job? Unfortunately, being any kind of a parent means spending some time disciplining the children. For one thing, it is likely there will be times when the children are acting up and your spouse isn't there, or when he or she is too tired or too busy with something else to deal with them appropriately. Perhaps you feel that this doesn't apply to your stepchildren; they always behave themselves. You've spent lots of time with them already and they've always been little angels (however, only those without their own children and who haven't yet married and entered a stepfamily could possibly think this).

It's a fact of life that *all* children misbehave at least occasionally. They have all kinds of reasons for misbehaving. Very young children often misbehave simply because they have little ability to control themselves and because they haven't yet learned the rules of our society. They want what they want when they want it; they don't understand the point of saying 'please' and 'thank you,' or why they should wait for their turn, or why they shouldn't hit their siblings when they're angry. They have to learn societal rules and self-control from their parents, and the more efficiently the children learn these things, the fewer problems the stepfamily will encounter later on.

Older children are more complicated. They have learned the rules, for the most part, but they are interested in seeing just how much they can get away with. They can control themselves when they know they have to, but without adults around to enforce the rules, their self-control is likely to break down. (The book *The Lord of the Flies* describes an extreme example of what could happen to children left entirely on their own.)

Children feel safer and more protected when adults are firm and consistent about the rules. They may complain and gripe, but they know deep down that they are totally dependent on their parents. If their parents have organized their children's world in a meaningful and fair way, life makes more sense and is more predictable to them. However, it's also quite possible for parents to get *too* picky and obsessive about the rules. Such parents often have problems of their own—they may feel frightened or insecure if they don't have a high degree of control over everything around them. The children of such parents are just as unlikely to learn self-control as those whose parents are completely permissive, for they have had little chance to take on responsibility and to practice the beginnings of self-discipline.

Another important function of discipline for children is that it shows that adults care about them. Assuming that the disciplining is done in a caring way, it gives children the message that what they do matters, that their behavior is important. Stepparents can't expect to develop truly meaningful relationships with their stepchildren unless they get involved in matters of discipline.

The final consideration in whether disciplining is actually necessary for a stepparent is the fact that you will most likely need some outlet to keep you from getting too angry with your stepchildren. Children of all ages can be extremely annoying at times, and all parents sometimes lose their temper when dealing with their children. This is not to say that forms of discipline are supposed to help you express your anger; quite the reverse. Disciplinary methods are meant to help you control your anger, not release it. They give you a way of handling the situation without having to resort to threats or physical punishment. Quite often, when you use clearly defined disciplinary techniques, you are able to diffuse and control your own anger as well as correct the behavior of the children. However, if you attempt to use disciplinary methods in an angry or punitive way, you will most likely make the children afraid of you, undermine your relationship with them, and damage your own sense of self-control.

DISCIPLINARY PITFALLS

There are several problems that can come up when a parent in a stepfamily tries to implement good disciplinary practices. These problems aren't unique to stepfamilies, but they can be more of a problem for stepfamilies than for nuclear families. They stem from the fact that parents may each have very different ideas about how to discipline the children. Let's take a look at some of the most common problems.

1. *Different styles.* It's highly important that the two spouses agree on how they're going to handle disciplinary problems. Some of our respondents suggested that the rules of the house actually be written down. Neill, a thirty-five-year-old man whose stepfamily included five of his own children from a previous marriage and his two stepchildren, wrote, "I would strongly suggest that anyone marrying someone with children think seriously both about how they want to raise their own children as well as how they feel about raising someone else's children. I feel they should write these rules down; they will serve as guidelines in the future and will have been written before personalities will have entered the picture. These rules should be discussed with everyone who is involved. I think that even the punishments that will be used when the rules are violated should be written down, again before marriage and before any prejudices arise." All rules should apply to all children equally, and these rules should be quite specific. You should avoid vague rules like "No horseplay in the house"; instead, focus on explicit things like "No throwing things in the house" or "No jumping on the furniture."

If you're already married, it's not too late. You can still sit down with the children, explain that you've decided to change the way things have been done in the past, and tell them you want to make a new set of house rules. Allowing the children input into these rules is a good idea, though you may fear that the children will be in favor of suspending whatever rules you already have. Many parents who have tried this have found that their children suggested much stricter house rules than the parents found necessary (though be prepared for the fact that when the time comes to implement the new regulations, children usually have all kinds of legalistic reasons as to why they should be exempt *this time*).

Discussing as a family what the punishments should be is also a good idea. Again, the children are likely to suggest absurdly strict consequences while you're discussing it on a hypothetical level, though you can count on plenty of begging and arguing when the time comes to mete the punishments out.

While you're discussing this as a family, please don't forget what is probably the most important thing—rewards. Children are far more motivated by rewards than by punishments, and it's very important to establish some desired good behaviors that should be rewarded. Some examples of good behaviors are: making their beds for a whole week without being reminded, helping Mom or Stepmom around the house, taking care of a pet, reading a good book, and so forth. The rewards should also be negotiated between parents and children ahead of time, should be commensurate with the good behavior (save the really good rewards—like going out for pizza and a movie—for especially positive behavior), and should be something the children really like (e.g., an extra half hour of Nintendo) without being something that's bad for them (two banana splits in one day).

2. *Inconsistency.* This is one of the biggest problems in any disciplinary program. You absolutely must be as consistent with the rules and consequences as you have time and energy to be. This won't be easy. Many a parent has discovered that it's less work in the short run to pick up their child's room themselves than to try to get the child to do it. The operative words here are *in the short run.* To abandon the rules for the sake of convenience is to teach the child that the rules don't really matter. Of course there are occasions when you can make an exception: when you or the child is sick, during a special holiday or a birthday, or during a crisis in the family. But for the most part, you must push yourself to be as consistent as you can possibly be (unless you are one of those people mentioned above who tend to be overly controlling and picky).

What you must do is insist on the rules that you've agreed on, without anger. You must intervene early, as soon as you notice there's a problem. For example, if your stepson has been asked not to tease his little sister, don't wait until the sister is crying and hysterical to implement the punishment. Act at the first sign of trouble. That will keep you calmer, will prevent your stepson from repeating an unhealthy pattern, and will teach your stepson that he's not going to get away with even minor infringements.

Unless the children in your family are all infants, you may notice a curious and unwelcome phenomenon when you start enforcing your new rules—the children's behavior may at first actually get worse. Don't worry, it's temporary. Children are too smart for their own good sometimes. They're testing you, seeing if you really have the backbone to carry out the new disciplinary rules. If you have the energy and patience to persevere with the rules, the children in your stepfamily *will* eventually obey them. If you've constructed a fair and effective set of rules, it's in their best interests to do so. But it may take time. Just try to get through one day at a time, and remember—this too shall pass.

What if your spouse is refusing to abide by your set of rules, even though he or she agreed to them initially? You need to sit down and go over the rules again. Find out if there's really a problem with the rules themselves. If not, the trouble may be that your spouse doesn't know how to be firm with children, or that he or she fears rejection from the children. In that case, you can help your spouse practice being firm. It may seem silly, but while alone in your room you can actually show your spouse how to talk to the children. First you can demonstrate, then have your spouse imitate you. Then you can pretend to be one of the children, and have your spouse practice telling you to go to your room, or to take a time-out (spending a few minutes sitting in a chair facing the wall). Then perhaps your spouse can give himself or herself an assignment to be firm with one of the children once each day (and not using the same child every day, naturally). It won't be easy at first, but after a while it will become so. In the long run, it's a lot easier than being a floormat.

3. *Reinforcement versus punishment.* If you've never taken a psychology course, or just never thought about it much, you may assume that rewards and punishments for children are pretty standard things. Typical rewards might be extra allowance money, being excused from chores, permission to go to the movies with friends. Typical punishments might be time-outs, spankings, restriction to the child's bedroom, loss of privileges. Some people think that all children feel pretty much the same way about these things. But the truth is, it all depends on the individual child. A child who is somewhat of an introvert and whose bedroom holds dozens of toys, books, a television, and a Nintendo game center (it's truly amazing how many children own all of those things) is not going to be very distressed at being confined to his or her room. On the other hand, a child who is very physically active and who spends every free moment outside on his or her bicycle is going to find that same punishment extremely onerous. You know the children in your

own stepfamily best, and you and your spouse need to sit down and carefully talk through just what punishment would have the greatest impact on each child.

In deciding what punishment to use, there are a few things to remember, however. First, spanking is probably one of the least effective ways to punish children. Unless you descend into the depths of brutality and really hurt your children, they probably won't mind being spanked that much, after the first few times. Research has shown that many children actually *prefer* to be spanked than to have privileges taken away. Spanking is soon over, and if it happens to children a lot, they just get used to it. However, if you're creative enough to come up with consequences your stepchildren will really dislike (based on your knowledge of their preferences and personalities), your disciplining will probably be much more effective.

Second, both spanking and scolding have the disadvantage that they are extremely negative ways of interacting with your stepchildren, especially if you spank or scold them when you're very angry. Instead of teaching them better behavior, you may be teaching them to be scared of you or to avoid you. This is not to say that you'll ruin your relationship with your children if you occasionally get angry and yell at them, but it's something to be minimized, not ratified into a code of discipline.

Third, the younger the children in your stepfamily are, the more quickly the punishment should follow the misbehavior. Young children have very limited understanding of time and are unable to think very far into the future. For them to make the connection between what they did wrong and the consequence, you need to act as soon as possible. So if the children in your stepfamily are very young (under age seven), you need to have available some form of punishment that can be implemented anywhere (in a grocery store, in the car, etc.). If you find yourself in a situation where it's absolutely impossible to discipline your children, take the first possible opportunity to do so.

Fourth, if the children in your stepfamily are very young and are already having trouble going to sleep at night or are having nightmares, it's not a good idea to punish them by sending them to bed. They may associate going to bed with punishment, and then have even more trouble sleeping.

How can you tell if the punishment you choose is the right one? A simple way is by observing whether or not the children's misbehavior is decreasing. You might even want to keep some kind of chart on specific behaviors that you're concerned about, such as poor table manners, talking back, or fighting with siblings. Your chart can be as simple as a calendar with one mark each day for each time the misbehavior occurs (if you're tracking more than one behavior, use a different colored felt-tip pen for each). If you've chosen the right punishment for the children in your stepfamily, the targeted misbehavior should gradually go down over time.

There's one further pitfall here. What if you notice your children's behavior is actually getting worse as a result of your discipline? As we mentioned above, that's the natural result at first, if the children are used to having things much more their own way. They're testing you, seeing if you're made of steel or if you're really just a marshmallow. But if time goes on (if you're being really consistent, a month should be plenty of time to see some changes) and things continue to get worse, you need to consider the possibility that what you're doing is actually rewarding your children. For example, the punishment you've chosen may be rewarding them by giving them extra attention. In that case, you need to reevaluate what you're doing, and come up with a consequence that will really be unpleasant for the children in your stepfamily.

You must also be creative when choosing rewards for the children in your stepfamily. Just like punishments, rewards should be tailored to the needs of the individual child. However, there is one form of reward all children respond to. They all love to be praised. Praise costs nothing, you have an endless supply of it, and best of all, it can make your relationship with your children much more positive. Praising others can even make you feel better about yourself. You don't have to save your praise for the perfect performance. One of the classic examples of this mistake is made by the parents who comments, after seeing a report card consisting of all A's and one B, "How come you got a B?" That's discouraging and deflating to children, and it makes them feel like they're never good enough.

Some parents worry that if they praise for anything less than the best, they'll be encouraging their children to be satisfied with mediocrity. That's just not true. The best way is to begin by praising the child's best *effort,* whatever that may be. Then, selectively praise everything that is on that level or is an improvement. Parents with young infants often do this instinctively. A common example is the reaction of the parents when their baby takes his or her first step. Though that first step is shaky and uncertain, most parents are tremendously excited about it, and communicate their delight to the baby by smiles, exclamations, and applause. But as the baby learns to take two steps, then three, then is toddling about confidently, the parents praise him or her, for the most part, only for the newest development. What has already been mastered can be taken for granted. The same principles apply with older children. A child who is extremely reluctant to share toys should be praised and encouraged even for allowing her sister to use some old toy she never plays with anymore (unless she charges her money for it). Each time she repeats that action, or something similar, she should be praised again. When eventually she finds it in her heart to share something more valuable, she should be commended particularly for that. Such praise should be as sincere and heartfelt as you can make it. As we all know, children are very good at detecting insincerity.

Aside from praise, the other rewards you use with the children in your stepfamily depend, like the form of punishment, on the child. What do your children like to do? What treats do they especially like? Of course, you have to use your common sense. Don't reward your children with food if they're overweight, and don't reward them with more television time if they're budding couch potatoes. Find something which they like that is good for them. We realize that this may be no easy task, but use your creativity. You and your spouse know the children in your stepfamily best.

One thing that's important to keep in mind is the difference between a reward and a bribe. A bribe, like a reward, is given to children for good behavior. However, a parent who offers a bribe usually places the primary responsibility for behavior change on the children. To tell a child "I'll give you $5 if you keep your room clean for two weeks" is to expect the child to monitor his or her own behavior with only the promise of a reward in the far future as motivation. Unless we're talking about a seventeen- or eighteen-year-old, that's too much to expect. For the parents to take primary responsibility for the children's behavior change, they must be involved daily in the children's reinforcement and punishment until the children have internalized self-discipline (and this usually takes years to accomplish). Otherwise, you will be setting yourselves and your children up for frustration and discouragement.

One thing you may be thinking at this point is that these principles require a totally unrealistic amount of time and energy to put into action. That is absolutely true. And there's probably no one in the world who could do it all perfectly, even if being a parent was their only job. The important thing is to make a start, and to do the best you can. You will find these procedures get easier as you and the children in your stepfamily get used to them; you will also find the improvement that will certainly result is more than worth the effort. In the long run, you will save yourself a lifetime of annoyance, aggravation, and maybe even heartbreak.

4. *"Splitting."* One way children attempt to get around rules is by trying to manipulate their parents. Of course, they don't do it deliberately and consciously—it's more of an instinctive reaction. It's one more way that children try to get what they want, when they want it. If their mother doesn't give in and give them what they want, they may go to their stepfather. Perhaps you think that if you've already agreed on specific rules, this shouldn't be a problem. Of course, your spouse won't give in if what the child is asking for is against the rules of the house. Right? Unfortunately, it's not as simple as that—there's an emotional element involved. Children are often quite aware of their parents' weaknesses and know how to get around them by using those weak spots to their advantage. This is a complicated problem because both parents rarely have the same weaknesses, they have different personalities and different relationships with the children. This is even truer for a stepfamily because the two parents have such different histories with the child. The effect that splitting has is to get one parent to bend or break the disciplinary rules, against the wishes of the other parent. That's why it is called "splitting"; the children are trying to split up the people in authority in order to get around the rules.

The children may play off the stepparent's need to be accepted and loved by the children by telling the stepparent that he or she is the only one that understands them and loves them. The children may make the stepparent feel that to be firm with them is to risk estrangement. Or, the children may be so sweet and winning that it's hard to resist giving them what they want. In each case, the children are using the parent's or stepparent's emotional needs to get what they want; if there are problems in the marital relationship, it can be even easier for the children to get one parent to go against the other's wishes.

Often it's very hard to recognize that your children are manipulating you because your own feelings are getting in the way. However, your spouse may be all too aware of the fact that you're being manipulated. Rachel, a forty-two-year-old woman who married a man with two teenage children, was able to see quite clearly how her stepdaughter was attempting to "split" Rachel and Rachel's husband, her father. "I did not anticipate how manipulative his daughter can be. My spouse can't see it as readily as I can, but my stepdaughter uses me, her father, and her mother very efficiently. She knows how to turn her father's anger away from her and toward her mother. Likewise, she knows she can often get her way with one parent by telling him or her that the other parent 'just doesn't understand me as well.' And she often tries to use me to 'break the tie.' " This gives you yet another reason to abide firmly by the motto *BE CONSISTENT*. You may be tempted to bend the rules "just this once" for the wrong reasons.

A related point is the importance of the parents maintaining a united front. Nora, a twenty-four-year-old woman with two sons from a previous marriage, soon realized that this was a problem for her stepfamily. She wrote, "Most people are most likely to fight about the children (discipline, etc.), so make sure you agree on these issues ahead of time. It was important to realize that my children and my new husband were now father and sons, and not interfere with that relationship in front of the children (i.e., if you don't agree with what your husband just said or did, you shouldn't undermine his authority with the children)."

The rule of thumb to remember is, *never* disagree with your spouse in front of the children on matters of discipline. If you do, you'll give the children the message that the rules really aren't all that important, and that your spouse is not to be respected as a parent. Feel free to discuss disciplinary decisions all you want to in private; you can even reverse previous decisions after the fact, as long as you do it together. If your spouse is the stepparent, it's particularly important to avoid interfering with his or her attempts to discipline, because your interference makes it that much easier for your children to reject his or her authority. Unless the children are extremely young, the stepparent has to work very hard to establish himself or herself as an authority figure with the children; your spouse needs your support, not your interference. The one exception to this rule is when your spouse is endangering the physical or mental health of your children by subjecting them to physical or emotional abuse. Then, of course, you must get involved.

DIFFERENT HOUSEHOLDS, DIFFERENT RULES?

Many of you have children or stepchildren who spend time in two different households. They may stay most of the year with you, or just visit you on weekends, holidays, or the summertime, or may divide their time equally between the homes of their two natural parents. This creates a different set of problems. It may be that the two households are run very differently. You may believe in strict curfews, cleanliness, and extensive chores for the kids; the other household may stress achievement in extracurricular activities and Sunday school attendance.

Consistency is of utmost importance in this situation as well. The differences between households are confusing for children, especially young ones. You will have to expect a period of adjustment each time the children return from living with their other family. Be patient with them, and go over the rules each time they return. Don't expect instantaneous absorption of the new rules, but don't keep making excuses indefinitely for them, either. Two weeks is probably a reasonable period of time for them to adjust to the new household.

If the children in your stepfamily are just visiting you for weekends or on holidays, the situation is a bit more complicated. Naturally, you're not going to want to be a heavy disciplinarian if you just see the children once a year at Christmas. You may have to modify the rules for the occasion, even if you have young children of your own at home. However, you should always enforce basic rules like no hitting, stealing, lying, or tattling. If you have at least a civil relationship with the adults in the children's "other family," it would also be a good idea to check with them to see if the children are currently on any kind of restrictions. This makes for continuity in the children's lives (though of course they won't like it much), and it will enhance their acquisition of self-discipline and self-control. Lillian, a thirty-five-year-old woman who got five stepchildren when she married Kenny, thought this was very important. She wrote, "It's important to get a *very* strong message across to all the children that all parents and stepparents should be respected because of their position by the kids, and by each other. My stepchildren, I think, have finally learned that I am not easily manipulated, because I respect their mother's position as mother. I stand behind all of their mother's decisions in this house, just as she stands behind them in her own house. That nips in the bud any ideas they might have of running loose around here even though their mother has them on restrictions at home."

Another of our respondents who mentioned this point was Eileen, whose stepfamily consisted of herself, her husband, Warren, her seven-year-old stepson, and her own three children from her first marriage. Eileen seemed to have an ideal relationship with her husband's ex-wife, and this actually made her job as disciplinarian easier. She wrote, "The most important thing I have done to make our new family work was to take over the job of communicating with my stepson's mother. When my husband did this chore, it put him in the awkward position of trying to please two people, and I never felt like my input was being taken seriously. So I started calling the mother over simple schedules, etc. It eased the tension between the two of us and got my spouse out of the firing range. Over the last two years, the mother and I get along fine and talk often about our child. We try to work together on disciplinary matters. It is nice to bounce ideas off each other. Because of this, my stepson does not play one family against the other, and I think it helps him to know we all get along." Not everyone can have this kind of relationship with their children's other family, but at least you can call and find out what ground rules the children are used to. As Eileen's story proves, to do so may even improve your rapport with your children's other mother and father, though it may be difficult at first.

THE PUNISHMENT THAT FITS THE CRIME

Not everyone is familiar with the disciplinary technique of "time-out," though many child specialists consider it to be the most effective way to punish misbehavior. Time-out means "time-out from rewards." Children are placed in a situation in which they get very little reinforcement. In other words, the children will be very bored in time-out. Most experts agree that the time-out should take place in a nonstimulating place: a hallway, a utility room, an empty dining room—a place where there are no toys, no television, and no other children to distract them. When they misbehave, children should be asked to sit quietly in a chair in the room which you've decided is the least stimulating for them. They should not be allowed to talk, sing, make noises, or move. It may be best to have them face the wall, to cut down on possible distractions.

How long should time-outs last? Child specialists recommend that each time the children misbehave, they should be given a minute of time-out for every year of life (i.e., a two-year-old should get two minutes for each misbehavior, a three-year-old should get three minutes, etc.). If the children persist in getting up, talking, or otherwise violating the rules of time-out, they should be quietly informed that their time-out doesn't start until they're quiet. They can get up as soon as they've completed their time-out properly, but you should tell them that it's up to them how long they have to stay there. This is better than simply giving them additional time-outs, because it gives them a sense of control.

At what age should children be given time-outs? Some experts recommend the use of time-out for all children over eighteen months; others recommend waiting until the child is three years old to begin using time-outs. It all depends on how quickly your children learn to speak and to understand what you say to them, and how much motor control they have over their bodies. They need to have the ability to understand what they've done wrong; they also need to have the physical ability to control themselves. Time-out should *never* be used with infants who haven't yet learned to talk.

If your children are very young (under five years) when you begin to use time-out, you may have to physically hold them in time-out at first. It's very important to do this as gently as possible, and to avoid threatening or scolding them. They have to understand that you mean business, but you should be very careful to avoid hurting or scaring them. You may have to explain the rules to them repeatedly; be sure to do so in language suitable to their age. Keep reminding them that they can get up as soon as they sit quietly for the designated number of minutes. You will need to be very patient with them at first, but if you are consistent, they will eventually get the message.

It's extremely important to explain this procedure to the children before the time comes to actually use it. Tell them that it's a way to help them control their behavior so they don't get into trouble. You should also tell them at this same time about rewards they can earn for good behavior.

Children should be supervised by an adult as closely as possible during the entirety of each time-out. If possible, both parents should participate when there are several young children in the stepfamily, because one parent needs to supervise the children who are not in time-out. Of course, there will be times when just one parent is home alone with the children. At these times, try to do the best you can. One solution is to place yourself strategically so you can see both the child who is in the time-out and the other children. To do so, you may have to ask the children who are not being punished to stay in one room together for the duration of the time-out; try to arrange this so that these children don't feel that they are also being punished.

It may sometimes be necessary to have more than one child in time-out at a time. When that happens, be sure to physically separate the children, and have them face opposite directions. Be sure to intervene quickly if one of the children in time-out attempts to distract the other. If one child is behaving properly in time-out and the other isn't, try praising the child who is behaving appropriately instead of scolding the one who is misbehaving. Remember to remind the children that it's really up to them how long the time-out lasts.

Other important points for time-out: You should use it early, at the first sign of trouble, and you should try to stay as calm as possible. You should also use it for specific behavior problems, and try to be as consistent as possible. Use it *every time* the problem behavior occurs. If you're in a restaurant, take the child into the bathroom to serve the time-out. It may seem an odd and artificial form of punishment, but it works because there's nothing children dislike so much as being bored.

There is one further point about time-out. You should set a limit on how long you're willing to sit with a child who is refusing to take time-out properly. You should invent a "Doomsday Penalty," something the child *really* hates (like no Nintendo for a week), to use if the child stays in continuous time-out for an unreasonable length of time. However, be sure to warn the child ahead of time that this is going to happen. Give your child a chance to pull himself or herself together.

The purpose of this chapter is to identify some of the most common disciplinary problems encountered by stepfamilies, and to suggest some general principles for dealing with them. A detailed discussion of how to discipline children is far beyond the scope of this book, and if discipline is a problem in your stepfamily, it would be a good idea for you to seek further information on this topic. There are many good books on child-rearing that offer additional information on the use of time-out and other disciplinary practices. An excellent one is *Families*, by Gerald R. Patterson.

We have covered a lot of ground in this chapter, and in summary we would like to give you a few general rules to remember. The following list may be helpful to you when things get hectic and you don't have time to sit down and think things through calmly.

SUMMARY: DISCIPLINARY DO'S AND DON'TS

Do's:
1. *Do create a set of specific house rules.* The whole family should be involved in this discussion, and it may be helpful to write them down.
2. *Do support your spouse in front of the children.*
3. *Do treat all children in the stepfamily alike.*
4. *Do remember to reward your child.* Praise the children for good efforts, and come up with rewards that they will especially like for good behavior.
5. *Do be consistent with both rewards and punishments.*
6. *Do discuss disciplinary practices with your children or stepchildren's "other family."*

7. *Do implement punishments at the first sign of trouble.*

DON'TS:
1. *Don't refuse to be involved in disciplining the children.*
2. *Don't interfere when your spouse is disciplining the children.*
3. *Don't let the children get around you by manipulating your weak spots.*
4. *Don't overuse spanking and scolding as a means of disciplining the children.*
5. *Don't use discipline of the children as a way to express your own anger.*

CHAPTER 12

Wounds That Don't Heal

ALMOST HOME. Carla could hardly wait. It was silly at her age, but she had been daydreaming all day long about Brian. It was so nice to have a husband to come home to again. Of course, home seemed even sweeter after spending the whole afternoon in conference with her most unpleasant client. Carla was a Public Defender, and her job required her to defend some people she could barely stand to be in the same room with. Her current case was a man who openly admitted that he often beat his wife and two young children. He was just teaching them a lesson for their own good, he said. Of course he hadn't meant to kill his four-year-old son, the boy had just slipped and hit his head on a water pipe.

As she turned into her neighborhood, Carla tried to wipe the day's unpleasant images from her mind and replace them with thoughts of her new family. Just a year ago she had been lonely and bitter, envying her married friends and trying to raise Jeremy, her seven-year-old son, all by herself. Now she had a loving husband, and they were a real family again. She had worried about how Jeremy would get along with his stepfather, Brian, but so far there weren't any real problems. Just a little arguing every now and then, nothing really serious.

She turned the corner to their street. She could see their beautiful new house. They had a whopping mortgage payment, but with their joint incomes they could afford it. She pulled up in the driveway. She didn't even have to worry about dinner tonight, because it was Brian's turn to cook. As she crossed the lawn, she could hear loud voices inside the house. Not another argument! She had assumed that all that was just part of getting used to each other. But by the sound of it, things were getting worse, not better.

She pushed the front door open. Brian and Jeremy were standing in front of the staircase. Brian was yelling, "Now, I tell you, now! Now!" As Carla watched, Brian grabbed Jeremy and shook him, hard. That was it. She dropped her briefcase on the floor and charged.

"What the hell do you think you're doing?" She glared at Brian as Jeremy ran to his mother, crying.

"I'm just trying to teach your son a lesson." Brian looked flustered and angry.

"A lesson! Is that what you call it?" She stared at Brian, feeling sick. Those were the same words her client had used. Brian knew perfectly well that she didn't believe in corporal punishment. He had agreed to live by her rules, even though he had been raised differently. But now, after only two weeks of marriage, his impulses were already getting the better of him. Even worse, he was trying to justify what he had done. What if this was only the beginning?

The Pervasive Problem of Physical Child Abuse

Carla, like most Americans, had heard a lot about child abuse. Her horror at violence against children was probably even more intense than most people's because her work had given her an appalling firsthand look at some ugly realities. Now, when child abuse apparently was entering her own life, she panicked. She had herself been raised by strict parents who had disciplined their children only by taking away privileges, and that was how she had raised Jeremy until Brian came along. She knew almost nothing about the psychology of child abusers, and she had no way of knowing if Brian had the potential to become one. She didn't know how she could prevent her husband from hurting her child without endangering her marriage.

Carla is not alone. An estimated 705,000 children are being physically abused every year in the United States. Unfortunately for those who are part of a stepfamily, many of those children are being abused by stepparents. Preschoolers are especially vulnerable to stepparent abuse. One researcher found that preschoolers living with a stepparent were forty times more likely to be abused than children of the same age living with both of their natural parents.

What is physical abuse? Many professionals define it as anything that leaves visible marks (bruises, cuts, burns, black eyes), causes physical damage (broken bones, injury to internal organs), or results in the death of the child. Most people find it very unpleasant to have to think about such things, but unfortunately there are many children for whom physical abuse is an inescapable daily reality. How can parents or stepparents do such horrible things to children? In many cases, abusers were themselves abused as children, and truly see nothing wrong about what they are doing. In other cases, the abuse may start out as spanking but then, as the adult experiences increasing stress and frustration, escalates into more harmful forms of punishment. That may be one reason why stepparents are more likely to abuse children; in many stepfamilies there is a high level of stress because there are so many people and so many needs that demand attention.

This issue has the potential to make or break a stepfamily, especially if the abuser is the stepparent. Parents who have loved and protected their children since birth will not be able to look on and say nothing while their new spouse hurts their children. But many, like Carla, just do not know what to do. Most are unprepared for the problem and are shocked and horrified when the abuse starts happening. Others discuss it up front, only to find, like Carla did, that their spouses cannot seem to control themselves in the heat of the moment.

What can you do if your spouse is physically abusing your children or stepchildren? How can you talk to your abusive spouse about it? How can you protect the children in your stepfamily without damaging your marriage? Does there come a point where your only option is to tell your spouse to get out?

It is important to address these questions because the consequences of child abuse are potentially very serious. Physical abuse of children can result not just in domestic stress, or the end of a marriage, but in the permanent disruption of a child's emotional and mental development.

WHAT PHYSICAL ABUSE DOES TO CHILDREN

Physical abuse can have both short-term and long-term effects on children. First, it models aggressive behavior for the child. That is, it teaches the child that it is okay for people to hit and hurt each other. Children are imitative creatures, who learn by copying the actions of others. Since parents are by far the most important influences in a young child's life, this lesson of violence is learned all too quickly, much faster than it is learned from television or comic books.

Children learn their system of values from the important people in their lives. If you want to teach children to respect others, you must treat them with respect; if you want to teach them to love others, you must give them affection. But unfortunately, if you physically punish them, you will teach them that violence is acceptable.

Abused children may have much less control over their aggressive impulses as a result of physical abuse. In extreme cases they may deliberately break their toys and hurt their pets. They may become bullies and torment children smaller than themselves. They may be hostile and defiant toward all adults. The games that these children play may be unusually aggressive in nature. The intense, violent rage often expressed in both words and actions by these abused children can be frightening to witness.

A child with all the behaviors described above is not very pleasant to be around. A parent who was abusive in the first place is likely to become even more punitive to try to get such a child's behavior under control. Unfortunately, all that is accomplished by this strategy is that the child becomes even more aggressive and hostile. It is tragically easy for a parent and child to get permanently locked in this vicious cycle.

Another way children may react to physical abuse is by becoming withdrawn. They may avoid other people, feel uncomfortable with physical contact, and have difficulty trusting others. This behavior also may lock abused children into a vicious cycle. The more they avoid other people, the more others perceive them as cold and uncaring; eventually no one may even try to get close to them.

Abused children may also become extremely passive, accepting whatever happens to them with a kind of tired resignation. They may appear listless and apathetic, with no energy to play or to make friends. They may seem to feel completely helpless, as if nothing they say or do matters. This defeatist attitude toward life often has a serious impact on their relationships, their education, and their emotional growth.

Physically abused children may also abuse themselves. They may bang their heads, hit themselves, or scratch themselves until they bleed. They may seem to take all their rage against their abusers and turn it against themselves. These children have internalized the abuse so it is part of themselves. Because their caretakers have hurt them, they seem to hate themselves.

A child may have any combination of the characteristics described above as the result of physical abuse. However, there is one characteristic that all abused children share: poor self-esteem. When a child is consistently hurt by one of his parents, by one of those who are supposed to love and protect him, he will inevitably begin to believe that he is a bad kid. Children learn about themselves from the important people in their lives. Physical abuse by a parent can give a child the message "You are insignificant, worthless, and unlovable." Once this painful lesson has been learned, it can be terribly difficult to unlearn.

LONG-TERM EFFECTS OF PHYSICAL ABUSE

What happens to abused children when they grow into adulthood? Research has shown that adults who have been abused as children often have serious emotional and behavioral problems. These problems can include recklessness, impulsiveness, chronic unemployment, poor interpersonal relationships, depression, anxiety, and drug or alcohol abuse.

Alcohol abuse is a particularly sinister problem for these adults. Adults who have been abused as children often use drugs and alcohol to drown their inner feelings of self-hatred, depression, and fear. Alcohol also has the effect of releasing inhibitions and can make it harder for such people to control their aggressive impulses; someone who is drunk has a greater likelihood of becoming abusive to his or her children. This is one way physical abuse is passed down from one generation to another.

Not everyone who has been physically abused as a child develops these serious problems; many factors contribute to children's emotional development. One of these is personal advantages, like talent, intelligence, and attractiveness. Children possessing these attributes are more likely to make friends and develop interests outside of the family; these friends and interests may become a refuge against the abuse, may help them believe in themselves, and give them hope for the future.

Another potential safety factor is other people in the child's environment. Even if both the mother and father are abusing the child, the child may receive emotional nurturance from a grandmother, an uncle, a cousin, a friend, or a teacher. These relationships can also be a refuge for physically abused children.

Finally, children will be less vulnerable to the long-term effects of physical abuse if they are not also abused psychologically. Psychological abuse, though it leaves no visible marks, is an insidious destroyer of a child's self-esteem, happiness, confidence, and trust. Young children believe what their parents say, and if they are told they are no good, they will accept that as gospel truth. A child who is occasionally slapped by a parent but is consistently given respect, attention, and affection will have a much greater chance of psychological health than will a child who is not physically harmed but who is habitually treated with ridicule, coldness, or contempt. Of course, the combination of both physical and psychological abuse is especially destructive to children's emotional health.

What to Do if There Is Abuse in Your Stepfamily

If your spouse is abusing the children in your stepfamily, you must first set firm limits. Make it clear to your spouse what you will and what you will not tolerate. Don't waste time on empty threats or ultimatums. If you do give an ultimatum, make sure it is one you are prepared to carry out without delay.

It is important to try to stay calm and in control while discussing the abuse. It will not help to get into an emotional uproar or to become accusing or tearful. If you are one of the many people who have trouble setting limits and saying "no," seek professional help to learn those skills. They are not all that hard to master (if you can't afford counseling, get one of the many books that have been written about assertiveness). It will probably be quite difficult to insist on your limits, especially at first. But remember, you are protecting the physical and emotional well-being of the children in your step-family, and that is worth the effort. In the long run, you are also giving yourself a better chance at happiness in your marriage and in your stepfamily.

Next, sit down and talk with your spouse (when you're both calm) about the abuse. Try to understand why it is happening. Perhaps alcohol or drug use is contributing to the problem. Perhaps there are emotional issues that need to be addressed that are causing extra stress and frustration. Perhaps there is a way to limit or supervise your spouse's interaction with the children so there is less opportunity for physical abuse. However, understanding why the abuse is occurring may help you feel more sympathetic toward your spouse, but it can't take the place of professional help. In most cases, it will not be possible to stop the abuse by understanding or by sheer willpower. And if the safety or health of the children is really at stake, professional help becomes a necessity, for there is no time to waste in going it alone.

A third thing you can do is teach your spouse about proper disciplinary techniques. Physical abuse is less likely to occur if your spouse has an effective alternative way to manage the children's behavior. These techniques were discussed at length in Chapter 11.

Finally, you may need to realize, as some of the people in our survey had to, that you are in a hopeless situation. You may find that your marriage is irrevocably damaged by your spouse's abuse of your children, or that your spouse is unwilling or unable to change his or her behavior. If you are the stepparent, you may find that your stepchildren are already too damaged by their experiences to be able to be part of a family.

Marjorie, a thirty-year-old woman whose three stepchildren had been severely abused and neglected by their natural mother, had to face this sad truth. She wrote, "The most difficult obstacle in at-tempting to make a family of his three children and my one child was admitting that it couldn't be done. That no matter how much time, attention, money, and effort were put into the attempt, it would not succeed. His three children had been too traumatized to want to create a family. The children have punched holes into walls and windows, destroyed furniture, our personal property, and their toys, pulled lights out of the bedroom walls, written on the walls, and abused their pets. The list could go on and on. Each child has been continuously in individual therapy and the family in family therapy. Each child has also had inpatient and partial psychiatric hospitalization. We still have defiant, lying, cheating thieves. These children have been given every opportunity in three years to blend into a family and they do not desire to be family even among themselves." Those of you who are trying to decide whether to enter a stepfamily, take heed. It is far better to discover these things ahead of time than to have to face them after years of time, effort, and emotional investment.

SEXUAL ABUSE OF CHILDREN

Sexual abuse has some of the same effects as physical abuse, but also has some unique problems. This form of abuse has been acknowledged as more and more of a problem in recent years, but many people still don't want to believe it exists. In fact, in our survey not one person expressed concern over the possibility of sexual abuse in their family.

Children in stepfamilies appear to be particularly vulnerable to sexual abuse, usually by a stepfather. One reason this may happen is because the stepfather does not have the opportunity to bond with the children in infancy as natural fathers usually do. Marylynn's story is an example of this problem.

Marylynn was not enjoying her usual Saturday morning shopping trip. She had found some wonderful bargains at a charming little boutique. A pair of beautiful black silk pants, and a couple of dresses that she really needed for work. She even found a pretty embroidered shirt for her daughter, Maggie. Now she was at her usual fast-food restaurant for lunch. A modest treat, but one she normally enjoyed very much. But her chicken sandwich tasted like paper and her coffee like mud. She couldn't get her mind off what Maggie, her fourteen-year-old daughter, had told her last night.

She had always had a good relationship with her daughter. When she had divorced Maggie's father, she had been able to comfort and nurture her child despite her own emotional loss and pain. When she married Dan four years later, she had worked very hard at helping Maggie and Dan build a good relationship together. She had been successful. Dan and Maggie had been like a real father and daughter. Until recently, she had gone to him with her problems, watched baseball games with him, and giggled with him about how silly boys were. Even the birth of Maggie's two half-brothers hadn't come between them.

But a few years ago, things had changed; their relationship became strained and uncomfortable. Maggie began to avoid Dan; when he tried to spend time with her, she seemed to overreact to everything Dan did or said. Marylynn had noticed that this started happening right about the time Maggie entered puberty, and had assumed that these troubles were just part of being an emotional adolescent. But after what Maggie had told her last night, she wasn't so sure.

Dan was out of town for a week, and Marylynn had taken the opportunity to ask Maggie, after the boys were in bed, how things were going with Dan. Marylynn was hoping to clear the air, and to give her daughter a chance to talk to someone who would understand. But to her amazement, Maggie had burst into tears. Marylynn tried to comfort her, but Maggie had only gotten more and more hysterical. Marylynn kept asking her what was the matter. Maggie finally sobbed out, "He keeps touching me."

Marylynn froze. "What do you mean, 'touching you?' "

"In bad places. On my behind. My breasts."

Marylynn literally could not believe her ears. Maggie must mean somebody else, not Dan. Some neighborhood boy. "You mean one of the boys you're dating?" she asked gently.

"No!" Maggie had almost screamed the words. "Dad!! Your husband!!"

Those words were still ringing in Marylynn's ears. But yet she knew it was impossible. There was no way Dan could have done anything like that. Probably Maggie had misinterpreted some casual, accidental touch that really meant nothing. Teenagers were so emotional, so intense. Everything seemed like such a big deal to them. Maybe Maggie had seen a movie about sexual abuse or incest and it had gotten her imagination working overtime.

Marylynn pushed her lunch aside uneaten. Maggie was probably wrong, but what if she wasn't? Just the thought of it made Marylynn feel sick and weak. She loved Dan, he was part of her, and part of her life. But if what Maggie told her was true, it would mean the end of their marriage. She couldn't live with someone who could do such a thing. Marylynn closed her eyes, trying to hold her fragile emotions in check, but a big teardrop escaped and slid down her cheek. She felt a terrible pain in her heart. It was worse than just a divorce. It would mean her whole relationship with Dan was built on a lie. He would be a bad person, an evil person. She would have no loving memories of all their years together, only memories of deceit and hypocrisy. If only Maggie was wrong! There had to be some logical explanation for it. She would call Dan tonight at his hotel room and see what he said. Surely he would be able to explain it all.

There's a saying that "there are none so blind as those who won't see." The reason that some won't see is because it is just too painful. Like Marylynn, many people who have the chance to stop sexual abuse are tempted to do nothing, because so much is at stake for them. To admit that sexual abuse is occurring may be to face the end of a marriage, the destruction of a family, and perhaps even the imprisonment of a loved one. Incest, in particular, is so forbidden and condemned by our society that it is very hard for anyone to accept it is really going on, even if they see it with their own eyes.

Recently there has been an increase in public awareness and information about incest and other forms of sexual abuse, and as a result the numbers of reported cases have skyrocketed. However, it is likely that there are still many, many cases going unreported (one recent estimate is 50 percent) because the children are afraid to talk, or because the people the children talk to are afraid to listen.

Maggie was unusually fortunate; the sexual abuse was confined to touching, and began when she was old enough to understand that it was wrong. She was also able to talk to her mother about it, unlike many sexually abused children. Ultimately, her mother was able to confront Dan and to get him into counseling. While Maggie will never be able to forget the abuse, the work the family has done in therapy has protected Maggie, while allowing the stepfamily to stay together.

Not all children are this lucky. Many experience much more traumatizing forms of sexual abuse, and have no one to turn to, because their mothers refuse to listen. What happens to these children?

WHAT SEXUAL ABUSE DOES TO CHILDREN

There are four major areas in which the behavior, emotions, and development of sexually abused children may be affected. The first is in the area of sexuality. A sexually abused child is often rewarded with attention and affection for sexual favors. They learn to relate to everyone sexually. This exponentially increases their chances of being abused again, for their provocative behavior may give a potential sexual abuser the excuse he or she needs.

These children also oversexualize their relationships in adulthood. They may feel that the only way they can relate to others is through sex, and may be driven by their natural desire for intimacy and closeness to offer themselves to everyone they meet. Without help, such people are bound to have severe difficulties in interpersonal relationships.

The second way sexually abused children react to abuse is with intense feelings of betrayal. This is a result of being exploited by someone whom they trusted, someone who was supposed to protect them and help them. These feelings of betrayal may extend not just to the abuser, but to other family members as well, who knew, or should have known, and did nothing. In fact, children may feel even greater anger toward these family members than toward the abuser, for often the abuser presents himself to the child as someone who does not want to do anything wrong, but just can't help it.

Because of their feelings of betrayal, these children may feel intense sadness, loss, and disillusionment. They may either begin to feel a chronic distrust and cynicism about relationships or else become extremely clingy and dependent. As adults, these children may have very poor judgment about who is trustworthy and who is not. They may be extremely vulnerable to relationships in which they are victimized just like they were in childhood. Their ideas about relationships may be severely distorted, for they are based on what they experienced in childhood. They expect and even invite betrayal; it is a way of life to them.

The third way that sexually abused children react to abuse is in feelings of helplessness. Their bodies and their personal space have been violated over and over, and there was nothing they could do to stop it. They often experience themselves as powerless, weak, and empty. This feeling is all the stronger if physical force has been used to make the child comply, or if the child has appealed to other adults but was not believed. Such children may struggle with constant feelings of anxiety and fear. They may have frequent nightmares and sometimes have unexplained physical symptoms. They may see themselves as victims and have little confidence in their ability to cope with new and strange situations. They frequently feel despair and depression, and may even try to kill themselves. However, some children try to overcompensate for their feelings of helplessness by trying to dominate others or by turning off all their emotions so they're invulnerable. In each case, the child's ability to learn and grow, to develop meaningful relationships, and even to function adequately may be seriously impaired.

The final way that sexually abused children react to being abused is by feeling shame and guilt. They feel, like all abused children do, that the abuse was their fault, that it happened because they are bad kids. Very often, the abusers themselves add to these feelings of shame by blaming it all on the child and telling the child that he or she will get in trouble if anyone finds out about the abuse. Sexual abusers will do almost anything to ensure the child's silence, and they sometimes feel that instilling shame or fear in the child is the best way to keep the abuse secret. Even when other people do find out, the child may be stigmatized. Sometimes the whole family blames the child because the father or mother has to be removed from the home. Sometimes the child is penalized by being placed for his own protection in an institution, where conditions are often even worse than in the family. Even if there is a safe refuge for the child to go to, children almost never want to leave their home or their parents. They love their parents, and they think they're being sent away because they're bad.

Because of these feelings of shame and guilt, sexually abused children have intense feelings of inadequacy and self-hatred. They think of themselves as damaged and spoiled. They feel set apart from everyone; they may think they deserve to be punished. As adults, they may be haunted by these same feelings of guilt, self-hatred, and a sense of incompetence and deficiency. They spend their lives trying to escape from their intolerable inner feelings of depression, emptiness, fear, and hopelessness. Drug or alcohol intoxication may be the only way they can escape from their painful emotional states.

This is the worst-case scenario. As in the case of physical abuse, how the child reacts to sexual abuse depends on many things, including the child's own inner resources, the amount of support available from the people around him, how old the child is when the abuse starts happening, how long the abuse continues, and who the abuser is. If the child has had a chance to establish a secure sense of self through nurturing relationships with people close to him, the damage will be less. If the child has someone to turn to who will listen to him and protect him, the damage will be less. If the abuse happens only a few times, the damage will be less. If the abuser is a stranger rather than part of the family, the damage will be less. The older the child is, the more chance that the damage will be less.

Some of you may be wondering just what "older" means. Doesn't most sexual abuse happen to teenagers? We wish that were so, but it is sadly true that even infants have been sexually abused. You might think that very young children would not understand sexual abuse enough to be hurt by it. They do not understand the pleasurable aspects of it, but they do understand that they are being exploited, threatened, and coerced. As people learn to express their sexual drives through their early sexual experiences, they also learn that to exploit sexually young children is okay.

The tragedy of sexual abuse is that it perpetuates itself. The sexually abused child is all too likely in adulthood to exploit a new generation of children, or to marry someone who will exploit him or her. Many mothers of sexually abused children were themselves abused in childhood. Somehow, they are attracted to men who later abuse their sons or daughters. And to them, sometimes, the tragedy of sexual abuse seems not quite so disastrous. "I lived through it, and so can they" is what they seem to think.

So if, like Marylynn, you have some reason to believe that sexual abuse is occurring in your stepfamily, don't close your eyes. No matter how much it hurts, you must confront the situation and do the best you can for your children. Yes, your children may be among the lucky ones. Your children may have the advantages we've described above. Perhaps they will escape almost intact from the experience and forget it with time.

But do you really want to risk it? Sexual abuse has the potential to stunt and warp a child's life past any later undoing. No father or mother would willingly saddle their children with the psychological burdens that we've talked about, but you may find yourself in a situation and not know what to do, or who to believe.

Whatever your situation is, it's important that you take action if you suspect sexual abuse. It will not be easy. The abuser may be someone you love very much, someone who you cannot believe would do such a thing. You may have to give up a relationship that you have come to depend on and that means all the world to you. That price is a heavy one, and very hard to pay. But if you do not pay it, the chances are that your child will.

WARNING SIGNS OF SEXUAL ABUSE

1. Preoccupation with vague physical complaints that seem to have no real physical cause (like headaches and stomachaches). Children sometimes represent their emotional pain symbolically through these symptoms, trying to let you know that they are hurting.

2. Recurring urinary tract infections and yeast infections. These can be sexually transmitted. And of course, venereal diseases of any kind are an unmistakable sign of sexual abuse.

3. Complaints of sexual abuse. Always take them seriously. Children almost never fake this, even when they are being urged to do so by one party in a divorce.

4. Premature sexual knowledge or activities, or a preoccupation with sex (e.g., compulsive masturbation).

5. Unusual clinging behavior, depression, anxiety, suicidal feelings, self-destructive behavior, etc., as described above. Carefully examine any sudden change in your child's behavior that seems to come out of nowhere.

If you do think you have a sexual abuse problem in your stepfamily, don't try to handle it alone. It may be very hard to tell someone else about it, but secrecy just makes it that much easier for the abuse to continue. Tell a friend, a relative, or a clergyman, and get their advice and support. Mental health professionals are trained to deal with these problems, and family therapy may be one of the few ways that you can correct the situation and still keep your family together. If you cannot afford a private therapist, go to a clinic where they will put you on a sliding fee scale. Above all, don't ignore the problem. It's not going to go away, not for you, and certainly not for your child.

CHAPTER 13

One Big Happy Family

THE PROBLEM OF CONFUSION

STEPFAMILIES can be very confusing for children. There are often many new relationships they must adjust to, and they sometimes have trouble knowing what all the relationships mean.

Wesley, a nine-year-old boy who experienced this problem, found it difficult to describe his new family. "I live with my mom, my stepdad, my stepsister Lottie, my stepbrother Donald, and my half-sister Frederica. My half-sister Valerie lives with Matt (who used to be my stepfather) and with her stepmother and her stepbrothers Wayne and Gary. My brother Charles and my sister Katrina live with my real father and my stepmother. Charles is my brother but Katrina is only half my sister. I have two grandparents in Ohio, and three in Delaware, and two in Maine, but only the ones in Delaware are my real grandparents; the rest are only step-grandparents. My stepuncle Billy lives down the street from us, and I play with him all the time because he's only a year older than I am. I have two real aunts in Ohio, but I don't get to see them much. I have three uncles and two aunts here in Maine, Natalie, Carol, David, Glen, and Murray."

If you found Wesley's description confusing, think how much more confusing things must be for the thousands of children who live with the realities of such a set of family relationships. Part of the problem is just trying to figure out what all these relationships mean, what these people expect of you, how you're supposed to act toward them, and what it means to be a stepfamily.

Our society is still geared toward the nuclear family; our language even lacks the words to express some of the relationships that are becoming common in modern society. What is the word for the stepbrother of a half-sister, for example? Even when the terminology is clear, the meaning may still be elusive. Children are taught what "mother" and "father" and "sister" and "brother" mean, but they are not necessarily taught the meaning of "step-uncle" or "ex-stepfather." Many children may have little to guide their behavior or their expectations in dealing with all these strangers who are suddenly part of their most intimate family life.

Even well-adjusted children are likely to become confused when confronted with so many new family ties. Emotionally healthy children have learned that good relationships are built on trust, on consistent support and understanding, and on respect that has been earned over a long period of time. When confronted with a large number of new relatives, all of whom they are expected to welcome into their homes and lives, it may be impossible for such children not to be resistant and suspicious. It is hard for children to be hypocrites. Unlike adults, children do not always understand the difference between socially constrained civility and real friendship, or why it is sometimes necessary to pretend for the sake of politeness.

When the children of a stepfamily are not emotionally healthy, the problem may be worse. Most stepchildren have been through a divorce, and as a result they may be struggling with questions about what it means to be a family or about why one of their parents doesn't live with them anymore. When these children are expected to welcome a group of strangers as part of their families, their confusion may be compounded. They may have doubts about the meaning of family love, or they may begin to believe that being close to people isn't that real or that important. Being children, they won't articulate these things to themselves in the same way that adults might, but their inner worlds may begin to take on a dismal and dreary color, and they may find themselves withdrawing from interpersonal relationships.

One indication that this may be happening is when children ask a lot of questions about their extended families. "Is Aunt Susan still my aunt now that you're not married to Chip anymore?" "Is Edmund my uncle already, or will he become my uncle once your wedding is over?" "Is Aunt Lilly the same kind of aunt as Aunt Wanda?" The questions of younger children may be more emotionally direct: "Do I have to love Uncle Brett now he's my uncle?" or perhaps, "Can you please make Uncle Brett not my uncle? I don't like him." Through these kinds of questions, children try to resolve their uncertainty about the new people in their lives, about the meaning of relationships, and about the meaning of love. It is important that you provide support, understanding, and guidance for your children through this transition. It is more difficult for them than for you, because despite whatever emotional pain and confusion you too may be enduring, at least your personality and intellect are mature and developed. In the course of becoming an adult, you have acquired a set of inner resources that guide the way you look at the world and other people, and you are able to cope with new situations in a consistent way. Your problem may be that you find it hard to change the way you do things; habits can be really hard to break. Your children, however, are still in the process of developing their resources and their outlook on life, and every new addition to the family is going to have an impact on that process. The more divorces and remarriages there have been, and the more people your children have had to adjust to, the more difficult it will be for the children.

In order to help the children in your stepfamily through this process, you should listen to both their questions and to the underlying issues, and try to reassure them on both levels. Let them know that there are different kinds of familial relationships. There are the relationships that have stood the test of time, that are forever—the relationship the children have with their natural parents is the best example. Others may be grandparents, or an ex-stepparent who consistently keeps in touch with the children, or a half-sibling that the children visit every year. The crucial quality is consistency. Anyone who unfailingly provides the children with affection, support, and attention is a living example of a forever relationship, whether he or she is legally part of the family or not.

The other kind of relationship could perhaps be called a "maybe" relationship. People in this category have some sort of legal connection with the children; however, they may or may not become a real part of the children's emotional world. They have the opportunity to establish a forever relationship with the children, but they have to do the work first. They have to invest much time and energy in winning the children's affection and trust before their relationship can become forever. Much of this your children will know instinctively, but you can help them by validating their feelings, and by giving them your support.

Reassure your children that they do not have to act a part just to satisfy the adults in their lives. If they feel uncomfortable when asked to sit on a new aunt's lap, or do not want to kiss a recently created grandfather, teach them to say, simply and politely, "No, thank you" or "I'd rather not." You may find it necessary to speak privately to the adults involved, to explain that the children need more time before they can feel comfortable in these new relationships.

You should do whatever you can to help ease your children's doubts and fears as they become part of a new extended family and try to maintain their ties with what has gone before. Listen to your own instincts; you know your own children best. With all the many problems and issues confronting you in this difficult and challenging time in your life, try to spend some time helping your children resolve their confusion about the extended family. If you are the stepparent, you can help them in another way. Build your relationship with them slowly, honestly, and respectfully; give them time and reason to trust you; don't force affection and intimacy on them till they're ready.

There is another way children may respond to confusion about the role of the new extended family in their lives. You may notice that they're being *too* affectionate with these new family members. The children may seem to be greedy for any kind of emotional involvement and seem not to care how or from whom they get it.

The children may be climbing onto their new grandmother's lap without an invitation, insisting on frequent hugs from everyone, or may kiss their new cousins every time they see them.

The reason for this excess of affection may be that the children are feeling insecure about the people in their lives. They may be afraid that the important people in their lives will always go away and leave them, and this can create in them a desperate need for closeness. They may be driven to clingy behavior by their need to ensure that others in their lives will want to stay close to them. Such children need extra attention and reassurance from their primary caretakers. They need to express their fears and be told that it is okay to be afraid. They also need to be told that other people's needs are important, too; that you have to have permission to get physically close to others.

THE PROBLEM OF REJECTION

Confusion of the children is not the only problem that the extended family can cause. Sometimes there is coldness, rejection, or outright hostility from the extended family. This is particularly common when the extended family views the ex-in-law as a victim. The classic example is the case of the man who leaves his wife for another woman; sometimes the extended family sees the former wife of their relative as the injured party, and regards the second wife as a homewrecker and an intruder. Should the second wife have children from another marriage, the children may also be included in the resentment and hostility.

To the extended family, these children are part and parcel of someone they greatly dislike. If there are also children from their relative's first marriage, this dislike may be strengthened further, because of the family's loyalty to the children from the first marriage. It may be painful for the extended family to see the new stepchildren take the place of the "real" children in their father's home.

Marie found herself in such a situation. She had met her husband, Walter, when he was still married to Claire. Marie had just gone through a divorce herself, and it was easy for her to recognize the signs of a marriage in trouble. She worked with Walter and couldn't help noticing how often he made derogatory remarks about his wife, how he seemed to make any excuse to work late and avoid going home, and how cold his voice was whenever he talked to Claire. Marie wasn't really surprised when Walter began to talk to her about the problems in his marriage. Soon he was asking Marie out to lunch more and more often; eventually his lunch invitations became dinner invitations. To Marie, it was only human nature—when one relationship failed you, you turned to another. But Walter's family didn't see it that way.

Marie would never forget her first meeting with Walter's family. It was about a week before the wedding. Walter had told his family about his plans to marry Marie several months before, but for some reason—Marie hadn't known exactly why at the time—something had always come up to prevent them from meeting each other. Marie and Walter had gone to his parents' home for dinner; Walter's two sisters, Angela and Nina, were there with their husbands and children.

When Marie walked into the house, she saw all of the family, tastefully dressed, arranged about the living room in carefully casual poses. There was an uncomfortable moment of complete silence when Marie entered the room. They all stared at her, and she was frightened by the coldness in their eyes.

The evening did not improve. Everyone was superficially polite, *too* polite. There was no getting past their arid courtesy. The conversation was restricted to such safe topics as the weather, politics, and recent movies. No one displayed the slightest interest in getting to know Marie on anything but the most superficial level; in fact, the few times she tried to talk about the upcoming wedding and about her wish that Walter's children from his first marriage would someday accept her, someone would immediately change the subject. Every now and then, when she turned her head suddenly, she met that same cold, unfriendly stare that had so upset Marie when she first came into the house. Worst of all was the moment when Walter's four-year-old niece, Emily, piped up: "Marie, Mommy says you are a bitch!" The entire evening was a nightmare; Marie couldn't wait to get out of there.

The situation did not get better over time. Walter's family continued to treat Marie, and Marie's children, as disagreeable outsiders who were only tolerated for Walter's sake. Walter was uncomfortable talking about this problem, and for a long time Marie tried to believe that Walter had the misfortune to come from a cold, uncaring family.

Then one day she stopped by Angela's house unannounced. From within she heard shrieks of laughter, and peeking in, she saw a large party which included Walter's children and both of his sisters. They were playing some kind of game which involved hiding behind the furniture and then jumping out with a loud scream when the person who was "it" came near; everyone was laughing hysterically, and the adults seemed to be having as much fun as the children. But as soon as Marie made her appearance, things immediately got very, very quiet. Marie left as soon as possible.

Most people who find themselves in Marie's situation find it hard not to become depressed or angry. When someone dislikes you and treats you with unkindness, the natural reaction is either to begin to dislike them, or to hate yourself and feel depressed. It is hard to avoid brooding about the situation; it is hard not to keep thinking over the various slights and snubs you've received. That is because for most people, it is very important to be liked by others.

When someone does not like you, it is natural to try to rationalize their dislike in a way that will protect your own self-esteem. People have various ways of doing that. "She hates me because she's a narrow-minded jerk" is probably the simplest. Some people can decide that, and then just forget about it. Others have to go through a much more tortured process before they have peace with their own souls. They may feel guilty: "She doesn't like me because I'm a bad person, or because I did something wrong, or because I made a mistake." They may feel rage: "How dare she not like me! Who does she think she is, anyway?" They may feel anxiety: "There must be something I can do to make her like me. It's all a misunderstanding, but if I don't do something to fix it, it'll only get worse. If I can make her like me, everything will be okay." Or they may feel an unhappy mixture of all three feelings—guilt, anger, and anxiety.

When people go over and over the past in this way, they are quite likely to communicate at least some of their distress to their children. This can be a serious problem. Children are very impressionable, and they identify with their parents. If the children get the message that their parents are continually at odds with part of their new family, they may begin to dislike these family members, too.

They may even begin to believe that all family relationships are inherently conflictual. They may begin to believe that there is something about them, or something about their parents, that is unlovable and unattractive.

Another problem is that if a parent is caught up in the painful ruminations about the extended family, they will have less energy to invest in having fun with their children and their spouse, and in supporting them and nurturing them. They also will have less "quality time" for themselves.

If you are encountering this kind of problem in your stepfamily, the best thing you can do is to minimize it. There is a strong possibility that there is not much you can do about the coldness and hostility, but you can try to put it out of your mind. Don't talk to your children about it. Don't pester your spouse with it. Don't spend those endless hours trying to figure out what is going on, and what you can do about it.

It will not be easy to do this. Many people obsess about such things habitually; it is part of the way they think. It may be very difficult for such people to stop their worrisome thoughts. But there are important reasons to try. If you want your marriage to work, you're going to have to establish some kind of truce with your spouse's extended family. Neither open warfare nor self-humiliation is an answer. You have to be able to live with yourself, and you have to have an acceptable way of coping with their bad behavior. You also do not want to alienate your spouse or put him or her in the position of having to choose sides.

If you behave with dignity and self-respect, and exert self-discipline to control the urge to ruminate and worry, those in the family whose regard is really worth having will come around eventually. As for those family members who cling stubbornly to their beliefs that you are an evil harpy, despite all the evidence to the contrary, allow yourself the luxury of pity. After all, those people have to live in their small-minded brains for the rest of their lives. They cannot escape their own bigotry and hatred.

The first step in minimizing the extended family problem is to distract yourself. When you suddenly find yourself a prisoner of unpleasant thoughts about your in-laws, concentrate on something else, on something pleasant. Use energy to do this, and keep trying for as long as it takes. If the in-laws have ever done anything that might be interpreted as friendly, think about that. If they haven't, think about going to a seafood buffet, making love, or winning the lottery. Visualize the face of someone you really care about. Indulge in a favorite fantasy of success. Call up one of your best friends. Listen to some inspiring music. Do anything that, for you, will stop the unproductive vicious circle in your head. Stop using up all your energy on self-defeating negative thoughts, and concentrate on things that will make you feel better about life. This is something you will have to do over and over, and there will probably be many times when you're completely unsuccessful. But if you persist, you will be successful in the end. You will break the cycle.

Second, you must modify your outward behavior. Don't allow yourself the indulgence of complaining about the problem ceaselessly to your spouse, your children, or your friends. In the case of your spouse and children, you can do actual damage to your relationships with them by talking about it too much, and talking also encourages you to continue thinking about it. Avoid the subject whenever possible. If someone says something nice about people you dislike, bite your lip rather than disagree.

Try to think of good things that you can honestly say about your in-laws, and slip them into the conversation now and then. Everyone has some good points. But be careful not to overdo it, or you may sound sarcastic. One benefit to this approach is that your in-laws may hear about your gracious behavior and that may improve their attitude toward you. The final step is to modify your behavior toward your unaccepting new relatives. Try to behave toward them as you would toward any new acquaintance with whom you expect to have a cordial relationship. The power of a self-fulfilling prophecy is amazingly strong in most social situations; our behavior toward others tends to call forth the behavior we expect them to have. If you expect them to be friendly, they'll be friendly. If you expect them to be obnoxious, they'll insult you. This may not be as true in the case of an already established relationship, for then expectations have become crystallized. But you can change them over time; it is a slow process, but it can be done. At least you may be able to improve things to the point that these in-laws are not a source of constant irritation.

Every time you see them, imagine how you would like them to behave toward you, and act accordingly. Try not to become discouraged. This process will take much time to accomplish, but if you are persistent, you will be successful in the end.

What if your family is the one that is being rejecting? JoAnn had this problem. Her parents had always been critical of the men in their daughter's life. JoAnn was used to the way they would pretend to like her new boyfriend after the first meeting, but then drop their little snide remarks. "It's too bad he doesn't have more hair." "It's such a shame how those acne scars stay forever." Sometimes the comments were even more direct: "I think he's a fine friend for you to have, but something about him makes me think he's bisexual." Or, "Don't you know any guys your age? He looks like he should be taking Geritol." Sometimes her parents made their feelings known by well-timed looks or sighs; that was probably the most annoying because it was hard to confront them about it. If she tried, all she got was, "You're so sensitive. Always imagining things. All I did was *look* at your mother!"

However, her parents' response to Chandler was worse than anything JoAnn had ever seen before. She now lived six hundred miles from her parents, and had come home for Christmas. She brought Chandler with her to meet them for the first time. Even though they had only known each other for two months, they were already engaged; her parents did not like him any better for that.

When they arrived at her parents' house, her mother met them at the door. She led them into the living room, where her father was relaxing with a beer next to a gaily decorated Christmas tree. JoAnn was always nervous when introducing her parents to the new man in her life, and she watched them like a hawk as she made the introductions. She was expecting their usual false affability with an underlying current of mockery, but she saw something very different. Her parents seemed cold, distant, openly disapproving. They looked uncomfortable, and they seemed to be having trouble thinking of things to say. JoAnn took an early opportunity of talking to her mother alone, by offering to help her in the kitchen.

JoAnn was not made happy by what her mother had to say. There was none of her mother's usual glee in finding out the flaws of her new man; there was just glum dislike. "I don't know what it is about him, JoAnn. I have a bad feeling about him. He's not the right kind of man for you." That was bad enough, but when JoAnn had more opportunities to see Chandler and her parents together, it got even worse. Her mother openly avoided, even ignored her daughter's fiance. Her father treated him with thinly veiled contempt. What was more, her parents were not slow in passing on their negative attitude about Chandler to JoAnn's sisters and to all the rest of the family.

JoAnn hoped that with time her family would get to know Chandler better and to like him. But after JoAnn and Chandler were married, things continued to get worse. Every time Chandler and JoAnn got together with JoAnn's extended family, someone there was sure to insult or snub Chandler. JoAnn was torn between anger and hurt. She couldn't disown her own family. What could she do to improve the situation?

There are some things you can do if your case is similar to JoAnn's. First of all, make it clear to your relatives that you will not tolerate any openly hostile behavior in your presence. If they want to see you, they have to be at least outwardly civil to your spouse and stepchildren.

Second, don't tolerate belittling remarks about your spouse which are meant only for your ears. "Love me, love my dog" has to be (figuratively) your attitude. It is also important that you try to be extrasupportive to your spouse and stepchildren during this time, even if you think they might be overreacting to your family's attitude. You may not have noticed all the little signals and innuendos that they have; it is also generally easier to dismiss someone else's troubles as unimportant than it is to dismiss your own.

A final in-law problem that involves rejection is when your spouse does not get along with his or her own family. He or she may refuse to see them, or become upset and agitated after every contact with the extended family. You will have to tread carefully here. It may be that years of fighting and conflict have taken their toll, and the damage is just too great to be repaired. Another possibility is that they really are unpleasant people, and it's in your best interests to steer clear of them. On the other hand, your spouse may be harboring resentment from years long past that no longer fits the reality of the situation. Evaluate the situation for yourself when you get the chance. Take your time about it, and don't assume that just because you are well intentioned you can change long-established negative patterns. It would be nice if your spouse could be reunited with his or her family, but you cannot make it happen all by yourself. Whatever happens, don't get caught in the middle. You are on your spouse's side, first and foremost.

DINNER WITH THE ADAMS FAMILY

Another extended family problem that some individuals have encountered is that of an extended family that is highly eccentric. There may be something about them which is hard to accept. Perhaps they let chickens run loose through their house and wash their dishes by putting them on the floor for the pets to lick clean (we did not make this up—we have actually known a family like this). Perhaps they have bizarre religious beliefs which are always the main topic of conversation. Whatever it is, you find it uncomfortable to be around them, and you may not want your children exposed to their strange ways, either. In this case, you will have to make a judgment call. Is their weirdness potentially life-threatening? Do you really think that your children will pick up odd habits and values from being around these people? Does it make you feel ill to eat food at their houses? Do they seem to be essentially goodhearted though eccentric, or do you think they might have corpses buried out in their backyards?

All things being equal, it is best that you and your children get to know your spouse's family. That will strengthen the bond between you and your spouse. However, the rewards have to outweigh the costs. There are things more important than family togetherness. If you feel that your in-laws present a real danger to your children's health, development, or emotional adjustment, you'd better keep contact to a minimum, and certainly do not *ever* let them stay with them alone without your supervision.

On the other hand, your in-laws may seem fairly harmless, but somehow they get on your nerves, or you cannot control your urge to laugh when in their company, or you think they are a bit tacky and low-class. In this case, let the attitudes of your spouse and children influence your decision more. If your spouse is attached to the extended family, and your children like them and seem to have a good time with them, you might want to overcome your prejudices to some extent. Who knows, the experience may even broaden your horizons. After all, your children are almost certain to share your values. They may go through a period of rebelliousness, but you will always be the primary influence on them. You can afford to let them experiment a little bit.

If *you* are the one with the peculiar family, you're probably used to others' reactions by now. You know what your extended family's good points are. Point them out to your spouse and do not try to deny that they have eccentricities. That will help your spouse realize that these peculiarities are not really that important.

THE PROBLEM OF SIBLING RIVALRY

The most upsetting problem for many stepfamilies is that the extended family makes an obvious difference in the way they treat different children who live together in the same household. Often one or more of the favored children are related to the in-laws by blood, and the neglected children are related only by marriage. An example would be a family which included children from both the spouses' first marriages and also two children from the present marriage. It is all too common for the grandparents and other relatives to feel that only the children who are blood relatives are the "real" grandchildren, and to make some difference accordingly in their gift giving and other attentions.

Sometimes the distinction is made between children who are blood relatives, but who are products of different marriages. Usually the fortunate children are those from the first marriage, which is generally looked on more favorably by the extended family. Jan and Robert, who have been mentioned in earlier chapters, had this problem. The oldest child, Todd, from Robert's first marriage, was treated very differently by Robert's mother than the three children Jan and Robert had together. Todd received many presents and phone calls which the others did not; the grandmother also caused a great deal of tension between Jan and Robert by accusing Jan of neglecting Todd in favor of her own children. While this certainly was not the only problem in Jan and Robert's marriage, the family atmosphere was poisoned further by Robert's suspicions that his firstborn son was being ignored and treated poorly. Robert and Jan's ongoing guerrilla warfare received further ammunition from the grandmother's behavior and complaints; Todd felt superior to his stepbrothers and stepsisters, and enjoyed the power of being able to come between his father and his stepmother; the other children felt that they were in some way inadequate and second-rate, at least compared to Todd.

There's no defending people who would go out of their way to hurt innocent children just because of who the children's parents are. Such people may very well be simply venting their own anger about past events on anybody within reach. This is even worse than the hostility which was discussed earlier in this chapter, because of the distinction between children. One or more children may be treated with affection and consideration; others may be ignored. The contrast makes it all too easy for the ignored children to get the message that there is something unlovable about them. A parent who sees his or her children ignored in this way often feels extremely angry. If your stepchildren are getting preferential treatment while your own children are being neglected, you will naturally feel somewhat resentful toward your stepchildren. However, indulging anger will only add fuel to the fire. You want to defuse the situation, not exacerbate it. Remember that the children must be considered first, because they are much more impressionable and vulnerable, and they will not benefit by angry talk and hostile discussions.

Unless things are very ugly between you and your in-laws, you might consider talking to them about the problem. Maybe they do not realize that the children (and you) notice what is going on. Maybe they think the children do not care. Don't be accusative or inflammatory—just give them the children's point of view. If you feel that you really cannot talk to them about such a sensitive issue, ask your spouse to do it.

If you are convinced that talking is not a good idea, another solution might be to ask the grandparents, aunts, or uncles of the children who are being neglected to pay them some extra attention. Explain to your children that sometimes it happens that you are closer to some relatives than to others, because you have more in common with them. Give them examples from your own past (most people have some) and don't let them think that just because one relative is less attentive to them, that they are disliked or overlooked. Be on the lookout for taunts between the children like, "Aunt Norma likes *me* best" or "Grandpa Murray doesn't like you." Children use whatever ammunition they can find in their battles, but you must be on the alert to discourage the use of such weapons.

Keep reinforcing the idea that some people have more in common than others and get along better than others. In all of these extended family issues, remember that children who have experienced divorce and are now part of a stepfamily are terribly vulnerable. They need security and consistency, and the parents have a responsibility to try to give them as stable an environment as possible. When confronted with these difficulties within the extended family, try to put your own needs second and consider those of the children first. They have the most to lose in the long run.

CHAPTER 14

Happily Ever After?

WILL YOUR SECOND chance be a fairy tale come true or a nightmare you can't wait to end? Either extreme is possible, as well as anything in between; the many different stories of our respondents certainly proved that. Some of them really regretted the decision they made to enter a second marriage. Connie, a thirty-nine-year-old woman whose stepfamily included her two children from a previous marriage and her husband's three children, wrote: "We dated two years before we married but I still didn't know him. If I had a close friend who was considering a second marriage, I'd tell her to just forget it!! She should just spend weekends with him. We've paid ninety dollars an hour for hundreds of hours of family counseling. Things are working well right now but the good times never last. I feel like we just keep putting band-aids on our relationship—I'm still not sure that we have a future together, even after eight and a half years."

On the other hand, other respondents felt very positive about their stepfamily. Sixty-nine percent of the people who responded to our survey believed that their marriage would last forever; 87 percent said that they would marry their present spouse again if they had to do it over. Ninety-nine percent of our respondents said that their spouse loved them, and 90 percent felt that their spouse understood them. Regarding relationships with the children, 76 percent of our respondents felt that their children from a previous marriage loved their spouse, 59 percent said that their stepchildren loved them, and 80 percent of our respondents felt that their children seemed as well adjusted as ever since the remarriage.

Rochelle, who was managing the task of blending her own two children and her husband's four into a stepfamily, was an example of someone whose second chance was happy and successful. "I have really been blessed to have this blended family—I can't imagine life without all of them. Sometimes life with all of them is great, sometimes it's the pits, but they are always there for me. I know that if I just hang in there for twenty-four hours things usually change—in one way or another!"

According to all of our respondents, however, there is one thing you can count on in your experience of trying to blend two families into one. It's not going to be easy. Sixty-six percent of our respondents said that blending families with their partners was more difficult than they had anticipated.

So how do you give yourselves the best odds for your second chance to be successful? Throughout this book we've discussed a variety of issues and problems that sometimes trouble people who are trying to make a success of their second chance. Not all problems apply to all people, of course, because there are so many different forms a blended family can take. Your second marriage may include no children, children from one or more previous marriages, or children from your current marriage; you may or may not have financial troubles, situational stresses, in-law or ex-spouse difficulties, loyalty problems, or disciplinary woes. Or you may still be trying to decide whether you should marry again. Across all this multitude of varying circumstances, are there any general principles to remember that could be rules of thumb in future times of trouble?

There are a few. First, if you're trying to make the decision to marry again, remember to listen to your head as well as your heart. Romance really doesn't last forever, and marriage needs to be built on something more lasting than feelings of sexual attraction. This is especially true in the case of stepfamilies, because there are so many people and so many needs involved. You must consider the practical issues and concerns first—whether your values and feelings are acceptably compatible, whether your financial situation will be at least tolerable, whether you will have the time and energy to build relationships with all the other new people in your life besides your spouse-to-be. Ask yourself if over the long term you can really live with things just as they are now; don't assume that once you're married things will change overnight through the power of love.

Michelle and John, whose story we've described in several previous chapters, are a good example of a successful second chance that was based both on romance and on reason. They moved slowly, got to know each other as friends, and made sure their values were compatible. Jan and Robert, on the other hand, rushed into romance willy-nilly, ignoring all the indications that there were serious problems in the relationship.

The second thing to remember is that, if you're already married, don't give up too easily if you do encounter serious problems. It's important to realize that blending a family is not easy for anyone. Don't anticipate that all will be smooth sailing, and it's important that you do not despair at the first sign of trouble. Your second chance is going to take a lot of work, no matter how compatible or financially comfortable you are. Even those of our respondents who appeared to be happiest had to work hard to overcome many difficulties. Chris and Stephanie, whom we discussed in previous chapters, are good examples of this. Though their feelings for each other were so strong that they each left a spouse to be together, their story didn't end with a simple "They lived happily ever after." They had to surmount many obstacles, not the least of which was their comparative poverty, once their divorces were final. However, their story is a testimony to what can be accomplished with dedication and hard work. Though their short-term struggle was very difficult, they were able in the long run to create a reality for themselves and their children that was very happy and fulfilling.

Like Chris and Stephanie, you will have to accept that what you are trying to do is difficult, but if you are successful, the rewards can be enormous. Susan, a thirty-two-year-old woman with one child of her own from a previous marriage and three stepchildren from her husband's previous marriage, had this to say on the subject: "I think it is important for people to understand that anything worth having is worth working for. With the stepfamily, you have two to three times as many things to consider. It takes a little extra planning, giving, and taking, but it can be a wonderful life with even more people to love than you ever imagined."

Keep in mind all the many, many things we've discussed in this book that you may have to work on. You or your spouse may have to slowly and painfully unlearn the lessons of a previous bad marriage. You may have to struggle with your resentment over unfair child-support payments. You may have to adjust to a less comfortable style of living than you're used to, and to living in cramped quarters, with little privacy. You may find yourself unendurably irritated by little things—like how your new spouse or stepchild chews his food—and have to exert yourself not to make too much of it. You may be persecuted by a vindictive ex-spouse, or be compared unfavorably to an ex-spouse. Your stepchildren may have trouble accepting you because of loyalty conflicts, or you or your spouse may may find it difficult to accept them. You may have difficulty establishing and enforcing rules of the household with your stepchildren. You may have to help heal the wounds of stepchildren who have been physically or sexually abused. You may find that you or your spouse is not accepted by part of the extended family. Yes, there are an unlimited number of ways that things can go wrong for a stepfamily.

The core of the problem is that everyone or almost everyone in the situation has been hurt in some way. They've been through a divorce, and no matter how amicable the divorce was, it surely left wounds. Those wounds can make it hard for all the parties in a second marriage to adjust and learn to be happy again. That's why so much work is required in this situation. But it's not impossible! If you have the strength and courage and hope to persevere, you can be successful in your second chance.

Third, it is important to put your marriage first, whether or not you have children living with you. This may sound paradoxical, in view of the fact that the most common problem for second marriages is the children. And what about all the chapters in this book dealing with the problems of stepchildren?

There's no question that the children in the second marriage will demand a great amount of time and energy. But how will you be able to devote that time and energy? You will only be able to do it if your marriage gives you security and support. If you are unhappy or dissatisfied with your marital relationship, you will have that much less strength to deal with problems caused by the children.

Research has shown that even your mental health can suffer when your marriage is in trouble—in particular, women who are not able to confide in their spouses are much more vulnerable to depression than women who can talk to their spouses and get support from them. What's more, the children will know it if there are marital problems, and they will feel less secure in their new family. They've already been through one divorce, and they may be quick to jump to the conclusion that there soon will be another.

Christine, a thirty-year-old woman whose stepfamily included her two children from her first marriage and her husband's son from his first marriage, wrote about the importance of putting the marriage first. "I feel that when you remarry, the relationship has got to be the number one priority. When that is strong and healthy, the other relationships (with your children and stepchildren) fall into line and become stronger and more loving."

Putting your marriage first means making time for you and your spouse to be together, no matter how difficult that may be in practical terms. Some of the people who answered our survey recommended a 'date night' once a week, when they would go out for dinner or to see a movie. Even if your financial resources are extremely limited, and it's impossible to pay for a baby-sitter, let alone a night out, you can still find ways to spend time together. Your time together may be as simple as eating popcorn and watching a movie on television after the children have gone to bed or having a drink together and talking about old times. The important thing is that you regularly plan time to be together when you have no stresses or responsibilities. You must *make* your marriage a priority; for too many people—when marriage is taken for granted—problems soon develop.

Another thing that was stressed by many of the people who responded to our survey was the importance of some kind of religious faith. We realize that this may not work for everyone, but it was mentioned by too many of our respondents for us to ignore it completely. Janice, a thirty-three-year-old woman who was the stepmother of two young boys, attributed the success of her stepfamily to religious faith. She wrote, "I don't think there is any *one* thing has made our family work. The most important factor, however, is God. He is a bond stronger than ourselves. We approach problems in a different way than people who don't have this common bond; we know we must at least try to understand each other. We are who we are because of the things that life has brought our way. We can learn from even the bad things in life; we can turn problems to our advantage by using them to make us more caring and less judgmental both of outsiders and of the people in our family."

We are not suggesting that any one religious faith is more worthwhile than others, or that any kind of religious faith is essential to the success of your second chance. But a belief in a higher power which in some way gives you and your spouse extra strength to overcome the daily problems and stresses can be extremely beneficial for some people. If you find that such a belief helps you, don't worry about the "psychological" explanation for it. If it works for you, don't change it.

There's one more rule of thumb that's extremely important. Once you've made the decision to marry, try to develop your sense of commitment to your marriage and your family as much as you can. We live in a culture that encourages us to start over rather than to persevere. We have disposable bottles, disposable razors, disposable contact lenses, disposable careers, and disposable marriages. And once you're been through one divorce, it's just that much easier to initiate another. Frances, who at the age of forty-one was dealing with the stresses of blending a stepfamily which included a total of eight people, made this point: "It's important to make the time to work through your difficulties. You have to be flexible, hang on to your commitment, and pray for wisdom, guidance, and understanding. When things get out of balance, we go for counseling to prevent walls of bitterness and resentment from building up. Warning: Don't do anything rash. Once you've been divorced and know you can make it on your own, it's a lot easier to give up on a marriage, but you can't go through life in and out of marriages."

Some of our respondents had to work very hard to conquer their urge to quit when the going got rough, especially when they'd already been through several divorces. Barbara, who at fifty-four was in her sixth marriage, had this to say: "The most important thing for me was to learn how to make a commitment. My husband and I both have multiple failed past marriages. I have five and he has three. We were lucky this time to find each other; we have a lot in common and both had a real desire to make this work, but—there have been many times in the past that we came close to giving up. I asked a lady I met a couple of years ago, who has been married forty years, what she felt was her secret to such a successful and productive marriage. She had one word: COMMITMENT. I believe many marriages that fail lack this. When hard times come along, we are so ready to give up. If you did not see divorce as an option, you would work so much harder to be happy together."

There are times when the best thing you can do may be to get out—if you become convinced that you've married someone with unchangeable character flaws; if you find that, after all, you and your partner have very little in common; if you or your spouse is still in love with an ex-spouse; if your spouse physically or sexually abuses your children. The story of Jan and Robert had many of these elements—Robert was grossly irresponsible with money, he had little in common with Jan, he was still involved with his first wife when he and Jan met, he was chronically unfaithful, and he was physically and mentally abusive to both Jan and the children. If you recognize your own situation in Jan's story, you'd better ask yourself why you're staying. Maybe you are so financially dependent that you can't (or think you can't) make it on your own; maybe your self-esteem is so low that you think you deserve the treatment that you are getting. There *are* times when the best solution is to get out. You may need the help of a mental health professional to take that difficult step.

Unless you're in one of those extreme situations, however, it's important that you hang in there and do the best you can. Have hope that things will get better; exercise all your patience and self-control; live one day at a time; go for counseling if you feel you can't handle things on your own. Yes, you've chosen to do something difficult, but that doesn't mean it's impossible. You may have hard times ahead, but all of your hard work, patience, planning, and devotion may be rewarded with a "wonderful life with even more people to love than you ever imagined."

You are trying to heal the wounds of past traumas, wounds sustained by you, your spouse, and the children in your family.

Don't give up. Don't let the memory of past failures affect your hope in the present and the future.

We wish you all success in your second chance. Good luck, and don't forget that you carry within yourself the strength, resolve, and courage that can make your new family work. Believe in your happy future.

STEPFAMILY QUESTIONNAIRE

How hard will it be to make your second chance a success? The following questions may help you understand both the strengths and weaknesses of your stepfamily, and give you ideas about what you need to work on. Each of these questions should be answered "True" or "False." The scoring key follows the questionnaire.

1. My spouse and I told each other everything about our financial situations before we got married.
2. I am proud to introduce my partner to close friends and family.
3. I admire my partner's ability to deal with difficult and stressful situations.
4. Either my or my partner's relationship with an ex-spouse remains strained and bitter.
5. My partner and I agree about how to discipline the step-children.
6. All the children in our home are treated alike.
7. An ex-spouse has caused my partner and me to have serious financial problems.
8. Our parents accept the step-grandchildren.
9. My partner and I were honest and open with each other about our previous marriage.
10. My partner and I got to know each other's children before we were married.
11. All the children in our family get along well.
12. The children in our family sometimes seem confused about where they should place their loyalties.
13. My partner and I have a good relationship with each other's children.
14. Either my spouse or I am still bitter and angry about a previous marriage.
15. It has been difficult to provide all the members of our family with the privacy they would like.

16. My present spouse is a better parent than my previous spouse.
17. My partner and I want pretty much the same things when it comes to our lifestyle and goals for the future.
18. My spouse and I have had periods in our lives when we lived independently.
19. My partner and I were very lonely for a relationship when we met.
20. My partner or I have been disappointed in relationships many times.
21. My spouse and I get along with most people.
22. I didn't seriously consider a divorce until my present spouse and I met each other.
23. My spouse and I get along well with each other's extended families.
24. My partner and I are compatible in the nitty-gritty details of everyday living.
25. Physical and/or sexual abuse has caused problems for our stepfamily.

Questionnaire Scoring Key

1. (True = 0, False = 1). If you and your spouse were honest with each other about your financial situations before you married, you were better able to plan for the future, and your trust in each other was probably enhanced.
2. (True = 0, False = 1). If your spouse is someone whom you respect and admire, you are more likely to become friends as well as lovers; your relationship is based on something more substantial than sexual attraction.
3. (True = 0, False = 1). Your partner's ability to manage stress effectively is an essential requirement for the difficult task of blending two families into one.
4. (True = 1, False = 0). A negative relationship with an ex-spouse can add to the stress and tension in your stepfamily and cause loyalty conflicts between parents and children.
5. (True = 0, False = 1). A united front is important in disciplinary matters. However, you must also agree to carry out your disciplinary strategies when the time comes to do so.

6. (True = 0, False = 1). It is extremely important that all the children receive the same treatment, both in disciplinary matters and in such things as gifts, clothes, and privileges. The only exception is when you must allow for age differences among the children (e.g., older children should be allowed to stay up later than younger children).

7. (True = 1, False = 0). Serious financial problems of any kind make life difficult for a stepfamily, but when an ex-spouse is the cause of these problems, there is an additional cause of stress.

8. (True = 0, False = 1). If your parents accept all the children in your stepfamily, your relationship with the extended family as a whole is likely to be much more harmonious and to be a source of support for your stepfamily rather than a source of stress.

9. (True = 0, False = 1). Honesty about a previous marriage creates higher levels of trust in a marriage over the long run, and is a good prognostic sign for your second chance. Such honesty often means that you and your spouse have taken responsibility for past mistakes and have learned from them.

10. (True = 0, False = 1). As many of our respondents indicated, getting to know each other's children before the wedding takes place can make the transition to becoming a stepfamily much easier.

11. (True = 0, False = 1). Tension and conflict between the children in the stepfamily can be a significant source of stress in a stepfamily, and can cause friction between the marital partners as well.

12. (True = 1, False = 0). Confusion about loyalties can create serious problems for the stepfamily; it is important that the parents try to understand what the children may be going through, and try not to make inappropriate emotional demands on the children.

13. (True = 0, False = 1). If you and your partner get along well with each other's children, there will be much less conflict in the stepfamily, and you will have that much more energy to invest in your marriage.

14. (True = 1, False = 0). Bitterness about a previous marriage may be an indication that you still have unresolved emotional conflicts concerning that marriage; it is important that you address these issues, or your current marriage may suffer.
15. (True = 1, False = 0). Living in close quarters can exacerbate trivial annoyances until they become unbearable.
16. (True = 0, False = 1). Being a good parent takes a considerable amount of emotional maturity, patience, and self-control; if your spouse is a good parent, he or she is likely to have other good qualities which will increase the happiness and stability of your second chance.
17. (True = 0, False = 1). Having similar values and goals is one of the best predictors of a successful marriage.
18. (True = 0, False = 1). If you or your spouse has never lived independently, you may be one of those people who has never developed the self-reliance and strength needed in adult life. In the long run, this may hamper your relationship, for each partner needs to give as well as to receive.
19. (True = 1, False = 0). Extreme loneliness can have an undue influence on the choice of a mate. Sometimes this can mean that you are so needy for acceptance and affection that you will accept any "frog." Unfortunately, every frog does not metamorphose into a prince or princess.
20. (True = 1, False = 0). Multiple failed past relationships may mean that you or your spouse is repeating unhealthy patterns and blaming other people for your own mistakes.
21. (True = 0, False = 1). Though no one is without occasional interpersonal difficulties, those people who can maintain relatively harmonious relationships with most of the people in their lives tend to be better adjusted and to have fewer problems in their stepfamily as well.
22. (True = 1, False = 0). If you or your partner left a spouse to be in your current relationship, you may be confusing marital love with sexual attraction and the desire for excitement. You may find that over the long run you may have to make some adjustments in your expectations of marital happiness.
23. (True = 0, False = 1). A good relationship with the extended family makes it easier on the children of the stepfamily, and makes loyalty problems less likely.

24. (True = 0, False = 1). The everyday details of life, trivial as they can seem on the surface, can over time assume considerable importance in the comfort level of your stepfamily. If you and your spouse have few problems in this area, your second chance will be much more free of stress.
25. (True = 1, False = 0). Physical or sexual abuse is a serious problem that should not be ignored or rationalized. Professional help is a necessity for those people who are trying to deal with abuse in their stepfamily.

After you have scored all your answers as one or zero, count the number of ones you have received, and compare that number to the scale below.

25–20: You have a lot of obstacles to overcome in your stepfamily, and you must work hard to make your second chance a success. Professional counseling may be necessary.
19–12: You have more problems than average, but with patience and commitment you can make your second chance work.
11–6: You have fewer problems than average; while blending your two families into one will not be easy, the odds are in your favor for a successful second chance.
5–0: You have fewer problems and more things going for you than most people who enter a stepfamily; while you shouldn't expect to automatically become the Brady Bunch, have confidence that with work the future of your second chance can be very bright.